Get Ready Version - Delroy Wilson
Ballistic Version - Leroy Smart
Belly Version - Clancy Eccles
John Left His Merina In The Arena - Ranking Joe
Fuss And Fight Version - Winston Jones
Gypsy Dub - Milton Henry
Fat Beef Skank - Dillinger
Easy Living Dub - D.E.B. Players
Revolution Dub - Jr Delgado
77 Festival - Morwell Unlimited

Folly Rankin' Version - Sly & Robbie
Number One Version - Wayne Wade
Back In My Arms Version - Jackie Edwards
Leave Yah - Jr Delgado
War In The City Version - Bob Andy
Render Your Heart

All Nations - Big Youth
I'm Not Ashamed Version - Culture
Every Nigga Is A Winner Version
- Prince Jazzbo
Dubs Of Thunder - Ras Michael
Babylon Fall - Jr Ross
Man In The Hills Version
- Burning Spear
Black Balcony - Dr Alimantado
Chant Down Babylon Version
- Jr Byles
Burning Satta - Bim Sherman
Natty Pass His GCE
- Shorty The President
Better Collie - Horace Andy
One Train Load Of Dub - Observer
40 Leg Version - Bunny Dimino

Run Aggressor - Ras Michael
Chapter 4 - Hugh Mundell
Free Man - Upsetters
Straight To I Roy Head
- Prince Jazzbo
I And I Are The Chosen
- Prince Far I
Farming Dub - Ranking Joe
Dub Money - Denny Hensworth
Straight To Jazzbo Head
- I Roy
Superstick - Sly & Co
All Gone - Trinity

Armagideon Man - Willie Williams
Entance To Jah World - Norris Reid
A Miserable Version - King Tubby's
John Lefy His Merina In The Arena
- Ranking Joe
Bald Head - Morwell Unlimited
Beating Version - Delroy Wilson
King Tubby's Time - Tubby's All Stars
Dub For All Black Man - Morpeus Players
Jah Never Fail ...

Murder - Tapper Zukie
Guilty Dub
Let's Have Some Fun - Jah Stitch
I Stand - Heptones
Double Dutch - D.A.T.C. Style
Trinity In Dub - Hi-Note Players
Cinderella In Black Version 4 - Augustus Pablo
Better Dread Version - Big Joe
Lightning Flash - Sons Of Negus

Cheating -
Earthquake
Detention O
Stepping O
In Cold Blo
We Want It
Quartie Ve
Ital Observ
Page One -
Stumbling
Lay Off -
East Africa - The Ethio
W-E-B-P-I-
Reggae Sti
Stampede -

BLACK STAR LINER

SIT DOWN! LISTEN TO THIS!

the roger eagle story • by bill sykes • foreword by elliot rashman

EMPIRE
PUBLICATIONS

First published in 2012

EMPIRE PUBLICATIONS
1 Newton Street, Manchester M1 1HW
© Bill Sykes 2012

ISBN 1901746 909 – 9781901746907

Printed in Great Britain by CPI Group (UK) Ltd, Croydon, CR0 4YY

Contents

For Steve Crook, Allan Frost, Jillian Cowie

Acknowledgements

I would firstly like to thank my family. I'd also like to thank close friends for their input and opinion and for putting up with the monomania and lack of conversational variety. I'd like to say a special thank you to all who went out of their way to provide contacts and context and for showing support, encouragement and love, and just for being brilliant. Thanks.

Thanks to: All at the Boogaloo, Connie Zeanah Atkinson Phd, Jeff Barrett, Bob Bellis, Andre Billington, Jayne Casey, Sarah Champion, Anthony Cond, John Crumpton, Kevin Cummins, Geoff Davis, Aimee Grundell, Penny Henry, Dr. Stephen Hopkins, Brian 'Planet' Jackson, Will Fulford Jones, C.P. Lee PhD, Kieran Leonard, Cathy Long, Alan J McCloughlin, John Marriott, Bruce Mitchell, Andrew Orlowski, Neil Pearson, Alex Poots, Elliot Rashman, John Robb, Ann Scanlon, Brian Smith, Barbara Sykes, Peter Sykes, Richard Thomas, the Walbourne family, Anthony H. Wilson and Pete Wylie.

Photo credits

My thanks to Maggie Backhouse, Steve Barker, Kevin Cummins, John Eagle, Martin Eagle, Dave Eaton, Jenny Hardcore, Dr Stephen Hopkins, Norman Killon, Bob Letsche, and Brian Smith.

Lastly I'd like to thank Roger Eagle for the influence he had on me, for being the maverick rock 'n' roll evangelist that he was, and for his huge influence on British culture.

Introduction

Roger Eagle is referenced in many music related books, his influence reaches far and wide. The idea of writing a book about him first struck me in 1994 when he lived a couple of doors away in the town of Whaley Bridge in Derbyshire. At this time I'd known Roger for several years, the band I played with having played at venues where he promoted gigs. He also got the band many gigs around the North-West of England, represented the band in a managerial capacity and in the way he did with many others, contributed to our musical education. So by this time I'd got to know him quite well.

In 1994 I conducted two (unpublished) interviews with him with the intention of including them in a biography - it didn't happen, as not long after conducting the interviews Roger decided he would do his own book, which was to my knowledge never finished. I presumed, given the man's intellect, great knowledge and contacts, that my efforts would be worthless. When he died in 1999 I automatically assumed that a biography of some kind would be forthcoming. By 2005 nobody had done it and I was told by a close friend to stop talking about it and do it - which is what I've attempted to do. I sincerely hope I have done the man's memory and influence a service.

AUTHOR'S FOREWORD

BANGOR CREMATORIUM

A BLEAK WELSH DAY WITH DRIZZLE,
WE'RE HERE.

THE SONGS:
Moonlight Bay - The Champs
Better Days - Carlton & The Shoes
It Keeps Raining - Fats Domino

Allan Frost and Billy Bennett are having a fag outside the building.

C.P. Lee delivers a wonderful, respectful and loving eulogy of Roger's life achievements and non-achievements starting off with a Lord Buckley monologue that paraphases William Shakespeare's Julius Caesar. Opening with the words "Hipsters, flipsters and finger popping daddies, knock me your lobes!"

I'd hung around at the back while the coffin was being carried to the grave, it's a family and close friends thing - I'm with Jillian, a close friend to Roger for many years. She'd kindly informed me of Roger's passing and invited me to stay at her cottage while the funeral was taking place. Although I am upset, my Englishness demands I show little or no emotion.

Jerry and Brenda Kenny remember me and say "hi", which is nice as there are many unknown faces, I think they'd been to the graveside, they are both tearful, Roger was an old friend and we're chatting, reminiscing, remembering rueing. Brenda says to me "Have you thrown some dirt on the coffin?", and no, no I hadn't.

The act of throwing dirt on the coffin is symbolic of the

burial itself, as if you are helping to fill in the grave, it's a laying to rest, a goodbye. It's meant to help with mourning and the idea of passing over, heavy or simple logic like that.

No, I hadn't, I was in denial, still am, I didn't want to let go, it's not as if there was unfinished business, it's like consigning someone to the dustbin. I didn't want to do that. Not until this man's story had been told.

Roger's whole skit was built on memory, the persistence thereof, and it's connection to the emotions. The Raw Emotive Power of Music. No, I won't bury him because the essence of this person and the lessons he had were important and should be passed on to other 'Heads', 'Diggers', 'Fanatics', 'Non-believers' and 'Could Be's' alike.

If you want to know how much this bloke means, ask his closest friends, not the ones who name-check him in the press. The people that knew his soul. Forget the ego heads - they were only ever there to line their own nests, with one or two exceptions. Not you by the way.

As a person Roger Eagle could come across as curmudgeonly, moody, overbearing and to some younger musicians frightening - with an accent that suggested an Oxbridge education, which was indeed the case. His mother Dorothy worked as an editor for the Oxford University Press and he was distantly related to George Bernard Shaw. At 6ft 4 and with an almost military bearing, you could quite easily imagine him screaming at squaddies on a parade ground. Once the barriers were down though, he became more personable. At the same time the educator's zeal became stronger - you were now one of his pupils and if you were receptive to the information being proffered that is now what you were. His main concern as far as his teaching was concerned was to honour the innovators, the pioneers, the unsung and unrecognised links in the rock 'n' roll chain, to better enable an overall understanding, a call to go to the source - the wellspring of influence.

For all his bluff and bluster, chiding and cajoling, bullying and encouraging, Roger Eagle was a very sensitive and private person, and because of the nature of his work as he got older he didn't let many people in to his personal world. Having spent years in the music industry and being exposed to games and get rich quick schemes, being taken advantage of by the trickster, the card sharp, the snake oil salesmen, the agents, the managers, the bands even. What could guarantee you an audience would be a genuine interest and love of music. A point that may not have come through in the writing of this book is how the appreciation of a flat, black piece of plastic with a spiral groove cut into it, could so inspire somebody. It was a way of life, a reason, an inspiration a... serious, dedicated appreciation of the roots of modern rock and pop music that seems to be a lost art.

He also had in his personality a definite element of the mother figure about him. His audience or the people that listened were his students. He wanted their education - be it life decisions, politics, art or his precious music, to have come from the source. He didn't want his pupils to be spoilt though - they had to work for it - nothing came on a plate.

To Roger music was foremost, his legendary record collection was in some ways also his children. He was never the sort of person to settle into a cosy domestic situation; his relationships were always rather short lived and with him being a sensitive and very private person it would seem he got hurt by people more ruthless than himself. This, I believe, is one of the major reasons he threw himself so wholeheartedly into the world of rock 'n' roll. It informed him as a person. It meant every thing to him. In conversation the way he'd describe a song was in the same way a child might; sheer joy, belief and an almost painful calling to play the tunes to others - having experienced some kind of religious reverie that had to be passed on - so that others could experience these tunes and their magical powers. Every track would have a story, right down to the minutiae. Every story told with a fanatic's passion, an understanding of every musician on the record, the producer of the song and personal details of the artist and their relativity to the story of rock 'n' roll. This man was, I believe, a true rock 'n' roll evangelist – there is nobody alive like him. An amalgam of Guy Stevens, John Peel, Bernie Rhodes, Harvey Goldsmith, Hunter S. Thompson and even a touch of John Cleese.

As for me – I'm just another of his pupils, we're dotted around all over the place, we love music, real music. We have studied at the school of Roger Eagle. Although in the interviews that I conducted I'm aware of the fact that it is easy to mythologise people, especially people who have meant a lot to us, we all have our own experiences and stories, and they are just as relevant and important as the next person's.

Another point that may not have come across in this book was Roger's sense of humour. Very English in essence, incongruous, sometimes sardonic, informed initially by The Goons, the Cambridge Footlights Review and Monty Python but also the more challenging and less appreciated humour of Lord Buckley, Lenny Bruce and certainly in the 1970's Richard Prior. I can remember being round at his house in Whaley Bridge – probably high, listening to dub or some obscure funk, rockabilly or whatever he had decided I needed to hear, and recall him leaning in and saying conspiratorially "It's all about shagging you know, Sykes." And you don't even have to think about it much, that is exactly what it's all about.

The tools of this master craftsman have been locked away with the secrets of the ages, there are only a handful of people alive skilled enough to use them.

FORWARD (sic)

An Imaginary Meeting With Roger Eagle
Inspired By a Photograph Taken By Mr Kevin Cummins

Nightclubs are otherworldly places during the day. Dark, empty, cool and quiet, the smell of disinfectant hangs in the air. The space is small, and at the edge of the gloaming, a solitary overhead mini spot is skewed to illuminate a table. There he sits, a pack of Reno Menthols and a Zippo in one hand, an almost finished cigarette in the other. One foot is frenetically marking some dark, dynamic rhythm booming out of the mighty internal Wurlitzer in his mind.

Roger Eagle briefly stands and barks, "Ah there you are!" A giant of a man.

He has the demeanor of an aged Teddy Boy Spiv and the stature and tone of a Grenadier Guardsman.

On the table there is a drained coffee cup and a large, half filled ashtray.

I spy a white shopping bag at his side, stuffed with Vinyl. Roger notices my curiosity.

"Lost Tubby's! Music Of the Bloody Spheres! Rare as Hell!"

"Fantastic! can you make me a copy?"

Roger snorts dismissively; request denied.

He reaches into his jacket pocket, pulls out a cassette and slides it over.

"You need some Crazy Rockabilly"

My heart does small skips. Eagle compilation tapes are treasures, Holy musical relics; fuck the format.

Without taking his eyes off me, Roger flips the Zippo, lights another menthol, snaps the lid shut.

"Well?"

"You mean The Book"

"Of course I mean The Bloody Book"

"It's great. Full of honest, thoughtful insights and recollections from friends and associates. It captures our love and respect for you and the fucking enormous effect and influence you have had on so many. Like it or not there is a special place in the hearts of all those you ordered, bullied, galvanised and enthused to Love Music Forever, especially Black Music"

Roger shifts uneasily in his chair and almost looks bashful, but not quite,

"Sounds suspiciously sentimental to me"

"Not particularly, but it is true and faithful to you in the best ways possible"

"So Bill Sykes 'Laid it down', as Buckley would say"

"And it stayed down. It's a labour of love, respect and devotion, with quite a bit of doggedness thrown in"

The X-Ray stare again.

"No muckraking or prying?"

"Jesus, Roger. You hid all your secrets and intimacies so well that we still don't know who the fuck you really are and what went on in most of your life"

"Bloody good show then. Always keep 'em guessing". He lets out one of his hissing sniggers.

I stand to leave. We don't hug or shake hands.

"Will I see you again"

"Don't bank on it"

"What if I manage to find a little piece of black hash?"

Roger harrumphs, "Well then, anything is possible."

Descending towards the exit, I shout back into the twilight,

"Stay Frosty Rog!"

"Dig infinity!" he commands finally.

I then trip, fall down the last few steps, and crash through the fire doors. I land awkwardly on my knees outside the club, blinded by sunlight.

Elliot Rashman
June 2012

1 - Roger Charles Eagle

Roger Charles Eagle was born on the 15th July 1942 at the Radcliffe Infirmary Oxford, to Dorothy and Charles Eagle. Martin is Roger Eagle's younger brother by 18 months. Martin and Roger could easily be described as complete opposites - in personal philosophies, political leanings and in artistic and musical tastes. It seems they diverged a short while after Martin was involved in a terrible life threatening accident in 1954. Martin was educated at the prestigious Magdelene College School in Oxford as was Roger. Martin would go on to be employed in the Aeronautical industry for many years. He now resides in County Cork in the South West of Ireland.

Martin Eagle: My Great Grandmother's name was Emily Carrol (nee Shaw) she had a family nickname of 'Fippy'. Her Mother, my Great Great Grandmother, was a first cousin of George Bernard Shaw. I don't think Roger showed the slightest interest in where he came from.

My father did all sorts of things. When he met my mother, or when my mother met him, she drove an old Riley car which I think was pre-war and not working very well. So she took it to this garage, and there was my Father, he worked on it and they sort of got to know each other. She respected him because he knew what he was doing. When my mother met my father he was a Petty Officer, She must have been in her late twenties, and she married my father. Although my father was very good with machines and objects like that he tended to treat people as objects rather. There's a name for it, have you heard of Asperger's syndrome?

Roger Eagle: I lived in Oxford until I left school, I lived in the country a bit during the war, that was in Charlbury.

My father flew Catalinas, he was in the Fleet Air Arm. I don't know if he was a pilot, I know he was in Catalinas, because there were photographs of them all over the place. I seem to remember some 303 machine gun clips holding together a photograph of myself as a baby, they seem to have disappeared.

I remember seeing the vapour trails, the con trails of the fighter planes, and everybody used to say "Is it one of ours or is it one of theirs?" It's a very early, very dim memory but it's there. I suppose at three years old you're just about able to remember a few things aren't you? A lot of tanks in the streets, the country lanes jammed up with boxes of ammunition, a lot of half tracks and stuff.

Martin Eagle: My father was an Inspector at the De Havilland Aircraft company. He had very strict standards in things and of course nothing that Roger and I did ever came up to his expectations. We didn't love him and he didn't love us, he didn't show any affection, and poor old Mum was caught in the middle. Mum divorced him shortly afterwards.

Elliot Rashman: The last time I saw Roger was when he came into the Blood & Fire office in Manchester, and he was already dying, and we knew that, and he was talking about, trying to explain where it all came from; this love of dynamic, because that's what it was about, top and bottom, not middle. He claimed it was when he was a little kid, I think in Oxford, a baby in a pram. In those days you were on your back looking up, yeah, and it was the RAF planes.

He said, "That was it! The noise of the planes! That determined my life. I had to have that noise. I had to have that sound, that dynamism."

I said, "Roger you were a fucking baby!"

He said, "I know, but from that moment on, I had to have that sound!"

Martin Eagle: I was run over by a large American Air Force lorry when I was 10. I was squashed in November 1954 when the lorry took a wrong turning. I'd come home from school to work on a little model aeroplane I was making. If I hadn't come home that particular day I wouldn't have been hit by this lorry. Things might have turned out completely differently.

Roger Eagle: Martin's accident happened in 1954, he was behind an American Air Force truck, the Queen Mary they used to call it, the one with a lot of wheels on the back. It was carrying a B47 jet engine at the time and it had stopped just past a roundabout. He was on his bike just immediately behind it and it was revving up, so he obviously thought it was going to go forwards and it came back on top of him. It wasn't until the driver felt the bump that he stopped and fainted immediately. His name was Flight Sergeant Gary Thacker and it turned out he was an alcoholic. In the long run my mother had to look after him more than anything else.

Martin Eagle: It's very sad because shortly after we visited the Air Force base the lorry driver who squashed me reversing came round to the house to apologise to my father, and my father hit him in the face, and he left. That was one of the things that turned me against my father.

Roger Eagle: Martin had most of his left arm destroyed, he was very badly smashed up, every rib was broken, he very nearly died. But off the back of that we went off to Brize Norton Air Force base and messed about – going mad with the yanks. I was probably what, 11 and a half, 12, they were letting us handle their machine guns and going in the plane cockpits, swivelling around the twin 50 calibre battle controls. They invited us up and he was made Colonel for the day and he had to take the salute or something like that. They were very generous, they had a whip round for him, it was near Christmas and he got a couple of cigar boxes full of money sent to him. He also got quite a lot of compensation, which over the years I've done my best to borrow off him.

Martin Eagle: I think Roger rather resented all the attention I was getting. It was most extraordinary, they made me honorary base Commander at RAF Brize Norton, they gave me a hat and there are photos of me being saluted. The Americans were very generous, they passed the hat round almost literally, they collected £139, I can remember counting it out on my mother's bedroom floor, I was absolutely awestruck, I'd never seen more than about threepence a week before that. On the strength of the money that was collected we went on holiday to Waterville the following year, that was the start of the connection with Ireland.

It wasn't long after the accident that he and I diverged, it's curious how we diverged, it happened around 1955. All sorts of things can bring about things like that, he went his way and I went mine. Also when I was squashed I was given £3000 as compensation, so Roger knew there was a ready supply of money to be tapped and I'm afraid that's what he did.

Roger Eagle: We're all totally different really, Martin's the scientific one, he hated me when rock 'n' roll started, I lost him as a friend. There's no doubt about it, rock 'n' roll split families back then in the mid fifties. He thought rock 'n' roll was the most horrendous thing he'd ever heard, for me it was salvation. Martin is very much a classical man. The opposite you see, this is what happens in families; brothers and sisters get split apart in their teens because they diverge sharply in their tastes. When you're in your teens a year or two makes a lot of difference, a couple of years is a huge gap. When you're in your twenties it's hardly any gap at all but when you're in your early teens, if you're born eighteen months apart, as we were, it does make a huge difference. John is ten years younger than me, Martin is eighteen months.

Martin Eagle: My father used to hit us, I remember Roger called him 'The Heap', this came from an American horror comic, one of the characters is called 'The Heap'. It was never really happy families, poor old mum. In fact mum was earning her living because my father was never able to contribute properly. She became an editor of the Oxford University Press. She was certainly working at the University Press in 1954, she would cycle to work everyday. My mother also worked at a hostel for midwives. At the time we lived in this large house on Abingdon Road, south of Oxford where all these nurses stayed who were training to be midwives. So when my parents wanted to go out somewhere there were always plenty of babysitters.

There were large parts of my early childhood when my father wasn't around at all, I never got to know him really, there was no love or affection, no sorting out problems together or that sort of thing. I suppose my father was the catalyst that made Roger and I different. Because I was younger I was brow beaten into the fact that you've got to do things properly, Roger rebelled against it. He wouldn't know how to put a screw into a wall or anything like that.

Roger was an arch scrounger, it's sad, he tried to get money out of everybody, he tried to get money out of my aunt, my mother's sister. With me, at first it was a loan in the hundreds, then it was a loan in the thousands. Roger always liked to think of himself as an action man, wanting everything now, don't worry about the details. Whereas I am a quiet, careful chap. If you screw an aeroplane together badly it falls apart in the sky and that's wrong. Roger didn't really care much for attention to detail.

Mrs Dorothy Eagle was educated at Central Newcastle High School and Edgbaston Church of England College. She read Sociology at Bedford College, London and worked as an Almoner in Oxford and at Ruskin College when it was used as a maternity hospital during the war. After working at the Clarendon Press as a part-time assistant, she worked as a literary lexicographer for the Oxford University Press, co-editing many official Oxford reference books including the Oxford Literary Guide to the British Isles, the Concise Oxford Dictionary of English Literature, the Oxford Companion to the Literature of Wales, and the Oxford Literary Guide to Great Britain and Ireland – amongst many others. Very highly regarded in her field for her meticulous attention to detail and an obsession with factual and stylistic correctness, she passed away in January 1990.

2 - Radio, Trad and early Rock 'n' roll

Martin Eagle: The Dragon school is a very highly regarded prep school in Oxford, Roger went there first. I remember I was struggling with Latin and my mother said, "It's costing ten shillings a day to keep you at the Dragon school," I thought that's more than I get for Christmas present money in a whole year. It wasn't until after I'd left that I learnt my Aunt had paid for Roger and me to attend the school, each for 5 years, that's an awful lot of money. She was a quiet person, she didn't trumpet her achievements. My Aunt Mary, mum's sister, lived in London, she was the only relative we had in London, Roger had a great regard for Mary and I think Mary regarded Roger as a protégé, kind of a son she never had, because Mary never married. Mary was brilliant; a genius, she was an entrepreneur and everything. She was one of the very first HMI's, a school's inspector. My Grandfather was a school's inspector as well.

The Dragon school was founded in 1877 by a committee of Oxford dons, the original remit being to provide a high standard of academic grounding and pastoral care to the children of professors of the University of Oxford. To give an idea of the kind of schooling Roger received, former pupils or 'Old Dragons' include former Poet Laureate Sir John Betjeman, novelist Nevil Shute, former Labour party leader the Rt. Hon. Hugh Gaitskill and playwright, barrister and novelist Sir John Mortimer.

Martin Eagle: I think in 1957 Roger was invited to go and stay in France, that was his first visit with Mary. Unfortunately Roger had this weakness for asking people for money, something

I would never do. He asked for a loan from Mary, and she thought 'well if you want something you have to earn it,' it was a strong ethic.

Roger Eagle: I lived in London before I left school, we'd go to London every so often. We'd get on the train, it was only 40 minutes away. I stayed in London on a houseboat for a few months. I would go to all-nighters in London in the late fifties at Ken Colyer's club and the Scene Club, to see traditional jazz bands more than anything else. I didn't go to the Scene Club when it was Cy Laurie's club in Ham Yard, Soho. That was a famous club that was open all night. It was a fifties thing to just to stay out all night and just go fuck it. There wasn't an awful lot to see, we'd go down to Eel Pie Island a bit but it was just like the very dawn of it all.

Brian Smith: The only tale that he ever told from when he was in Oxford, was from having been at a party which evidently got a bit wild. There was a load of lads and some local girl who gave her favours to a whole bunch of them. She turned out to be underage and I think they actually ended up in court for it. He always considered himself to be very, very lucky not to have gone down for it. Whether it got into court, or whether they were all cautioned I'm not sure. They were certainly charged and it certainly got as far as them being interviewed. I think it's possibly that there were so many of them, there was no suggestion of rape or anything like that. Obviously they didn't take as serious a view as they might have done. That is the only story he ever told of his youth.

Roger Eagle: The first musical thing I remember was the mambo, as I recall it in the early fifties, like the big dance was the mambo. I've got a Picture Post somewhere, dancers throwing each other in the air. I think one of the first records I ever bought was 'The Stone Age Mambo' by The Ivor and Basil Kirchin Band. It was like latin, a heavy sort of latin rhythm. "Hot potato mambo, my baby told me to go, scrambo!" you know that kind of stuff.

"My baby dropped me boing, like a hot potato, when she found, I don't know, how to do the mambo". Then there was 'Mambo Italiano'. But the first major influence on me was Alan Freed on American Forces Network Frankfurt.

The Ivor and Basil Kirchin Band released 'Stone age Mambo' in 1955 on the Parlophone label. A British based big band calling itself the 'Biggest Little Band In The World', playing hotted up mambo's. They appeared on TV wearing animal skins for the performance of 'Stone Age Mambo'.

Roger Eagle: Alan Freed was the man. That's where you heard your Chuck Berry, LaVern Baker and everybody else. Way before it came out over here. He was good. Then there was Gus Goodwin, who no-one's ever mentioned since, which I think is a shame because Gus Goodwin was a very powerful DJ on Radio Luxembourg. He used to spin around on his stool. He would open his show with 'Basin Street Blues' by Louis Armstrong, with the incredible Gene Krupa drum break that starts it. A real battering drum solo started the show, and then he would play every rock 'n' roll record he could lay his hands on, yelling and shouting and things like that. He was the only British equivalent of any American DJ, he seems to have completely faded from everybody's memory.

Martin Eagle: Roger was the tallest chap in school, Magdalen College school, and he seemed to have different kinds of friends, more tearaway types. There was one chap called Marcus Champ, he always had his hair slicked back in a DA style and I think he rode a Ducatti. At 16 you get your first Motorbike, and it's street cred business, you've got to have a decent motorbike. Roger got one eventually. In fact Roger had a bad crash near Weston-on-the-Green, I don't think he was terribly hurt, it upset mum but it didn't stop him getting another bigger motorbike. The old one remained in a heap in the garden getting covered in weeds and grass.

Tommy Smith originally met Roger Eagle in the late 1980's, here he tells of a story told to him by Roger about one of the first tunes to have an effect on his taste in later years.

Tommy Smith: As far as I'm aware the first song that got him into rock 'n' roll was 'Bad Penny Blues' by Humphrey Littleton, he may have told everybody a different record but that's what he told me. It's a great record, kind of the end of trad, more your jazz R&B if you like.

The first recognised all-nighters with music and dancing in Britain in the modern era were held at Cy Laurie's club in Ham Yard on the Junction of Great Windmill Street and Archer Street in London's Soho. Opened in 1951, it was a basement club with a hardwood floor, the decor would have been rather drab, the toilet facilities likewise. The bar would serve soft drinks and crisps to an art student clientele dressed in cheapish beat fashions. The music played at this club and others such as the Eel Pie Island Hotel came to be known as traditional or trad jazz. By 1955 these 'Raves', as they were then known, were frequented by teenagers or a younger crowd and trad was considered to be a relatively new phenomenon at the time.

In 1954, trumpeter Ken Colyer launched a successful jazz club at 10-11 Great Newport Street, which had originally opened in May 1951 as Studio 51. Another major club in London catering for trad jazzers was the 100 Club on Oxford Street. The music played in these clubs would have been romanticised British versions of a New Orleans style of music from decades earlier, a retro genre where artists such as Louis Armstrong, King Oliver, Fats Waller and singers such as Bessie Smith were idolised. The prime movers were Chris Barber, Kenny Ball, Ken Colyer, Humphrey Lyttelton, Acker Bilk and George Melly.

Out of the trad jazz movement came another offshoot, the British version of rock 'n' roll, a mixture of folk, blues and trad jazz which came to be known as skiffle. With an emphasis on faster rhythms, a do-it-yourself ethic and a younger, more rebellious attitude, which would pave the way for the American rock 'n' roll explosion proper. The trumpet player Ken Colyer was extremely influential in bringing skiffle to the attention of the British public. Within his trad based band he would perform a set of American folk inspired songs whilst playing guitar, with the proviso that he was educating the audiences to the roots of jazz.

From playing banjo with the Ken Colyer band to singing with The Chris Barber Band, Lonnie Donnegan became extremely successful with a string of chart-topping tunes with his version of the skiffle genre. He, probably more than anyone, came to define the style. As well as providing a launchpad for The Beatles in the guise of The Quarrymen, skiffle was the precursor of the British R&B and beat boom and many of the artists who later went on to find success started their musical careers in skiffle bands.

It also gave people who had witnessed this music the idea that anybody could do it, in that it had energy, it was exciting, and anybody, with a bit of practice, could learn to play the guitar in that particular style; you didn't have to be classically trained and probably more to the point the concept and idea of appearing cool in and amongst one's peer group was born, at least as far as youth and the working classes were concerned. Also the possibility of earning a living while doing something which is essentially enjoyable must have been, and indeed still is, enormously appealing.

Roger Eagle: I remember going to London listening to jukeboxes, like the one in The Freight Train, which was a coffee bar run by Chas McDevitt and Shirley Douglas, also the 2 I's, which was like the rock 'n' roll place, where all the hard cases used to hang out. I wasn't particularly into skiffle, it was alright, it was

American based of course. It was all based on Woody Guthrie and Leadbelly. The Vipers were ok, there were one or two that were good. It was all a bit home made. It was alright, happy-go-lucky sort of stuff.

The advent of rock 'n' roll had a radical social and cultural influence on the whole of British society, the reverberations of which are still being felt today. Roger had many interesting, well-informed ideas and opinions on the phenomenon, which ultimately played a large part in moulding his interest in music and the entertainment industry. The fact that he experienced and participated in these cultural changes makes his opinions all the more interesting. In cinemas all over the UK American rock 'n' roll was making an impact and the public's reaction ranged from fear and loathing to fanatical appreciation.

Roger Eagle: You couldn't see the 'Wild One', you weren't allowed to. I don't recall it being on release at all, we'd heard about it. The films that did the damage were 'Rock Around the Clock', 'The Girl Can't Help It', 'Rock, Rock Rock', 'Mr Rock 'n' roll', 'DJ Jamboree', stuff like that. Those were the ones that did the damage, because for the very first time you could see and hear this incredibly powerful music. If you can imagine what it's like in a cinema with rock 'n' roll being played through a cinema sound system, it was extremely exciting, because there's a huge bass resonance there.

With Bill Haley and the Comets, archaic as they are seen by a lot of people, they had an enormous impact because of the very powerful dance beat, which is no different, the basic principle that's going on throughout most of it. It's just that enormously powerful backbeat, which is the basic thing of it all, it's not the same beat, it's the same principle. This is what will move a lot of people in a big building, all of a like mind. That's what it does, because there's nothing like a lot of people jumping up and down to the same kind of music.

It's not tribalism, well it is in a sense. It's like the DJ's used to say in the States, the people are pushing against it, it's just the beat, you can see it on those old movie clips. It's the beat, it's the beat and that's right, the excitement and it was very powerful. Nobody thought it was going to last, they thought it was an abberation. I saw it as, I don't know what I saw it as, but I didn't think it was gonna fade away, because the effect was so dramatic.

Martin Eagle: Roger had a holiday job on a building site and because that was quite a formative thing for him he took some photographs. There was a slum area called St. Ebbs in Oxford, southwest of the centre and it was completely raised to the ground and these new buildings were put up. Roger got a job humping blocks and cement; labouring. I think that helped reinforce Roger's worldview, he worked alongside people who were quite left-wing and anti-establishment.

Roger Eagle: One of the first rock 'n' roll records I heard and we didn't get them out in the right sequence in this country, we got them all arse about face, was probably 'Maybelline' by Chuck Berry. I was just a rock 'n' roll fan until I heard Little Richard, then I knew I was a fan and I had to have everything the man ever did, Little Richard was the cornerstone for the whole thing, this was 1955/56. Then I heard Ray Charles, the 'In Person' and 'Live At Newport' LP's from around 1958/59 – they really converted me. Rock 'n' roll died in 1958. Ray Charles was the first to see the possibilities of mixing different types of music. He mixed rock 'n' roll, R&B, jazz and even country. There were other releases from that time that were a great influence. Fats Domino, a lot of R&B releases on London Records, Gary US Bonds' 'New Orleans' had an enormous sound for the time. Arthur Alexander, LaVern Baker. Chuck Willis' 'The Sultan of Stroll' that was a very, very important LP, I love Chuck Willis.

Martin Eagle: Roger's music is essentially a kind of protest music isn't it?

By 1954, two distinct jazz scenes had developed in London's West End, the trad scene already discussed and the modern jazz scene. One point that cannot be understated in regard to the fifties British jazz scene is the importance of clothes and fashion as a way of identifying oneself. The kids who were into trad jazz dressed down with a kind of knowing shabbiness; heavy sweaters, duffle coats, sandals and baggy corduroy trousers. Quite drab on the whole, they became known as beatniks or beats, many being political activists. Membership of CND was almost compulsory, the total opposite to the modernists. Modern jazzers were the early incarnation of the 1960's mod movement; style and attention to detail were the bywords of this new scene. The London-based jazz musicians of the time would copy the dress styles of the visiting American musicians, this would also influence the fans and followers of the modern jazz style.

The term 'Modernist' was first used by *Melody Maker* to describe the people that frequented modern jazz clubs such as The Flamingo. Situated downstairs from the Whisky A Go-Go on Wardour Street in London's Soho, it first opened in 1958 and became synonymous with the rise of the early mod movement.

The sounds the early modernists sought out were by artists such as Tubby Hayes, The Modern Jazz Quartet, Dave Brubeck, Miles Davis, Mose Allison, Jimmy Smith, Jimmy McGriff and the rhythm and blues of Ray Charles.

Another important factor in the progression of the later British mod and rhythm and blues scene were the musicians Cyril Davis and Alexis Korner. In 1956 they opened The Blues & Barrelhouse Club, the first dedicated British blues venue, opened specifically to promote black American music. Located on the first floor of the Roadhouse pub on Wardour Street, where Cyril Davis had earlier run a club called The London Skiffle Centre, it was by all accounts a modest affair but it hosted the debut of England's first proper blues band – Alexis Korner's Breakdown Group, who later became Blues Incorporated. From 1958-60 this early incarnation of Blues Incorporated would build up a following touring London's environs, then head back to the club to play into the early hours. The reputation the club gained earned them visits from respected American blues musicians such as Big Bill Broonzy and Otis Spann.

The club met its demise after Davies & Korner purchased a 10-Watt guitar amplifier in order to emulate the guitar styles of Muddy Waters and Elmore James. Apart from upsetting the purists who attended the club, it upset the landlord who sacked them for being too loud. The Blues And Barrelhouse was a big influence on the next generation of British R&B musicians but by 1960-61 mainstream acceptance was still elusive.

Roger Eagle: The fifties and sixties were plagued with cover acts; there'd be a black American original and there'd be some white boy. I mean Pat Boone for God's sake! There's this famous story about him on TV and he's singing Little Richard songs, 'Long Tall Sally' and stuff and he doesn't have the slightest idea what the lyrics are about. He just sings them as if he's in a Sunday school choir that's turned up to sing a couple of pop songs. Georgie Gibbs recorded some black stuff, she was a white singer, there's a whole stack of 'em, Bill Haley did 'Shake Rattle & Roll', Big Joe Turner stuff. The person who was interesting was Elvis, because he totally warped black and white music into his own thing, now that is interesting.

John Eagle: I think Roger left home in about 1959/60, so I must have known him for the first 6 years or so.

Martin Eagle: Roger disliked my father a little bit more than me, I was afraid of him. Mum divorced him and that must have been around 1957/58. Then Roger left home in about 1959.

Roger Eagle: It's the music and the eras, most people who know me don't know the first part. They talk about The Wheel, or they talk about The Village, or they talk about The Stadium or they talk about Eric's or they talk about The International. But what they don't know about is what actually set it all off, which was the fifties. Because it was about freedom and independence. I mean I was riding a big motorbike at the earliest opportunity. As soon as I was old enough I bought a 350 Royal Enfield, and I was off, I used to go down to Cornwall, over to London, wherever, and it was rock 'n' roll you see, that was the thing.

National Service ended in the UK in November 1960. If Roger was born in 1942 he would have reached the age of eighteen in July of that year, making him eligible for service for 4 months. His whereabouts at this time don't seem easily traceable, he seems to have already left home by the time his parents had divorced in 1959, the next definite date that can be traced is 1962 when he arrived in Manchester with a friend on his motorbike.

Having just missed National Service, Roger would have been part of a completely new generation of young people, unburdened of their duty to Queen and country, freed from rationing and austerity and staring into a new optimism. Britain's cultural and social climate was now being very much informed by what was happening in the United States. This was starting to be felt at creative grassroots levels with musicians beginning to write their own material rather than allowing established songwriters to do it for them. Roger Eagle and young men and women of his generation and outlook were about to start moulding British culture and society to suit themselves.

3 - The Brazennose Street Twisted Wheel club

The British music scene in 1962 was still pretty much ruled by Tin Pan Alley; songwriters churning out songs to be recorded by three or four different artists. Beat bands were the order of the day and many of the groups popular at this time were former skiffle groups. If you wanted to be successful as a musician it was imperative that you moved to London.

The Folk scene was in a boom period, or going through a revival, and any night of the week you could catch up and coming singer songwriters in London's Soho at venues such as Les Cousins and the Blues & Barrelhouse club – a Manchester equivalent being perhaps the Chorlton Folk and Irish club.

On the British Folk scene the influence of black American folk/blues music could be felt, and artists such as Big Bill Broonzy, Leadbelly, Woody Guthrie and Josh White were having a big impact on young folk musicians. By the early sixties, consciously politicised lyrics in folk performance were becoming common in the US, Bob Dylan being a prime example, this political awareness was also starting to influence a generation of songwriters in the UK.

The BBC, ever the innovative presence on the radio, had nothing to offer the youth of the country except the 'Light Programme'. To the BBC the concept of 'The Teenager' and a specific market for that demographic was a new concept. The youth market was catered for by pirate radio stations such as Radio Caroline, Radio London and the ubiquitous Radio Luxembourg. It was 1967 before the BBC deigned to cater to the demand for youth radio – Radio One was launched because of the threat from pirate radio.

Guy Stevens was the extremely influential R&B and rock 'n' roll fanatic who began DJing at The Scene club at Ham Yard off Great Windmill Street, Soho in May 1963, in the same venue that Cy Laurie's club had been the trad jazz epicentre in the 1950's. Also DJing at the Scene club was James 'Doctor Soul' Hamilton who, with the help of Stevens, was responsible for breaking many great records. This pair were the first British club DJs to play imported R&B and soul music.

The Scene club became the mod club in London. So much so, that people would travel from all over the country, and even Europe, for Stevens' Monday night sessions. Stevens celebrated black American music in a way, and with a fervour, that had not been witnessed before in Britain, and he wasn't in the least bit precious about his musical knowledge. With the success of The Scene club, along with his enthusiasm for rock 'n' roll, R&B, ska, jazz and soul he drew a large number of devotees. If you were out in London looking for black R&B in 1963/64, you would be heading for The Scene club. Anybody and everybody who liked black music at the time would go to check Guy Stevens' club out; from The Rolling Stones, The Beatles, Eric Clapton and The Spencer Davis Group to bands such as The Who, The Animals and The Small Faces who used his extensive knowledge and record collection as a source of material and inspiration. The Scene club was so influential that at one point Atlantic Records and Tamla Motown would send records over for him to sample and play.

Guy Stevens' knowledge of R&B and DJing secured him the job of running the UK division of the Sue record label for Chris Blackwell of Island records in April 1964. He used the label to release obscure American singles not only from the US Sue group but also with and for smaller independent labels such as Kent, V-Tone, Fury, Ace and some of the larger ones. He also advised Pye

International about the records they should release from their deal with the legendary US Chess/Checker label. It was with Guy Stevens' patronage that Chuck Berry first played in the UK. He also went on to produce records for Free, Mott the Hoople and The Clash.

The problem, if you could call it a problem, with the Scene club was that the clientele became very fashion-oriented, and consequently very cliquey but then again the whole modernist movement was about being separate, better, constantly evolving, elitist even. You wouldn't spend time there if you weren't part of the mod scene. The whole mod world revolved around Ham Yard and Soho, for a short while…

Roger Eagle: Before moving to Manchester I went to The Scene club in London's Soho, which Guy Stevens ran. It was the first sort of R&B club to take it away from live gigs and the kind of thing that Alexis Korner and everybody were doing. He was the first guy to turn it into a record thing really.

Guy Stevens' influence on the British music scene and more specifically the rhythm and blues scene in Britain, as Roger suggests, really cannot be underestimated. His Monday night sessions at the Scene were popular, plus his love of and enthusiasm for black American music must have been inspiring to many young music fans in the UK.

Martin Eagle: Roger had a series of motorbikes, he got one motorbike then he got a bigger one and eventually he took off up to Manchester and that was the last we heard from him for a long time.

Roger Eagle: I moved to Manchester in 1962. I suppose I didn't have anything to do after I left school, and my mate Ray Dodgson said he'd buy my motorbike off me. So I drove it up, with him on pillion. He was going to university in Manchester and I'd no idea, I just thought I'd see a different city, that's all. I'd never been north, apart from Newcastle-upon-Tyne – so I just thought I'd take a look at Manchester because he was going there. I started kipping on floors and stuff and got a job at Belle Vue, clearing tables. I also got another job at Kellogg's as a quality control line inspector.

Judy Williams: I think when this new music was filtering through, there wasn't anywhere to kind of do anything with it in Oxford. So he got on that bike and buggered off in search of something and it had to be less comfortable than that Oxford life. That, in a way, was uncomfortable for him, to be allowed to be liberal and free, with all those challenges at that period in time, it was quite risky to do that. You weren't supposed to do that. He said he stopped in a place called Manchester and it happened to be raining, and he thought 'This is the right place'.

Roger Eagle: I got to see the Kinks, the Beatles, Bo Diddley whoever was around really. I'd go to the Oasis off Albert Square, the Jungfrau which was a bit further north of the centre, near Fennel Street I think, (24-36 Cathedral Street at the back of Manchester Cathedral) and the Three Coins, which was a club on Fountain Street, which is where I saw the Beatles. (The Beatles played The Three Coins on Fountain Street in Manchester on January 27th 1963). It was just after 'Please Please Me' came out and there was a real buzz about them, we had to get down there about 5 o'clock in the afternoon. At the time all the poppier groups were around, you know Brian Poole and the Tremeloes, that kind of thing. They weren't licensed these places though, they were just coffee bars but it was still pretty cheap to go in.

As the beat band scene declined, American rhythm and blues became popular in the UK and a host of home grown bands started to appear. Initially copying their American heroes, these bands established a scene in the South-East of England. Clubs such as the Crawdaddy in Richmond hosted bands such as the

Rolling Stones, Zoot Money, Graham Bond and The Yardbirds. London clubs such as the Marquee, The 100 club and the Flamingo put on acts such as The Who, John Mayall's Bluesbreakers, Georgie Fame, Chris Farlowe, Geno Washington and The Animals - all influenced by American rhythm and blues.

Although not a huge fan of homegrown British R&B, it must have been inspiring for Eagle to observe black American music having such a huge influence on the popular music being made by artists in his native land and of course he formed opinions on them and went to gigs by the bands he considered interesting.

Roger Eagle: The best band by far from over here were 'Them', when they did 'Baby Please Don't Go' they really turned it into something different. That was Van Morrison's secret, he could do stuff and make it sound totally individual. They were part of a long tradition of very good bands from Ireland. I've nothing but the greatest respect for Irish bands on the whole. They are very good to work with, very professional, never had the slightest trouble with any Irish band I ever worked with.

Locally The Hollies were making some noise, but people round town were saying that Bobby Elliot, the drummer, was the main man in the band. The Hollies were like lightweight pop. In fact I had a mild sort of row with one of them, I can't remember which one, about their cover of 'Searching' which was their 2nd record (The Hollies version of 'Searching' was released in August 1963 and reached No 12 in the UK Charts). I thought it was a load of crap, and I told him, I said, "Why don't you do your own stuff?" I don't know if it was Allan Clarke, I'm not sure which one it was. He said what they all say, which is "Yeah we get to do our own stuff but the record company wanted us to do this," which is what they all say when you catch 'em out.

If you're going to criticize there's got to be a point to your criticism. You can't just say that was a load of shite then walk away. You've got to say what they may not like you to say, but they go away and think about it afterwards. I didn't do it for any particular reason, I didn't go up to him. I was sitting at a coffee bar table and he was sitting opposite me, and I said "look this 'Searching', it's not good enough you know. The original was by the Coasters, I mean you can't improve on the original, or Alvin Robinson's version which is even deeper and rougher, well heavy, that's a real black rock 'n' roll record of the highest quality. What's the point in covering it in a sort of silly lightweight pop kind of way. It's already been done to perfection."

Roger Fairhurst was a friend and fellow R&B enthusiast for approximately three years. Here he explains the circumstances under which they came to meet and how he and his friend from Bolton, Mike Bocock, taught Roger how to import rhythm and blues records from the U.S.A.

Roger Fairhurst: There was a weekly music magazine called *Disc* in the early 60's, and it was full of stuff like Herman's Hermits. I only used to buy it for the reviews because occasionally real music came in. I wrote a letter to the magazine because I was a bit pissed off with what was in it, you know these perfumed tossers they had on the television. I said, "People like Bo Diddley and Chuck Berry write their own songs, if some of the people featured in your magazine could write their own songs, rather than stealing other people's, then maybe they'd be a bit more interesting to listen to."

Anyway they printed this letter for some reason, they must have been short that week, and strangely enough I got a reply from Roger, who I'd never heard of or met and who lived in Manchester at the time. He wrote to them and they passed his letter on to me, I wrote to him and we ended up corresponding. He suggested we meet up in Manchester and I said "Ok". So we met at Barry's Record Rendezvous and he told me what records he had and I told him some of the stuff I had.

He said "How did you get hold of them?" I told him that a

friend of mine, Mike Bocock, worked in a bank and I used to go and buy dollars from him. I would send dollar notes to Chess Records in the U.S. and they would send me a record. If you simply sent a dollar note to Chess or others we dealt with such as Duke and Peacock they'd send a record back. Chess actually sent me their 1960 catalogue, which I still have, it's the size of a small birthday card. There's 4 LP's, 4 EP's and the rest are singles, because that was their market. Black music was for black people, to them black people didn't have enough money to buy LP's, they bought singles. So there's a lot of social stuff comes into this.

So I'd visit his flat on Wilbraham Road in Chorlton, we'd play music and we got on very well and we got this bee in our bonnets about the fact that there was nowhere you could listen to this stuff, nobody played it. All the clubs, of which there were dozens and dozens in Manchester at the time, were all playing Cliff Richard type beat/pop stuff. The Beatles had started by then, and it was Ok in it's own way, but it wasn't our thing y'know? We'd heard about Guy Stevens and The Scene club in London, and we were thinking why can't we do that?

So, on Friday and Saturday nights I think it was, we used to get an armful of records each, it was unbelievable this – and walk round the centre of Manchester, going in all these clubs and saying "Why don't you play this stuff?" and these people looked at us as if we were absolutely out of our fucking minds and they told us we were. Roger did more of this than I did, because I lived in Bolton, which is 10 miles away, but I did some of it with him. The response we got was, well negligible, because nobody wanted to try anything new.

Although Manchester's club owners didn't welcome the two Roger's at the time, it was a different story in some of the city's coffee bars. At the Cona on Tib Lane you could take in records to play on the house music system. Roger would take his records in to play and also listen to other people's, consequently meeting like-minded music fans. Another meeting place was the Town Hall pub.

Not far from the Town Hall pub was Manchester's Brazennose Street. In 1962 it was a generally nondescript street in the heart of the city, a minutes walk from Albert Square, office workers, sandwich bars, and a thoroughfare to Deansgate. On the left hand side walking towards Deansgate was a three storey building, at the end of the row on the right hand side, number 26, was a coffee bar named the Leftwing, a place frequented by jazzers, beatniks and hipsters. John Rowlands, who played trumpet with John Mayall's band Blues Syndicate would put on all-night jazz sessions.

A year later the Leftwing had gone into liquidation and the place was bought by five brothers by the name of Abadi. Their idea was to open a coffee dance club and put on beat groups from 7:30 in the evening and closing at midnight. The club was opened on Saturday 26th January 1963 by Karl Denver who played with support from Dean West & the Hellions. At the time Denver was performing at the Palace Theatre in town and had had chart hits with amongst others Wimoweh and Mexicali Rose. Until September 1963 the club was to open five nights a week. The very first DJ at the Wheel was Geoff Mullin.

Ivor Abadi: We were five brothers. My older brother Jack came back to England in '62 after being in the States and the Philippines. We found a place in the centre of Manchester and decided on wheels as the theme. That involved collecting all kinds of wheels—from cartwheels to bicycle wheels. We even had a ship's wheel from Paris. That formed the club's décor. It was just brick walls painted black, white and red in the basement, with lots of little, cavernous rooms. It really had a character all its own.

Jack Abadi, along with Danny Betesh, Sydney Sagar and Johnny Sueke had already been involved in one of the first coffee dance club venues in the UK - the El Rio in Macclesfield, a small club famous for early appearances by The Beatles and The Ronettes.

Along with his brothers, Jack was considering turning the downstairs area into an all-night club.

Roger Eagle: At this time I was buying up every R&B album I could lay my hands on. So I'd ordered all the Chuck Berry and Bo Didley albums on import from the States (Chess and Checker albums bought from Barry's Records on Blackfriars Street a.k.a. Ancill's). I just happened to have them there in front of me, on the table in what was the Left Wing coffee bar. If the albums hadn't arrived that day, if I hadn't gone to that particular coffee bar and if I hadn't taken them out of the box and been looking at them, none of it would have happened.

Ivor Abadi: I think we were at the right place at the right time when we opened because The Beatles had just started to hit. This was the baby-boom generation - people born in 1946/47. There were a lot of young people, and they wanted something different.

Roger Eagle: They said, "Do you know anything about rhythm & blues?", I said "Yeah", and he (Ivor) said, "Well we've just bought the place, we're gonna call it The Twisted Wheel, do you wanna come and play some records on Saturday night?", so I said "Yeah", the whole thing was a bizarre chance. My only DJ experience was taping tracks on one of those reel-to-reel tape recorders and taking them along to parties to play.

The Abadi's went for R&B because it was what was happening, they had a friend in the business down south somewhere, a guy called Johnny Sueke at The Place club in Hanley, and they were of the early sixties entrepreneurial class of people and they were a bit hipper than the fifties business men. They'd buy a coffee bar and turn it into a youth-oriented club as a way of making money. It wasn't because they liked black music, they knew nothing whatsoever about black music. That's how I got the job.

Roger Fairhurst: Ivor and Jack Abadi being good businessmen, thought to themselves if we can fill this place with Mindbenders fans until 11 o'clock, then throw them out, then open up with this loopy black stuff at midnight, some of them might come back in, at least we might get it half full.

Ivor Abadi: There would always be a queue outside because we'd have to empty the club from the early session. We'd let them in usually about midnight. They'd pay their money, take off their coats and there'd be a coffee bar on the ground floor area. They'd meet up there, hoping to run into friends from all over the place and they'd have a coffee. Then they'd take their bags to the clubroom and maybe at that stage they might start exchanging records, which was a popular thing to do at the club.

Roger Eagle: The first night I did was an all-nighter, I had quite a lot of tunes, but not enough, I mean I was just playing anything, I was playing R&B, I played rock 'n' roll, I played early ska, whatever I could lay my hands on - bit of jazz, bit of gospel stuff, I just chucked it all in there. Ninety nine point nine nine per cent of it was black music and that was the difference. The other clubs were very pop oriented, stuff that was in the charts.

Ivor Abadi: Musically, we started with jazz and blues, which slowly became rhythm and blues, which became soul music, and then, eventually, Northern Soul. We didn't want to be as commercial as everybody else. So we were playing different music even in the early days. It wasn't pop-based.

From the time of the very first Twisted Wheel all-nighter, Brian Smith made a detailed photographic record of the happenings at 26 Brazennose Street. With only the most basic of cameras, Brian managed to capture the feel of the place and the people. Beautifully observed and framed, his work is an excellent documentation of life at the Manchester club. Brian's photographs have also appeared on many artists' album covers including Howlin' Wolf on the Chess label and Muddy Waters. Here Brian explains how he first came across Roger Eagle.

Brian Smith: I was in the basement of Hyme and Addison's record shop just off John Dalton Street in Manchester, which was run by Noah Ancill, buying some EP or other, a rhythm and blues thing, when suddenly this sheepskin coat on legs bounded across the room, snatched it from my hands and said "Ah yes you should come to the Twisted Wheel, we play all this kind of stuff, in fact we're doing an all-nighter this week, you'd better come along." He started going on about Screamin' Jay Hawkins and I said I had a record by him and he's like "What!? What!?" I think I was the first person he'd come across that had one. I had a 78 with a piece out of the rim. He said "Right, fetch it round, here's the address" and he scribbled down this address on Wilbraham Road in Chorlton, "Come round, I'll expect you around 7 o'clock." Of course, I went round because that's what you did. I went round to his pit on Wilbraham Road, and then to the very first of the all-nighters, with Spencer Davis, on a Saturday.

On Saturday 28th September 1963, the Abadi brothers opened the Twisted Wheel for the first of its legendary all-night sessions. The main band was the Graham Bond Quartet supported by the little known at the time Spencer Davis, who played a 12 string acoustic guitar and harmonica blues set. At his first all-nighter at the age of 21 Roger Eagle played records, rhythm and blues records, that had never been heard in Manchester before. 'Help Me' by Sonny Boy Williamson was the first record to be played at a Twisted Wheel all-nighter.

Roger Eagle: This was the first time that there was ever a place that played almost 100% pure black music, that was the point. And it was danceable and became a sweat. I mean I had to keep people dancing for seven hours, with a break for the band. Seven hours is a long time and there weren't that many soul and R&B records available at the time. The bands played for 3/4 of an hour, they came on about midnight.

I played Little Richard, I played good black rock 'n' roll, I've still got the same records I used to play down there. The Little Richard American EP's are the ones I used to play mostly for some reason. But in the early days at the Wheel it was rhythm and blues, which was basically rock 'n' roll anyway, it just depends which shade of it you took.

I wouldn't have played a Bill Haley record there or an Elvis record, no I wouldn't play that! But black rock 'n' roll certainly was played. You see the Wheel was originally a rhythm and blues club and there were blues singers, famous blues singers, great legendary names who played at the Wheel.

At 21 Roger Eagle's image was more the 'rocker' look; his hair modelled into a quiff of sorts and for the tough Mancunian winter months a big sheepskin coat. Maybe a tie, certainly a shirt but not really the flash Italian style look of the youths he was playing the gutsy rhythm and blues to. Here, Roger talks about his impressions of the clientele in the early days of the Twisted Wheel.

Roger Eagle: Scruffy, some of them were black, it took a month or two but it actually took off like a rocket, full almost from the word go. A lot of them were scruffy kids who were into blues, who had combat jackets with Little Walter stencilled on the back, things like that. This was just as the Stones were getting off the ground.

Brian Smith: It wasn't the dressed up mod scene it became later at the Whitworth Street club, it was more the dosser end; they wore parka's and were quite scruffy, pretty awful really and they danced these strange snaky dances, a bit odd you know?

Roger Fairhurst: I honestly don't remember the first two or three weeks, I was there at all of them, it was fuller than the Abadi's expected and they were quite pleased. Then the word started to spread.

Ivor Abadi: We had two distinct sessions at the club: the ordinary session—four nights a week on Tuesday, Thursday, Friday and Saturday, when it would be open from 7:30 p.m. until midnight—and then the all-night session on Saturday, which drew people from a much wider area. They'd come from 100 miles away. This is the scene that ultimately developed into what we now call Northern Soul.

Roger Fairhurst: Roger and I would sometimes go and have a drink before the all-nighter started, we'd come out of the pub about half ten - eleven and walk down to the Wheel with arms full of records. I'll never forget, it was about the fourth week and there was a line of people right down the street and there was a coach that had come from somewhere in the Midlands, full of people. I thought, Christ, you know? This is really doing something and it was absolutely mobbed that night, packed out. You know the old saying 'the sweat ran down the walls', well it did. There was no air-conditioning, it stank, there'd be people asleep, all kinds of stuff.

Brian Smith: It was good because you would get an early and a late show. It had two sort of club lives, it was a typical beat club in the evenings, from 8 or 9 o'clock, then they'd chuck people out. It wasn't licensed, they'd sell coke and orange juice, hot dogs, that was it. It was always a bit of a dump, it had whitewashed walls and very little else, the only concession to anything were these cartwheels set in the wall, that gave it its character. But it did have a lovely atmosphere, real hot and sweaty.

The all-nighters would kick off at 12 o'clock and a lot of these people had been out earlier, and a lot of them would go into the unlit rooms in the middle and most of them would be asleep. I'd go round and take these pictures, for the Abadis mainly, and you couldn't even see to focus, I just went click, click, click and occasionally a couple of young girls would come up and say "What's going to happen with that photograph, and can we have it? We're not supposed to be here."

Ivor Abadi:When we first started doing all–night sessions, we used to close at about 3:00 or 4:00 in the morning. But because a lot of people came on public transport, they had nowhere to go until their public transport started again. So the local police came to us and asked us if we'd stay open a little later so that people weren't wandering the streets. The police weren't pleased that people were coming from other towns and cities.

It wouldn't have been unusual to find people asleep after a few drinks before getting to the Wheel. With no trains or buses out of the city centre until much later, it was the most natural thing to do. Roger would have been aware of this when the dance floor was empty.

Brian Smith: How many DJ's would play an entire side of Jimmy Smith at three in the morning? He'd play something like 'The Sermon', things like that, Blue Note tracks that I actually couldn't handle then, I got into those things much later. He'd play stuff by Mose Allison, Percy Mayfield – 'River's Invitation', 'Natchez Burning' by Howlin' Wolf, a quieter slower track, or Hooker doing 'Tupelo Flood' where he talks all the way through it, he played this stuff and they listened.

From an interview with John Crumpton in 1994 Roger talks here of his admiration for the legendary Howlin' Wolf.

Roger Eagle: I'm still astonished at the fact that Howlin' Wolf managed to record, because if you listen to Howlin' Wolf in the context of what was going on at the time he was a very rough and raw sounding man. What a wonderful human being. I had the fortune of meeting him and talking to him, a very nice man indeed. He was sitting on his hotel bed in Manchester, he was wearing yellow socks with no shoes on. He was talking about his children back in Chicago, I asked him what they were into, he said "The Beatles". Howlin' Wolf's children being Beatles fans to me was a glimpse into a different world, it's a whole different thing.

Another accomplice of Roger's, and a fellow rhythm and blues fanatic, was Neil Carter. For a short time Neil was a major part of Roger's circle of friends. By the time he encountered Roger at the Twisted Wheel, Neil already had experience DJing himself, and would later go on to DJ at the Brazennose Street Twisted Wheel. Neil was also assistant editor on the *R&B Scene* magazine as well as, like many others, Roger's chauffeur. Later Neil worked for 'Uptight and Outta Sight' – the Atlantic records appreciation society. He also joined the Stax tour of Britain in 1967 as a photographer.

Neil Carter: When I first met Roger I was working as a DJ in Stockport at the Kingfisher and the Manor Lounge clubs, I was keen on blues, rhythm and blues and rock 'n' roll. The Kingfisher was where I started off really, they had a jukebox there when I first started going, then they put in a turntable with a pile of records for people to just play. So I tried that and then they asked me to do it as a DJ, that's how I started on that.

So I went down to the Twisted Wheel to the rhythm and blues all-nighter, pretty much when it first started and Roger was the DJ and I just got talking to him and found that we liked a lot of the same sort of music. So that's how I got to know him; this was at the time that he was living on Wilbraham Road and went there to see him regularly.

Roger and myself were good mates for a year or so. After a while I DJ'd at the Twisted Wheel all-nighter on Brazennose Street, Roger and I would do alternate nights, he would DJ one week and I would do it the next.

Ivor Abadi: We brought over a lot of acts from the States for two or three week tours. Every Friday and Saturday night we'd have a group on. We had to have English groups because there weren't always American groups around. Even though we opened in January 1963, we didn't host any American groups until probably September or October when we started the all-night sessions.

As the Twisted Wheel club was taking off it was not the only club to host live rhythm and blues in Manchester, although the Wheel was exclusively R&B based, other clubs went on to take advantage of the general interest in the music at the time.

The Bodega Club on Cross Street was the first Manchester club to feature R&B when it put on Alexis Korner's Blues Incorporated in March 1963. In the first months of the Wheel opening as an R&B club, The Bodega booked bands such as Long John Baldry and the Cyril Davis All Stars, it also went on to feature regular R&B only nights on Wednesdays, but it was mainly a jazz hangout.

The Oasis Coffee Bar, situated on Lloyd Street, was specifically aimed at teenagers and the pop market, providing a venue for the many Manchester based beat groups, who appeared there on a regular basis. The Beatles made the first of several appearances there on February 2nd 1962, this was their first professional gig in the country outside Liverpool. By the summer of 1963 it was easily the most successful club in the city, with a membership of more than 32,000. With bookings such as The Beatles, The Rolling Stones, Bo Diddley, Gene Vincent and Little Richard, the idea of a shift of clientele to a different club seems ridiculous with hindsight. But then the Twisted Wheel began to hold weekly R&B all-nighters and the ever increasing crowds began to get a taste for the powerful music Roger Eagle was playing just around the corner from the Oasis.

Another club to take advantage of the Wheel's burgeoning popularity was The Jungfrau on Cathedral Street which opened on 30th November 1962 as a club catering to the teen beat phenomenon. Pre-Wheel meeting places in the city were The Cona coffee bar and also the El Mogambo which was on Mosley Street.

Roger Eagle: You see what we're talking about here is how Manchester split itself off (musically) and became a separate society and that's why it happened. Otherwise it would have been a pop city like everywhere else. If it didn't have a black music club it was just mainstream pop with a few R&B and ska things thrown in at the edges – if the DJ's had heard of it. It was the first time there was a really serious movement, it became a friendly, welcoming movement but still exclusive. It was very much a certain prouder person.

The Abadi brothers quickly realised how lucky they had been to gain the services of Roger Eagle. Artist selection was now greatly influenced by his recommendations. By the start of 1964, in regard to membership and reputation, the Wheel had become the fastest growing club of its kind in the north of England, with only London's Flamingo and Marquee clubs as its main rivals.

Ivor Abadi: I knew we wanted to have non-stop music. I didn't want interruptions from the DJs, who always wanted to talk. I wanted musical continuity. You have two turntables and when one record is finishing, you blend it into the next one. We always wanted that. It was like magic and we're not quite sure how that happened but it was a big hit from the very beginning.

Roger Eagle: They were the meanest employers I've ever had; incredibly tight, mean people. I made them a fortune and they treated me like shit. But I didn't know any better in those days, I was not a promoter and I didn't really understand, but they were very, very mean. I wasn't a particularly high profile DJ, I didn't have the ambition and I certainly didn't have the patter. I was happy playing the music that I loved. I would play six or seven hours solid, single-handedly, with just an hour or so's break for the band – for £3 a night.

Along with the rapid rise in popularity of rhythm and blues, the Twisted Wheel had other allies to popularise the club's scene. The BBC's Top of the Pops, first broadcast from Manchester on 1st January 1964, was to bring together all the disparate elements that make up the popular music chart, and put it onto television screens throughout the Britain – thus giving the record buying public a performance, with video and sound, to experience new and not so new artists. Top of the Pops, along with Ready Steady Go, which came into British homes in 1963, would go a long way towards influencing the way whole generations of music lovers dressed, thought and conducted themselves.

In this instant, the dawn of British popular music television would have a large impact on the younger generation, introducing them to mod culture i.e. sharp suits, Italian styling, scooters and the appreciation of black rhythm and blues music.

Roger Eagle: I was always a pretty smart dresser but some of the kids down there were years in front of anything I have ever seen since. We kind of had a mutual respect. They loved the records I used to play and I reckon that's why they liked me. I never invented the mod scene down at the Wheel, it just happened. Saying that though, I'm really glad I was part of it all. I never booked any of the acts, I would recommend acts but I didn't know the first thing about booking them. I was surprised at how much attention they paid to me. I didn't realise it but in the States DJ's were very important people. I mean as far as I was concerned I was a badly paid menial at the back putting records on, you know? But I twigged after a while that the American music business took you very seriously indeed and so they should, because the club DJ's that existed in England at that time led on to enormous sales for American artists, absolutely gigantic.

I mean Guy Stevens broke some records just out of club playing and that's one club alone. 'Shotgun Wedding' by Roy C got into the Top 30, he played that, and it was a hit just out of club play, that was the first time that I knew of that happening. No one at the major record companies had heard of it, it was on Island Records, it was certainly one of their very first hits. I've got the original Island pressing, still play it, it's a classic. So of course DJ's were influential, you couldn't hear that stuff on the radio, no chance whatsoever.

Roger would get records sent to him from Guy Stevens to add to his already large collection, Stevens would also visit The Twisted Wheel and supply Roger with records and advice whenever he visited.

Lists of available music could be found in the small ads columns of the weekly music press. To add to that auction lists were available, postal lists were mailed to you from the US. In the period 1963-67, singles or 45's were released and deleted at a huge rate in the States. Roger would check the Billboard chart listings and if tracks appeared and disappeared rapidly, he would bid for them, keeping him ahead of the game. Roger would also receive 45's directly from American record companies such as Ronn and Jewel. With his enthusiasm for R&B and what would later become soul, Roger would write to US record companies and request records that hadn't been released in the UK.

Brian Smith: Cyril Davies All Stars had been appearing live with Long John Baldry as their second singer and were booked to play the Wheel in January '64.

Cyril Davis' All Stars were considered to be the best and most authentic sounding of the early British R&B bands, they were around for only a relatively short while, releasing two singles on the Pye label, 'Country Line Special' and 'Preaching The Blues'.

The band were booked to appear at the Twisted Wheel on Saturday 11th January 1964 but between the Wheel booking and the actual gig Cyril Davies died from what was later confirmed to be leukemia but is to this day reported variously as endocarditis, pleurisy and a pneumonia related heart attack after waiting for hours in the rain following a gig.

After attending a gig at Eel Pie Island on Sunday 5th January, Long John Baldry met Rod Stewart on Twickenham railway station playing harmonica and singing Howlin' Wolf's 'Smokestack Lightning'. Impressed, Baldry asked Stewart if he'd like to sit in with the All Stars at their Tuesday night gig at London's Marquee club. That same night, January 7th, Cyril Davies collapsed and died.

Brian Smith: This band was what became Long John Baldry's Hoochie Coochie Men and they dragged in a virtually unknown Rod Stewart to sing with them. The night was an all-nighter and it was packed, it had been sold out for weeks for Cyril Davies. I think 50% of the audience arrived not knowing he was dead, largely due to the communications network at the time, he'd died literally days before and it wasn't national news.

I've got mates who've never bought a Rod Stewart record in their life but they have a bit of a soft spot for him for that night because it was bloody electric, they hadn't rehearsed anything and Rod came out with a guitar and he sang something like a 40 minute version of 'The Night Time Is The Right Time'. It was just him, a few guitar licks and perhaps a bit of rhythm behind and it was absolutely electric.

In an Interview with Austin Scaggs for *Rolling Stone* magazine in 2003 Rod Stewart recalled the gig at the Wheel.

"It was at a place called the Twisted Wheel in Manchester. I was in Long John Baldry's Hoochie Coochie Men and I did a song called 'Night Time Is The Right Time'. I was only eighteen or nineteen and one of the older guys gave me a pill called a 'Black Bomber'. Being young and gullible and indestructible I took it, and I made this one song last half an hour. I just wouldn't get off the microphone and kept singing the same verse over and over."

On Saturday 8th February 1964 the Pop/R&B band Manfred Mann had been booked to play the Wheel. By coincidence they were at No 5 in the pop charts the same week and consequently guaranteed a good crowd on the night of the gig. On the night, with the club packed to well beyond capacity and with the queue still growing, the Abadis were told by the local police to lock the doors while mounted police were called to disperse the growing crowd. Open as a club for just over a year, and not even 5 months into the regular Saturday all-night sessions, the Twisted Wheel had broken all attendance records for any club in Manchester. That night an estimated 6,000 people were locked out.

Roger Eagle: The Abadis always got me to look after the black acts, I just don't think they got on with them, that wasn't racism, well it was racism in a small sense in that they just didn't understand them, they didn't talk the same language. Black people used to make them nervous, Sonny Boy Williamson gave Ivor Abadi real cause to be nervous...

On 15th February 1964 the legendary blues singer, harmonica player and Chess recording artist Sonny Boy Williamson II made his debut appearance at the Twisted Wheel.

Arriving in Europe in 1963 as one of the performers on the 'American Folk and Blues Festival' concerts, Sonny Boy spent most of the three trips he made from the US to Europe in England. Playing gigs to hugely appreciative mainly white crowds and recording with British groups such as The Animals and The Yardbirds, Sonny Boy became a sensation not only at folk/blues revival gigs but also on the teenage beat club circuit.

Described variously as a womaniser, mysterious, sly, moody, suspicious, bitter, even evil, many rumours, myths and stories surround the man. His birth date is shrouded in mystery with several dates between 1894 and 1912 reported; the fact that Sonny Boy lied about his age hasn't helped matters. Also the fact that he would tell differing stories of his life and background each time he was interviewed has contributed to the confusion and indeed the legend. At one point married to Howlin' Wolf's sister, he was present at the gig where another blues legend Robert Johnson was taken ill and ultimately died, from what was thought to be poisoning from drinking whisky out of a bottle with a broken seal.

When Sonny Boy first played the Wheel he, along with 10 or 11 young blues fans, went back to Roger's flat at 540 Wilbraham Road in Chorlton. The experience of socialising with a bona fide Delta bluesman must have been like some sort of rite of passage for this gang of rhythm and blues fanatics. It must have turned Sonny Boy's head too, not only playing to appreciative, primarily white audiences, having not experienced that in the States; but also being invited into white people's homes. Saying that, the racial climate in Britain was very different in 1964 to what it is today.

Roger Eagle: Sonny Boy Williamson stayed at my flat one night, I had to take him back there because he was with a woman from Cantrell Farm in Liverpool that he'd met at The Blue Angel and the hotels wouldn't admit him with her and he also refused to go on stage at the Wheel. He wanted to get his leg over with this woman, pure and simple. So we had to ferry him backwards and forwards in taxis and things. It ended up we took him back there. I remember trying to show him how the gas meter worked before we left and he said, "No, no, no, no, no! Clear off, clear off!"

So we all went back down the Wheel and returned about 8 o'clock in the morning and that's when that photograph was taken - the one where we're all standing round. That's Roger Fairhurst, who did *R&B Scene* magazine with me. Chev and Earl, a couple of black guys who came to the Wheel, Gloria who I met Little Richard with, and a couple of other people. That's me at the back, and I'm holding up the record 'Walkin' the Dog' by Rufus Thomas because Sonny Boy had just explained to us what 'The Dog' was all about in the most graphic possible terms, so I'm just pointing at it. "It's about shagging, do The Dog motherfucker!" and that there is the girl from Liverpool.

Sonny Boy put a great big wodge of cash in her hand when he said goodbye to her at Piccadilly Station. I went round to her flat to pick him up once or he picked her up from there once, and there's this Liverpudlian family in this tiny little flat in Cantrell Farm and Sonny Boy Williamson comes in and takes their daughter away. The randiest man I have ever met, bar none, I think I can safely say that. A great harmonica player, but err… he did like his pussy.

He was 67 and it wasn't long before he died. I got a letter from his widow, I wish I'd kept it. Mattie, saying 'I regret to inform you that Sonny Boy Williamson has passed away in St. Helena, Arkansas, and is there any money owing to him?'

Of course there wasn't. He blew the whole lot on Johnny Walker Red and hookers, but that's a blues man for you, they don't make 'em like that today.

Roger Fairhurst and Brian Smith, both friends of Roger Eagle at this time, were present when Sonny Boy Williamson played his first Twisted Wheel gig.

Brian Smith: Well that was one of the great nights that, because he was touring with The Animals and they played The Wheel on the Saturday night. I don't know where he was playing on the Sunday but whoever was running the tour, they got Roger to look after him for the night, y'know, put him up at his pit. So at very short notice and with hardly any film in my camera we had Sonny Boy to ourselves for a few hours at Roger's flat with that lady. I don't know if anybody's tried to track her down, she was certainly costing him £40 a day or something for her services, which I think she worked hard for.

There was one point in the afternoon when I was taking a few photographs and he called me over and he said, "I want you to take a picture with my woman holding my rod." I don't know where the hell I would have got it processed, anyway it never happened.

There was one point where he spoke to Roger and Roger gathered us all up and ushered us all out of the room and we all sat out on the stairs in the lobby, while he gave this woman one on Roger's pull down bed. The bed's creaking away there and, you know, he says we can go back in, Sonny Boy's there in a pair of full length long johns and she's sat in the chair doing her nails.

He gave us yards of time, we never had a tape recorder or anything in those days, if I'd known I'd have had a fistful of film. I was using an old Ilford Sportsman with a fold out flash in those days, I just took what I could.

He was giving us all these lurid tales about going round Chicago nailing all these people that had done him wrong and shooting them in the bollocks, all sorts of stuff, some of the stories possibly even true.

Roger Fairhurst: When Sonny Boy was there I think there were 10 or 11 of us that stayed there that night and there was a blonde haired lady of the night with Sonny Boy. I have to give her credit, she was the best cook out of all of us there.

The following morning, bearing in mind this was a Sunday in 1964 and no shops were open, a few of us went to a Jewish supermarket which was not far from Roger's flat. We got a couple of chickens, potatoes, rice and some other stuff and came back. They then set to, to cook a Sunday lunch on Roger's two hot plates. The girl who was with Sonny Boy did the chicken and it was bloody brilliant, we ate out of cereal bowls, Roger didn't have a great deal of cutlery.

Neil Carter: I was at Roger's flat when Sonny Boy went round there, he had a young lady with him. He was just a total character, the impression he gave was I want to drink my whiskey and have sex with this woman, that's what he was interested in. An unbelievable harmonica player and a great showman as well.

Roger Eagle: I met Muddy Waters, Little Walter, I don't care how good a harmonica player you are technically, Little Walter was the king, always will be. The amplified electric harmonica, he did it for the money. Years later people may have raved about his harmonica playing in context of all the other harmonica players but at the time Walter was just trying to be a bit different and earn some money. When he started he was playing for white folks as much as black folks. He was playing at waltzes, polkas anything, then he'd go to Chicago and play blues because that's what they wanted to hear. But the guy produced this wonderful stuff, the high watermark for harmonica players. Sonny Boy Williamson was a more accomplished harmonica player with a much broader range but he didn't have Little Walter's edge. This is me speaking as a critic again because young people will come to me and say, "What do you reckon? What do we listen to? What do we buy?"

Throughout his life Roger's tastes developed to encompass many different rhythm based styles of music but quite a substantial number of artists from his youth remained important to him right until the end. 'The Pioneers' as he liked to call them. These included, in no particular order, Little Richard, Bo Diddley, Chuck Berry, LaVern Baker, Ray Charles, James Brown, Otis Redding and Elvis Presley – a little later it would be Captain Beefheart & the Magic Band, King Tubby and Lee Perry. These artists were part of his personal philosophy, part of his person, part of his legendary record collection and part of his being. If you were party to his teaching he would have insisted you listened to these artists. If you understood these artists – not just aurally but actually felt their influence – you'd be a lot closer to understanding Roger Eagle.

Roger Eagle: I've always been there with the pioneers, I admire the pioneers, I mean look at Bo Diddley for fuck's sake. Anyone who's playing blues on the streets of Chicago anyway they can, just to get a few dimes and stuff in, and comes up with this incredible rhythm, that nobody had done before, he didn't originate the rhythm, it's a very old rhythm, but he did it and no-one else had done it like that. He must have torn people up!

Bo Diddley, when he first started, he must have really ripped 'em to fuckin' pieces. The wailing harmonica, the Bo Diddley guitar, the beats and the shaking maracas, it must have been really something out there on the streets of Chicago in the late forties/ early fifties. He would have been competing against guys who were doing like country-blues, that's the way it evolved.

Look at Chuck Berry, he wanted to be like Nat 'King' Cole, he wanted to be a ballad singer but trying to sell records and stuff, he pinched Tiny Grimes' guitar licks, vamped them up and away he went, fuckin' great. This was in the forties, Tiny Grimes and his Rockin' Highlanders, they used to wear like Highland dress with kilts – a black band from New York! Screamin' Jay Hawkins used to sing with them, in fact I must re-aquire myself some Tiny Grimes, that is where Chuck Berry's guitar riff came from.

Not long after the release of their first LP, The Rolling Stones turned up at The Twisted Wheel. According to Ivor Abadi it took some convincing to actually let the Stones in as they were considered 'trouble'. The band were probably staying in Manchester on the Saturday night with either gigs or television commitments to attend to. Roger Eagle described the Rolling Stones as a "bloody good backing band".

Roger Eagle: The Stones came down to the Twisted Wheel about the same week as their first album was released (April 17th) and I got a copy of it and I played every original track off the album. I played 'Walking the Dog' by Rufus Thomas, I played 'I'm a King Bee' by Slim Harpo and so on, I just played all the originals, and they stood there at the coffee bar surrounded by people just looking at them, not talking to them, looking, because they were quite big by then. They knew exactly what I was doing and I suppose most of the kids did as well. I just felt like doing it you know, played all the originals in the same order as the LP, bang, bang, bang, bang, bang because I thought The Stones were being real lazy, just copying other people's songs and doing a very feeble, white, puny version of them.

It was me saying there's a north/south thing. I'm a southerner by birth – but a northerner by emotion. I prefer the north. I'm not saying I don't like southerners, but they do tend to be so temporary down there. To me if something is solid then it's worth looking after. Whereas they're into it and out of it – which is really not the northern style.

I actually got on ok with The Stones. Brian Jones bought a copy of *R&B Scene* off me when I was in London. I'm one of the DJ's that has publicised the music and when The Stones went to The States they got Howlin' Wolf on prime time national television. Fucking hell, that's the thing to do! I admire them for doing that.

Brian Smith: The Stones certainly never played at the Wheel to my knowledge. I saw Brian Jones and Keith Richards in there, I never saw Jagger but others reckon they did. I've got a photograph of Jimmy Reed in the bogs. At the time I never saw it blown up and a few years later I did an exhibition and when this photo was blown up you can see scratched in the brickwork on the wall of the bog – 'Mick Jagger, Archway, London'.

A point that crops up time and again throughout Roger's life is his determination to educate or teach people, generally musicians, about obscure or classic tunes of every genre. To Roger it was almost a religious calling. This is one of the reasons he is remembered throughout the British music scene so fondly. He wasn't just a DJ, he wasn't just a promoter, he wasn't just a band manager, he was an avid music fan with an inherent need to turn people on to music they had not been exposed to, therefore helping them with their musical education, also this knowledge was passed on to others. If you had experienced one of Roger's many music lessons you didn't forget it.

Bruce Mitchell: While he was at The Wheel, he also preached R&B singles to everybody, in the Roger Eagle style. He did this to everybody, the visiting London groups would frequently go back to his flat in Chorlton and he would play them what they should be playing and they would take that on board. The Spencer Davis Group single 'Strong Love' was one of Roger's suggestions, an obscure blues thing. This evangelism never stopped, all groups and musicians fell under his spell, he had that enthusiasm that's infectious.

In an interview with *New Breed* magazine at his home in North Wales in February 1999, just three months before he died, Roger talked about some of the younger rhythm and blues bands and musicians he befriended at the Twisted Wheel. Eric Clapton has personally verified Roger's account of him visiting the flat in Chorlton.

"I used to be friendly with Stevie Winwood, he used to come round to my place when The Spencer Davis Group played the club. Eric Clapton was a good friend at that time. I remember one Sunday morning after he had played at the club, he brought a good-looking mod girl round to my place and she got completely pissed off because all he wanted to do was listen to Freddy King records."

After writing to Don Robey at Duke Records to sing the praises of Bobby Bland's voice, Roger received in return a demo version of Bland's 'Yield Not To Temptation'. Don Robey made sure that Roger's praise for Bland was quoted on the record sleeve for Bobby Bland's next album on Duke Records 'Ain't Nothing You Can Do', released in the UK in 1964 on the Vocalion label. The words quoted on the cover of 'Ain't Nothing You Can Do' from a twenty-two year old Roger Eagle were:

'Bobby... a prime example of a sophisticated rhythm and blues singer'

After getting a taste for rhythm and blues while living in London in 1962, Brian Rae moved back to the North-West and subsequently became one of the DJs at the Twisted Wheel after Roger Eagle left. It would seem that Brian took over Roger's job. Being slightly younger meant that Brian was almost a student to Roger, a position which Roger always felt more than comfortable with. Here Brian recalls his first encounter with Roger.

Brian Rae: I first met him at The Wheel, he was the disc jockey standing behind the wheels that were a framework made up for the disc jockey to stand behind. Behind this framework there were two decks, where the disc jockey would stand and immediately behind the disc jockey they'd have a load of shelves, these shelves had the Wheel record library on them. He used to bring in his own stuff, well basically he used to get his music from all over the place. No end of people would help, he used to hear what people wanted and he had a good ear for what he wanted to play. Subsequently, the Blue Beat stuff he used to play was from Moss Side and so on. Most people wouldn't go down there at that time because there was a stigma attached to Moss Side. Roger was very much his own man, he had a great feeling for certain records that most people would have shied away from. I think he got that feeling from being well into his blues type stuff, rockabilly and rock 'n' roll. It gave him a good feel for what was subsequently to be American pop, R&B or soul. His taste was immaculate.

Ivor Abadi: We also got a lot of records from the US Air Force bases in England. There was one not too far away. The DJs used to communicate with airmen and we would get the music they were playing, some of which became northern soul. Manchester also had Jamaican music shops. So we had this mix of Jamaican-style music, soul, and blues to produce a new overall sound.

Brian Rae's first club experiences were in London venues such as the Marquee and the Flamingo. Having experienced both the London and Manchester music scenes of the early 60's, his opinion is significant.

Brian Rae: The Wheel and the Flamingo were running neck and neck, although the selection of records at the Wheel was far better than you'd get in the Flamingo.

While the club's reputation was built on not just the R&B acts that played, but also the music played by Roger, by the summer of 1964 the mood of the club and tastes of some of the newer members was changing. Rhythm and blues and black music tastes amongst white teenagers was going over-ground, the club was attracting a larger mod membership, who began to demand more of what was then a new term 'Soul'.

Roger Eagle: I didn't see the word 'soul' until the Solomon Burke album 'The King of Rock and Soul'(1964), that was the first time I heard it mentioned and then R&B became soul, and it became the thing to stay up all night dancing.

Within six months of The Wheel all-nighters starting, Roger had gained the awesome reputation as one of the most influential DJs around; his energy, enthusiasm, dedication and allegiance to black music transformed The Twisted Wheel from a mediocre coffee bar to the number one rhythm and blues club outside London.

The music at The Twisted Wheel in the early days, as Roger explained, was very eclectic; lots of different beats, rhythms, styles and performers. American Sue records imports were among the first danceable soul records to be played at both The Scene club in London and the Brazennose Street Twisted Wheel.

Roger Fairhurst: When I was involved we played all sorts of speeds of stuff, and I think that we always thought that it varied the thing and made it more interesting. There were a large number of people who used to go there to listen, they didn't all go to dance. But as Northern Soul appeared there was a lot less listening going on and a lot more dancing, hence places later on such as Wigan Casino, as long as it went 'clonk, clonk, clonk' they were happy. I think Motown had a lot to do with that, because Motown was sort of regimented and formulaic in every way – they weren't doing anything interesting. That, to me, was totally uninteresting, I wanted to hear the Coasters being funny and witty and clever, I wanted to hear King Curtis sax solos, stuff like that.

Eagle's love of rhythm and blues could not prevent an unusual event occurring at a gig by John Lee Hooker. After being introduced by Roger from his DJ booth, Hooker was just about begin his set when a group of young mods coolly turned their backs on the stage and walked away from the great bluesman and into the recesses of the DJ room which was separate from the performance area. This act would not have been intended as disrespectful, it was simply that they wanted to dance and have a good time. This single event can be considered important as it seems to foretell the switch in Wheel club goers' tastes from the tougher R&B sounds of Chicago, to the polished and slick soul sounds coming out of cities such as Detroit.

Roger Fairhurst: Neil Carter DJ'd at the early Wheel all-nighters sometimes but Roger was the main man, he did most of it. If he wanted a break or wanted to go to the loo, or have a bowl of soup, I would help out and do half an hour or an hour, now and again. I used Roger's records, Neil would do the same, I think he did more after I stopped going. I stopped going for other reasons, namely the poor quality of the backing bands for American visitors. They couldn't bring their own bands and the bands they were given were in the main absolutely dreadful. There were honourable exceptions; John Lee's Groundhogs were brilliant, and the 5 Dimensions were superb. John Mayall was absolutely fucking atrocious, not that he couldn't play, he just wouldn't stop playing, he was too loud and he tried to drown out who he was backing, which was dreadful, ill-mannered, terrible.

You see people like T-Bone Walker or Little Walter are very heavily jazz influenced, and they improvised a lot. How can you improvise with somebody who only knows two chords? You can't, so it diminishes what you are able to do on the stage quite drastically.

Neil Carter: Little Walter was a real character, I sort of acted as his chauffeur in Manchester, I was only a young lad and not very wise in the ways of the world. He was such a character, he wanted me to take him to places where he could get girls and booze and all the rest of it, but he was still very pleasant. I didn't feel threatened by him at all. You do hear some stories about him carrying a gun and all that, I never saw that side of him, he was always on his best behaviour.

Stan Hoffman is a musician who got to know Roger in the earliest days of The Twisted Wheel. As a musician he played in various bands at The Magic Village. He also played Liverpool's Eric's club with assorted bands from the era including Gyro and Tosh Ryan's Rabid records roster. In the 1970's and 80's Stan also played flute and saxophone in Dougie James Soul Train.

Stan Hoffman: I go back to 1963 with Roger, when The Twisted Wheel was still called The Left Wing coffee bar. I would describe him as a personal friend, he nearly got me nicked loads of times, he wasn't very street savvy. He was an old beatnik, he was from the beatnik days, but I tell you I thought the world of him. He was writing to Chess Records way back in the early 60's and getting all that stuff and helping to get the acts over. One of the first records I heard him play was 'Spoonful' by Howlin' Wolf in The Twisted Wheel in about 1964. The way he announced it and then played it, he was right into it. Nobody else was doing it, he was into jazz as well. At the time most people were into trad but he was right into be-bop. He loved the really obscure stuff and some of that stuff he was getting from the States, they probably only pressed about twelve of them.

In 1964 in Manchester the teen dance styles were still based on

Roger Eagle & Family, RAF Brize Norton c. 1955

oger aged 15
oth photos
rtesy
Martin Eagle.

*Right: Roger aged 15
Photo Martin Eagle*

Roger Eagle circa 1964 - Photo Brian Smith

Sugar Pie DeSanto, Roger Eagle and Howlin' Wolf

Roger Eagle and Howlin' Wolf - both photos courtesy of Brian Smith

Roger with Hubert Sumlin and (below) Willie Dixon - photos Brian Smith

Sonny Boy Williamson II at Roger Eagle's flat, with some of the Twisted Wheel regulars, February 196

Sonny Boy Williamson II with Roger Eagle, Roger Fairhurst
and some of the Twisted Wheel crowd (see p.37)
Photos: Brian Smith

Roger with Lightnin' Hopkins (above) and Little Walter (Below) - Photos: Brian Smith

the jive, a fifties partnered style. With hardly any examples of contemporary R&B dance styles to go off, such as James Brown or Jackie Wilson, from TV or film, it's unusual that the later expressive styles developed at all. It must be remembered though that people were now travelling the country to visit all-night music venues and it's possible that these styles developed from fans who travelled to Manchester.

Roger Eagle: It would have a been a lot of the early mods that came down to the club, the original mods. They didn't have that much money, you either spent your money on a scooter or you spent it on records and travelling to all-nighters and stuff.

Neil Carter: I think the mod scene came into its own when The Wheel moved to Whitworth Street. It became more of a soul club rather than R&B. At Brazennose Street it was very much the harder R&B sounds such as Jimmy Reed, Muddy Waters with some rock 'n' roll such as Chuck Berry, a lot of Bo Diddley and a lot of Chess stuff.

Roger Eagle: There were many imitators, two or three years in there was the Mojo club in Sheffield that Peter Stringfellow used to run, he used to come over to The Wheel and write down the name of every tune I played. Then there was the Golden Torch at Tunstall in Staffordshire near Stoke.

R&B SCENE MAGAZINE

Brian Smith was a good friend to Roger Eagle and his photography was featured in the magazine *R&B Scene*, on which he contributed along with Roger Fairhurst and also Dave Wagget who did the artwork. Roger produced and edited the magazine which was the first dedicated rhythm and blues magazine of its kind in the country. The magazine was first published in June 1964 and was aimed at teenage R&B fans who, up until then, had to manage with just LP sleeve notes to learn about the music.

Brian Smith: It was the very first glossy illustrated blues magazine.

Neil Carter: I worked on the *R&B Scene* magazine with Roger as well, I was sort of the assistant editor if you like, so I helped Roger put it together. I helped with interviewing people, writing articles and such like.

A point that seems to repeat over large parts of Roger's life is his inability to deal sensibly with money. His sympathies generally seemed to correspond with that of the artist and the artist's inability to do lucrative business deals while concentrating his energies on creative concerns. Consequently, he lost money on deals that, while satisfying his own personal taste, could not be considered sound monetarily. Still, his personal taste has been proven to be immaculate and taking chances is gambling and Roger certainly knew about that.

Brian Smith: I think his poor old Mum bailed him out on more than one occasion. She did with the magazine more than once. He talked the Abadis into doing *R&B Scene* and they published the first one, but he had no distribution. He was just taking it round in Neil Carter's car boot, selling them a dozen at a time to record shops – that was it. It lost several hundred pounds on that one issue, and this is in 1964. The Abadis panicked and he bought it off them, or rather his Mum did. I think he took it on to about 7 issues, and then his Mum paid off the £1000 accumulated debts, mostly print bills. I've still got the copper printing blocks for the photos. To do those kind of big run photos they used to engrave a piece of copper, and they were inked and that's how it worked.

Neil Carter: As far as the Abadi's were concerned I DJ'd and they paid me at the end of the night, that was it really. Whereas Roger knew them pretty well, they helped fund his *R&B Scene* project, so he knew them a lot better than I did.

Around the same time that Roger and the guys were setting up the *R&B Scene* magazine, they also formed a club of sorts which they named the 'Northern Blues Appreciation Society'. Membership cards were printed and a venue sought to air tunes to blues fans around the Manchester and Salford area. It would seem Roger set up the club as a way of making contact with similarly minded blues fans. With so little information available about American blues music and with his experience of the enthusiasm for it at The Twisted Wheel, it made sense that he would try and bring the music to as many people as possible.

Here Brian Smith tells his story of Roger Eagle's first foray into music promoting in mid 1964.

Brian Smith: My recollection is that it kicked off at the Pack Horse in Bridge Street. I couldn't say how long it was based there but after that it moved to the Crown on Blackfriars Street and eventually moved to the Black Lion on the corner.

It was a glorified place to play records. We had a small membership of what we called the 'Northern Blues Appreciation Society' and we had cards printed, all fairly amateurish stuff, there may have been a couple of bob to pay on the night. I remember Roger playing records and sending a little round-robin asking for record requests that people would like to hear and we'd try to get hold of them, although that didn't get very far as people started writing down made up artists and songs. I also remember one or two people using it as a rehearsal gig, I don't think Roger paid them though. I would say John Mayall certainly played there, Victor Brox and Annette and the original St. Louis Union, which was then very much a soul type band.

It probably started in '64 but it wasn't to be a paying gig because with Roger still DJing at The Wheel, he wasn't sure how the Abadi's would react. It was Roger's idea but we did it with him. I'm sure on the club membership card it mentions Neil

Carter and Dave Waggett as being involved in the running of it.

In 1964 Brian Jackson was working as a Tax Officer at the Department of Inland Revenue. Here he explains how he first came across Roger Eagle running a blues evening at a pub in Salford. Roger and Brian were to cross paths many times over the coming 35 years. Brian is now a campaigner for 'Friends of the Earth'.

Brian Jackson: I wasn't interested in what my friends were interested in, like Billy J Kramer & The Dakotas or whatever was in the pop charts. I was listening to John Lee Hooker and Howlin' Wolf with Hubert Sumlin on guitar. I'd also discovered Bob Dylan, this must be circa 1964–65.

I'd heard there was a club in Manchester in a room over a pub where they had this R&B and blues scene going on. So me and a friend went down there to check it out, it was at a pub called The Black Lion Hotel, which was on the corner of Chapel Street and Blackfriars Street in Salford. This pub had a curved frontage, it was late Victorian and it had, along with the public bar rooms downstairs, an upstairs room which had a curved wall along the front of the building, shaped like a piece of cake. You went up the stairs and there was a guy taking money and putting it in a tin and this was of course Mr Roger Eagle. I'd never met him before, a big bear of a man. He said, "If you like blues, you've come to the right place", he used to talk in a staccato kind of manner, it was like an order. "Yes, we do like blues", I said, so we paid him, it was something like 2/6d, we went in and there's five people and a dog in there, and there's a bloke at the end of the room playing guitar through a little amp, singing white boy blues. His name was John Wilkinson and he called himself John Inson, I've not seen him from then until now.

Over the next two or three weeks I took friends of mine to this club, we'd decided it was a nice place to go to, because at least they were playing blues. As a big folk fan at the time I regarded blues as black folk music, that's the way I saw it. So I kept moaning at Roger, I said "Why not put some folk acts on as well? We could have an open mic and a singer's club." Now he didn't even have a PA system, he didn't play his records there, it was just a room. I said, "I can bring a turntable, a valve amp and some speakers and we can play some music before the artists come on." So he kind of ummed and ahhed. A couple of weeks later, on a particularly bad night, there were only three people there, it was rather glum and cold and I got the impression the landlord didn't even want him there. I said to him again

"Get some folk music on, we can get a buzz going," Roger lost his temper this time, he just threw everything into the tin, threw it into his case and said, "alright, I've had enough, seeing as you can do it better, you take the club, I'm off!" and he stomped off.

So I found myself proprietor of the Black Lion Folk and Blues club. What I did was contact the *Manchester Evening News* and another publication called *The Rocket*, had a chat with reporters, told friends and got some acts in. We got a turntable in and played some records and within a fortnight the place was heaving. I thought to myself, Roger you're such a bloody fool, why didn't he just hang on?

Further up that street was a record shop called 'Barry's Record Rendezvous' where they used to sell really rare records, I was one of their biggest customers. I met a lady who worked there called Patsy Robinson who I think turned out to be Roger's girlfriend at a later stage. She chatted me up, I'd never been chatted up before. I really fancied this lady as well, but within quite a short space of time she snared Roger. I don't think it was the other way round. She dumped him eventually and left him a rather unhappy man.

For Roger Eagle and the people working on *R&B Scene*, it became an obsession in the Autumn of 1964 to locate the whereabouts of the outrageous and theatrical performer Screamin' Jay Hawkins. Roger was always drawn to enigmatic and unusual entertainers such as Link Wray, Travis Wammack, Lord Buckley and Captain Beefheart to name just a few. So to get Jay on at The Wheel became a prime concern. That August Jay was tracked down to Honolulu, Hawaii where he could be found working as MC/in-house pianist at a downtown club. Everyone working on *R&B Scene* was now on a mission to persuade Screamin' Jay Hawkins to come to England and play at The Twisted Wheel. The letters sent from Manchester finally reached Jay and in October Jay's manager John Cann contacted *R&B Scene* and it was agreed that the magazine would help publicize a tour and Jay would appear at The Wheel.

In 1982 Roger Eagle was asked to write the liner notes on a Screamin' Jay Hawkins L.P. on an Edsel/Demon records release entitled 'Frenzy'. This is what he had to say:

'The secretary of the Carl Perkins Fan Club - Brian Smith, and myself, had gone to the Midland Hotel in Manchester to meet Little Richard. Unexpectedly we also met Don Harris and Dewey Terry who were employed at that time as Little Richard's bass player and guitarist. Don and Dewey were immediately cross-examined by Brian and myself for information concerning various rock 'n' roll legends who at the time were only known to us via their wild and rare recordings. Brian mentioned Screamin' Jay Hawkins. The affable Don and Dewey replied that Jay was still on the scene and working, in of all places, Hawaii. We wrote to Hawaii. Jay replied. Jay in fact replied from his hospital bed where he was recuperating after a certain lady singer had seen fit to plunge a large knife into the person of one of the wildest, most outrageous figures who ever stomped through the pages of rock 'n' roll history.

'Not only did Jay send us all manner of press cuttings and details about himself but we also received an album from the desk of a man named Jack Cione, who employed Jay in his night club and who also ran a label called the Sound of Hawaii. Included on the album were two tracks by our man - 'The Whammy' and 'Seems Like You Just Don't Care'. Next thing

that happened was a phone call from a nice man in New York called John Cann. Could we recommend anyone who might be interested in bringing Jay over to England? I suggested the agent who booked a lot of the soul and R&B acts into The Twisted Wheel, where I was the DJ at the time. Before long a welcoming committee from the Wheel had gone to London Airport to meet Jalacy Screamin' Jay Hawkins in person. Jay emerged at 6 in the morning, setting fire to his beard as he made his entrance, "You don't have to keep us amused all the time," we murmured and led him away for questioning. A master of true-image rock 'n' roll musicianship, Jay appeared in a cape, turban and shades, carrying with him a skull called Henry. Palm concealed flash paper, ignited by cigarette smoking Henry, heralded his entrances.

'FLASH… a series of images… Jay backstage at The Wheel concealed behind a door, the featured artist of the evening was T-Bone Walker; Jay having last seen him fourteen years previously when there had been some trouble concerning a trombone fired from an Arkansas hotel window at 3 am. Jay leapt from behind the door as T-Bone was making his way to the stage, utterly destroying the bluesmaster's sense of reality… later Jay joined T-Bone on stage for a stunning version of 'Mumbling Blues'… Jay driving Neil's Anglia at full throttle down Wilmslow Road, left wheels touching the kerb, singing at the top of his voice… a burst of opera when interviewed by Jimmy Saville on TV… Jay enhancing some lucky young couples wedding, when, appearing in the afternoon sunlight, they were greeted by the sight of Screamin' Jay Hawkins leaning from his hotel window opposite the church waving Henry and firing blanks from a .32 shouting "Shame on you"… memories of tours in the States with Chuck Willis and Nappy Brown… each in their Cadillacs with a case of scotch, bourbon or brandy in the trunk of their cars stopping by the side of the road to set up a bar… Jay appearing at the Apollo - emerging scratched and torn from his coffin; the man had had a monkey with him at the time and the release catch had stuck…A nightclub owner in Chicago who had been reluctant to part with Jay's fee, being asked to ignite the gunpowder in the special effects box at the side of the stage - Jay had thoughtfully primed it with three times the

normal amount of powder - nightclub owner losing eyebrows... Jay onstage... the stage in pitch darkness... a terrifying bang which scared the audience silly... Jay emerging into the spotlight over the, 'I Put A Spell On You' riff, Henry smoking a cigarette (you know smoking's bad for you, look at Henry).

'FLASH... Jay's rich baritone coming as though from the back of a swamp-filled cave... howling, screaming, grunting the lyrics, Jay suddenly pulling out a battered tenor sax, blasting the enthralled audience with all the power his lungs could command... the red spotlight, white turban, shades, a skull on the end of a pole, BANG!... FLASH!... 'I Put A Spell On You... because... you're mine...SCREAM... all mine... CRASH!'...

Brian Smith: When we went down to meet Screamin' Jay in early '65, we dropped in on an aunt of Roger's who worked for the BBC as a producer or something, I assume she was single and she lived in this beautiful place in Chelsea. We also stayed at a place in Cheshunt with an old friend of his from when he was a kid. He was a Met. PC, quite plummy, he seemed too upper crust to be in the Met.

Neil Carter: The main player in getting Screamin' Jay Hawkins over to England was actually Brian Smith. Jay was working in Hawaii at the time and this album came out that was recorded at the club he was working at – he had just a couple of tracks on it. I think Brian got hold of a copy of that and as a result Roger got in touch with the club.

He was absolutely fantastic, I think I was lucky knowing him at a time in his life when he had a very stable relationship. He came over two or three times during the mid-60s and he was happily married to Ginny, his Hawaiian wife. I think he left everything to her when he died. I don't know what happened between them. I was in regular contact with him then suddenly I got a letter saying "I'm moving, don't contact me again" and that was the last I heard of him. Certainly when I knew him he was great fun and all this business later about 'Are you one of Screamin' Jay's kids?' was quite a surprise really. He used to come round to our house regularly, he loved my Mum's apple pie, he was just great.

Remember this was the mid-sixties, he was just treated like anyone else, over here the idea of colour was never really an issue. I mean we never really thought about it to be honest and I think that was quite an eye-opener for him. He was very much aware of the black/white divide in the States but he didn't really see much of that over here at all, I think he appreciated that a lot.

CP Lee: You know the great story about Roger getting Screamin' Jay Hawkins to play in this country? Well it takes them a while to find the manager, long distance phone calls, you could be bankrupted with a long distance phone call in those days. Just before he's to meet Screamin' Jay, Roger gets a telegram and it's a bit sort of obtuse, and it says 'Don't forget that before he plays, Screamin' Jay likes to smoke'. So Roger is a bit baffled by it and then realises he's worried that he can't get American cigarettes. So he gets somebody to go to Burtonwood airbase and they buy 200 cigarettes off somebody and then they come back. When Screamin' Jay arrives he goes, "Screamin' Jay, I've got your cigarettes." And Jay goes, "When I said smoke I meant dope." We were all naive, we knew nothing of this... but imagine the surprise of Roger putting him into the car for the drive from the airport to Manchester city centre, and they've just about reached Fallowfield when Jay rolls down the window and pulls out a revolver and starts firing. This is, of course, in the days before anyone gave a shit about how you travelled. Whether it was blanks or what to wind Roger up I don't know.

Roger says "What the fuck do you think you're doing?"

Screamin' Jay goes, "Just keepin' 'em on their toes man!"

Have you heard the story about them driving through town with Lightnin' Hopkins. Lightnin' shouts through the window,

"Come on over here baby, I'm gonna teach your pussy to whistle" and Roger's going, "We don't do that sort of thing" and Lightnin' is going, "Hell man she was smiling." As you can imagine, for us lads this was a completely different world.

The hard work that Roger and the guys at The Wheel had put in to track down Screamin' Jay finally came to fruition when Jay made his first appearance on Friday 19th February 1965. He also played the early and late sets on Saturday 20th, his backing band were a local group called the Falling Leaves. Jay would go on to play one more set at The Wheel on Monday 19th April 1965. Sadly, while in the UK, Jay became involved with a certain booking agent of questionable morals and after a disagreement over money or unfulfilled dates it's said that a gun was held to Jay's head, and Jay understandably fled the country.

Neil Carter: It was really the two Roger's, Brian and myself, we were regulars around 1965, we used to go everywhere together, we'd go to all the shows and we'd go backstage at all the shows as well. If it was a big show such as Bo Diddley we'd tend to all go together, in fact it was only the American blues, R&B type acts we were interested in.

I had my own car, but I had very little money, well this was really why Roger and I fell out. I was a teller in the bank at the time and the salary was peanuts. Roger grew to expect me to drive him everywhere, I just felt I was being taken advantage of more and more. Eventually I just sort of cut the tie and didn't see him again, which is a shame really, but I just felt he was taking advantage too much. I couldn't afford it anymore.

By the Easter of 1965 the buzzword at The Twisted Wheel was soul, the mod scene had mutated and Motown was massive. The clothing styles were becoming more casual and a younger dance-oriented crowd were taking over the dancefloor. Soul was going overground, you couldn't escape it. The first Motown tour or the

Motortown Revue landed in the UK on March 19th 1965.

Roger Eagle: I went to see the early Motown tour, there was only 150 people in the audience, a great line up of acts including The Supremes and The Miracles, it must have been '65, it was empty, just really badly attended. It was at the Manchester Odeon, the bands actually applauded the audience for coming. I remember The Miracles, The Supremes and The Contours. It was a big tour but it just didn't work, it was a year too early basically.

Many consider the last 6 months of the Brazennose Street Twisted Wheel to be the best times in the club's short history and by April 1965 The Wheel was at a peak and it's claim to be the number one R&B club in the country at the time would be difficult to dispute. It was considered to be a major venue by touring black American artists who were visiting the UK with increasing frequency. The club had the best dancers, a hip clientele and with Roger Eagle, the best DJ in the country. Rivalled only by The Scene club in London, The Wheel had it all.

But things were not plain sailing behind the scenes. The owners of the club, the Abadi brothers, were struggling with the short twelve monthly lease and an increasing interest in the club being shown by the Manchester police. With this in mind the Abadis decided to move the club across town to 6 Whitworth Street, which was on the opposite side of the road to the Fire Station.

4 - The Whitworth Street Twisted Wheel club

Towards the end of the Brazennose Street Twisted Wheel and from the start of the Whitworth Street Wheel, the club's essence merged with the significant rise of the Detroit record label Tamla Motown.

Starting his music career as a record producer in the 1950's, Berry Gordy started the label in 1960 with a loan of $600. He first named the label Tammie then later changed it to Tamla. With the publishing arm of the company, Jobette, already in place, it was the first exclusively black record company. The key to Berry Gordy's and Tamla Motown's success was in appealing to both white and black audiences. Smokey Robinson, in Gerri Hershey's book 'Nowhere To Run', stated, "Berry wanted to make crossover music, and crossover at that time meant that white people would buy your records, Berry's concept in starting Motown was to make music with a funky beat and great stories that would crossover, that would not be blues, and that's what we did."

Tamla Motown Records, on Berry Gordy's insistence, became a company with a close-knit family feel about it. Each act to record for the label had to go through what could be described as Gordy's prep school. Each act went through the same kind of nurturing or training, and this brought them closer together.

Maurice King coached the young stars in harmony singing, while Cholly Atkins took care of the choreography, teaching the slick dance moves, the back drops and spins. With chaperones at live gigs, the young stars were groomed to play anywhere and to anyone. In-house competition was actively encouraged, the writers would produce songs, producers write, singers would produce and vice versa.

The real star of Motown, though, was the sound; a stylish, sophisticated version of the rhythm and blues genre that proved to be hugely popular with both black and white audiences the world over. The actual sound of Motown was influenced in many ways by the church. The style of the label's singers was grounded in gospel. The accompaniment also borrowed from the church, the tambourine was placed forward in the song mixes and almost became Motown's calling card. The clapping, the simple steady uptempo four beats to the bar rhythms, the call and response harmonic structures and lyrical proclamations, in some cases resembled eulogies from the pulpit.

Above the craft of the songwriting, it was the production team of Eddie Holland, Lamont Dozier and Brian Holland that paved the way for the success of the label. Their work not only epitomised the Motown sound but, for 6 years, 1963-68, Holland Dozier Holland were the company's most central component, providing America with it's strongest challenge to Lennon and McCartney's domination of the pop music marketplace. The fact that the Beatles mentioned Motown to reporters wherever they went, did no harm at all to the Motown cause.

The influence of the Motown Corporation ran deep into the core of American society and culture, the echoes of which could be felt in the UK. The music proved to be some of the most enduring, stylish and popular ever committed to tape.

All over the US, in every major city, small independent labels began starting up, striving to imitate the Detroit label's success. For each of the small labels achieving success by emulating the Motown sound, there were hundreds, possibly thousands, of total failures. Some would be pressings of perhaps only 1 or 200, released and distributed to just the immediate locale. Many of these obscure releases would go on to become the staple of the so called 'Northern

Soul' scene of the 1970's. The scene, generally a retrogressive one, is still around today, and no doubt there are tunes, unsuccessful at the time, still to be discovered.

The Whitworth Street Twisted Wheel club opened on Saturday September 18th 1965 with a performance by The Spencer Davis Group, the later all-night session was DJ'd by Roger Eagle.

Roger Eagle: I was at the first place for about two years – that's where I started meeting the stars. I was at Whitworth Street for about a year – to my mind it was slipping a bit because we had some real giants on at the early Wheel but it was still capable of throwing up some good stuff. Ricky & the Vibrations were good, 'Hang On Sloopy' was a big record for them. Ricky out of the Vibrations gave me 'I Spy For The FBI'. When he got to know you he'd bring records over.

For the regulars at the Whitworth Street club the musical landscape was starting to change, rhythm and blues was going overground, becoming more popular with white audiences in the UK and the US, consequently its very essence was being diluted.

Roger Eagle: Over here, as in the States, they kicked the bluesmen out, and the slicker suited guys came in, you know, the guys who sang harmony and had the urban beat, the Motown beat. When that stuff started happening the blues singers were very much relegated back then. They just did concert tours and the blues fans went and sat there and clapped politely at the end of the numbers. Before, a blues artist would play at the Wheel to a packed club and the people were away with them, they weren't mods, they weren't into songs, they just liked what they were doing, and then it changed. I found soul very boring later on, I must confess. A year or so, 18 months was great, it was really good. Then it became just a question of a fast dance beat to keep people up all night. Most of them would be taking a lot of pills, that's all they wanted to do, in fact they didn't really want the bands on. The

Inkspots played there one night (June 1966) and the crowd were desperately trying to get them to play dance music and the Inkspots were completely baffled by it all.

As the urban Tamla Motown sound became increasingly popular, Roger's views on the Detroit record label were beginning to diverge from the popularity the label was gaining.

Roger Eagle: I played a bit of Motown, I played the Contours, I played some Marvin Gaye, I played one or two of the usual things, you couldn't avoid playing it really, Junior Walker of course, by far and away my most played Motown act was Junior Walker and the All Stars.

I would say it was seen as very high quality pop music with a great dance beat, but people became addicted to Motown and they didn't progress really. Because they liked that sound, 'The Sound of Young America' and it was a brilliant sound. But for me there's only so many times I can listen to the Temptations sing 'My Girl'.

I'm talking about the early stuff, before they concocted the botched up Tamla Motown label, their music was released on 'Oriole'. 'London American' had one or two Motown things but the label I was used to from Motown was 'Oriole'. Later it was 'Tamla' or 'Motown', or 'Soul' or 'V.I.P.' or whatever. But, er, a little too polished really and that summed up the way soul was going for me really.

Roger's musical tastes were always diverse, his knowledge and awareness of different genres and the different moods each record could create were what set him apart from the beat and pop DJ's working the Manchester clubs at the time.

Roger Eagle: There's always been popular soul and the deep soul, the club soul. It all split into so many different sections, DJs carving off their own different areas and calling it this, that and the other. I'm a roots man, I always have been, I just like adding layers to the roots. The roots of soul are tremendous, there are some enormously wonderful early soul records.

What it is, is the competition, it's the edge, the shoving and pushing by a new wave of artists, eager to establish themselves against fierce competition. What happens then, and it always happens it's the same cycle, is that money then appears, and the record companys usually don't have a clue, and they start spending money on people that aren't quite as good as the initial wave, and they're not as difficult to deal with. They're not as difficult to deal with because they want a career. They turn out records that sound better to the public ear because they're sweeter but to the connoisseur they sound bland, they kind of float off the surface because the pioneers have done their work and gone. The moment the money comes in, look at what happened to Stax, it went bust for millions, if not billions, they got too slick and they just started sounding like any other product. It's the law of the jungle, you grow too fast, you topple over.

One of the major points about the Twisted Wheel, and the whole mod scene as it developed in Manchester and all over the country, were the stunning dance styles that evolved; a free style that was a million miles away from the fifties partnered dance styles. The more expressive dance styles took off at the Whitworth Street club.

This was about self-expession, it was about communicating attitude, it was about cool, it was about transforming the energy and performance coming from the speakers into something that was your own and could maybe go some way toward explaining how you felt. Leg splits, knee drops, spins, back drops, slides – you had to make it up, there was no precedent, just the chance to rise above the drudgery of the working week, a dead-end job – a dead end life. To lose yourself in the music and claw back some personal pride. The more flamboyant dancers would have to be almost gymnasts to execute some of the acrobatic moves.

To dance for five or six hours takes super-human exertion, not to mention physical fitness, and there's no doubt that some dancers at the Whitworth Street Wheel were indeed super-human. But for mere mortals, whether to just stay awake or to have the staying power to dance energetically for long periods or simply to get blocked out of your skull, all-nighters became synonymous with uppers. Call them what you will; 'Pep pills', 'Speed', 'Blues', 'Purple Hearts', 'Dexys' or 'Black Bombers' – amphetamines were as much a part of this scene as your haircut, your clothes, the way you danced or the people you were seen with.

The music at the Brazennose Street club in the early days, as Roger explained, was very eclectic, with lots of different beats, rhythms, styles and performers but as the crowds grew so did the demand for a fast beat.

Be it chemical or natural, when you're speeding you sync with the beat and there's no feeling quite like being on a dance floor with a bunch of like minded people, dancing to a tune you love. The up-tempo tunes were requested, if not demanded, frequently from the regulars so that the faster beat became part of the scene, and the essence of the club. The faster tunes would later become known as 'Stompers'. These faster tunes, or as Roger described them the Urban or Motown styled beat, became the foundation for the future Northern Soul scene.

Ivor Abadi: Northern soul music is typically fast and very danceable. The dancing itself is also fast. The young people, especially the boys, would do acrobatic-type dancing, so they'd need a lot of space to do it. Sometimes one or two of the boys would take over the whole dance floor to the detriment of other people dancing. They wouldn't quite be doing somersaults but you'd see them spin around on the floor.

Brian Smith: What Roger didn't like was the fact that the stuff played in the club was becoming very repetitive, it was only played because it fitted a particular beat.

Les Hare: Amphetamine soul was what he called it, it was either a Motown record or a Motown soundalike record.

Roger Eagle: I remember playing the advance US copy of the Four Tops' 'Reach Out I'll Be There' (UK release Oct. 1966) for at least six months before it was released in the UK.

Along with the success of the club came unwanted attention from the press and Manchester's vice squad. Reports of rebel teenagers, amphetamine abuse and all-night dance raves became commonplace on TV and in the national and local newspapers. Their activity was tied in with a number of pharmacy robberies of prescription Drinamyl otherwise known as Purple Hearts.

Amphetamine Sulphate was first synthesisized in 1887 by Lazar Edeleanu but was not used medically until the 1930's, mainly to counter high blood pressure and enable asthmatics to breathe more easily. It was later prescribed for a large range of ailments including migraine, epilepsy, depression, sleeplessness and hyperactivity in children.

An estimated 72 million amphetamine tablets were issued to British forces during the Second World War with the express purpose of delaying fatigue and enhancing alertness. In the 1950's and 60's the drug was widely marketed as a slimming aid. Until 1956 many amphetamine based tablets could be bought in Britain over the counter and without a prescription. In 1964 the Drugs (Prevention of Misuse) Act was passed to control Amphetamine use in the UK.

Roger Eagle: The first two years were fun but into the third it became boring quite frankly because the music became too similar all the time, it was just a fast dance beat to keep people dancing all night. They were blocked out their heads on 'Blues' or whatever they were taking and you were just a human jukebox. You'd put one record on after another and if you tried anything different they would yell at you because all they were interested in was dancing. They're having a great time but for a DJ like myself – and I used to be a bit creative – it's just boring you know. So the other DJs that followed me capitalised on it and made a fortune. I don't begrudge it because I didn't have the mind to go on with it and do it, because I didn't think it was that brilliant anymore.

What separated Roger from other DJs working in Manchester at the time was his musical judgement and fine tuned appreciation of what could be considered a classic piece of music. The musical plagiarism and poor productions he must regularly have come across were immediately recognised for what they were, second rate, and these acts and labels were rarely given a second chance. He would have been looking for something different to what was making the charts, and to what other DJ's would have been playing. Also in many record shops in the 1960's, listening booths would have been common but Roger, like many other DJ's, will have purchased music without even hearing it a lot of the time, especially if he'd liked a previous release from the artist, or if the record had been imported from the US. It seems Roger developed his own personal filter, a gold standard filter and only these tunes would be allowed on what he would later term the 'Twentieth Century Jukebox'.

Ivor Abadi: Roger Eagle worked with us but he's passed away. If anything, he was a little too way out. He was more interested in the purity of the music and was happy for everybody just to sit and listen. But that's not what the crowd wanted, or what we wanted, for that matter.

Brian Rae: When Roger was doing it I think he got fed up with the fact that everyone was off their heads on pills and they just wanted up tempo stuff. I remember him playing one or two really good Fats Domino things, 'On Broadway', the Drifters, Esther Phillips stuff and so on. I'm one of the guys who was DJing at that intermission stage, where it wasn't what Roger was playing.

I was playing a huge assortment of uptempo soul. Not particularly Detroit based or anything, all that appeared with the Detroit thing a lot later on.

Roger Eagle: It's a strange thing; you could talk about drugs and music for a long time, different eras and different drugs and the different types of music. There's nothing more boring in this universe than not taking drugs and DJing to a crowd of kids who are blocked out their heads on pills. They are very boring people when they're speeding on their chemicals and you've got to put up with a lot of earache and they have no memory whatsoever, it's like instant memory loss, it takes about half an hour to organise a light for a cigarette. They're in a pleasant frame of mind; they're high, they're up, they're having a great time but unless you are there with them it's totally boring. I took pills twice, 'Blues', what the world at large used to call 'Purple Hearts', the standard amphetamine based pill at that time. There were other drugs around like 'Bombers', 'Green and Clears', Mandrax and some horrible yellow things going round, but mainly it was 'Blues', they were perfect for the music, perfect for the time and for those kids that wanted to do it and risk the damage they were doing to themselves, which was considerable. There'll be a lot of people out there today who got their reproductive systems and kidneys fucked up, particularly the women I think, because they just didn't know what they were doing. Some of them were taking unbelievable quantities. I had two twice, and I was off my head, speeding like crazy, and I knew kids that were doing sixty, eighty it's unbelievable.

Eagle's candid views on the uppers culture at the Twisted Wheel were informed by first hand knowledge but he was totally aware of the dangerous implications of getting involved. Here he speaks about his experience of the seamier side of the club and his concern for some of the clientele's future well-being.

Roger Eagle: It was alright but it got a bit frightening, it was too much, I mean it was speed on top of speed, because when I'm working I'm speeding anyway. Your heart goes, I know the symptoms, I can identify it immediately when someone is speeding, they're talking too fast. It's just that when kids are 16, 17, 18 and they fill themselves full of chemicals and they don't know what they are, then 10 or 15 years go by and they suddenly start developing all kinds of ailments, nobody's done a survey on that and perhaps they should. Liver and kidney damage would be what would concern me most with what I call the chemicals, the pharmaceutical products, the man made stuff. I've never really read much about the effects of drugs, I just see it. I tell you there was no sadder sight than to see a bunch of Wheel kids on a Sunday evening coming down off the pills from Saturday night. I mean just sitting there crying, mascara running down their faces, just totally depressed, and they've got like four or five days to get through at work at some fucking horrible little job before they've made enough money to get high again on Saturday night. The whole thing was about Saturday night, getting everything ready, spending all the money on everything connected with it all and going out and getting lost for 24 hours you know, 36 probably.

The popular impression of the Twisted Wheel is that it was a haven for amphetamine use right from the start of the all-night sessions. There's no doubt that as the club gained popularity and the membership grew, this certainly proved to be the case and a problem for the owners of The Wheel, the Abadi brothers.

Brian Smith: If anybody talks about the Wheel they always assume it was synonymous with the drug scene, yet to my certain knowledge, I may have been very naive, I never saw anyone in there doing anything. Apart from a couple of times when a couple of packets of something were found and the Abadi's heavies grabbed hold of them, took them outside and gave them a dusting, then took them to South Street police station about two minutes walk away.

Roger Fairhurst: I think a lot of the pills stuff has been very much exaggerated. It was gradual, mainly the dancers I think.

Ivor Abadi: We got blamed for everything that happened because we attracted all the people. And of course there was a little pep-pill scene in the sixties – amphetamines – and obviously some of them took pills but not everybody. We got blamed for something that was happening all over the place, including schools and universities. Suddenly the pep-pill scene was portrayed as something we'd created, but that's another story.

As part of his PHD thesis, CP Lee put forward the argument that the Manchester police of the 1960's systematically shut down the city's thriving and diverse coffee bar and live music scene. An extremely important piece of historical detective work, it uncovers the power and corruption that lay at the heart of the city's cultural demise from the late 60's through to the late 70's.

It was all brought about by one man with the assistance of an unprecedented Act of Parliament; Chief Superintendent Alan Dingwall and the Manchester Corporation Act (1965), which came into operation on 1st January 1966. CP Lee published his findings in the book 'Shake, Rattle And Rain'.

As an example of the effects of the youth/beat generation, the writer Alan Lawson in his book 'The True story of Manchester Music' listed over 200 clubs in Manchester which catered for this demographic between 1963 and 1966. By 1967 this was down to around a dozen, by 1971 there were three. The reason for this cultural desert, according to CP Lee, was police action, with allegations and rumours of corruption within the police force and stories of protection money being taken from clubs along with refusals to renew licenses.

CP Lee experienced first hand the emptying of clubs by the police and the resulting crowd in the street outside being threatened with charges of obstruction. This police harassment wasn't just common to club goers, the same went for young persons gathering in small crowds around the city centre.

While it is undeniable that drug use around Manchester in 1964-65 had escalated, it is also true that a criminal fraternity existed in the clubs of Manchester. Some clubs and coffee bars would undoubtedly have been used for the selling, procuring and taking of drugs. This would not have gone unnoticed by the police.

The first official police acknowledgement of Manchester's club scene came in the Chief Constable's Annual Report of 1964. In this document Chief Constable J.A. McKay referred to the growth of licensed and unlicensed premises and problems created by the 'Coffee club'. By August 1965 Chief Constable McKay was moved to almost single-handedly create outrage throughout the region via the press, TV and media. The panic created was severe enough to warrant the passing of a special Act of Parliament that allowed the police extra powers to deal with the perceived problems created by the coffee bars and clubs of Manchester. By using spurious links to local teenage deaths and mishaps totally unrelated to Manchester club culture, Chief Constable McKay began his campaign to decimate the Manchester club scene. Press interest was already there, it just needed a nudge and in the Chief Constable's annual report of 1965 it stated, 'Press interest was encouraged and interviews were readily given to the press and BBC reporters.'

Chief Constable McKay's club cleansing campaign was complete when he appeared before the House of Commons and presented Chief Superintendent Dingwall's special report. In August 1965 the Manchester Corporation Bill received royal assent and became the Manchester Corporation Act. It gave the police formidable power in regard to controlling and shutting down coffee bars, clubs and live music venues. In essence no-one could own, operate or run a club without express police permission.

Some clubs closed immediately, others moved around the city attempting to find permanence, many turned to the older, safer market of late night supper clubs and cabaret bars. Club nights were interrupted, music stopped, people's livelihood's disrupted. By 1967 drug raids became common, only a handful of venues survived, none were brave enough to hold all-nighters. By 1968 only two venues were left that catered purely for younger people, these were The Twisted Wheel and The Magic Village, both venues integral parts of the Roger Eagle story.

Brian Rae was the DJ that replaced Roger Eagle when he left The Twisted Wheel, his style was influenced by Roger and he was one of the first DJs to play Northern Soul style R&B at The Wheel all-nighters.

Brian Rae: I went to the Whitworth Street club when he was the disc jockey. Subsequently I did an audition for the Abadi brothers on a Tuesday night and I got this job and I was part of the disc jockeys that were set up at The Wheel. There were three DJ's as far as I can remember, occasionally the Blackpool thing (Twisted Wheel club Blackpool) would finish early and the guy from Blackpool would come down and do a bit. My spot was in the middle of the night, occasionally I'd do the end of the night.

Years and years later, it never dawned on me at the time when I did the audition at The Wheel for the Abadi brothers, but it was to replace Roger. It didn't hit me at the time, it was only years later that we worked it all out. I was showing him these old posters I had from The Wheel, and one of them was from a Tuesday night which was when I did my audition and 'Ugly' Ray Terrett was on, I had to play half an hour of soul stuff and there was no competition so they gave me the job.

As rhythm and blues and rhythm and blues influenced music became more prevalent, in clubs, on the radio and on television, the more it became an integral part of the national psyche, ingrained in the social fabric of working class life and culture. Blues music and blues influenced music became more British than it's own indiginous folk music heritage of lyres, lutes and madrigals, in a similar way to the modern consensus that certain styles of Indian food have come to be considered 'British'.

The term 'Northern Soul' was introduced by writer and soul archivist Dave Godin, who made a major contribution towards the understanding and awareness of American soul music worldwide. Godin founded the Tamla Motown Appreciation Society and also became Motown's consultant in the UK. In 1968 he founded 'Soul City', a record shop and label based in Deptford, South London. In an interview with Chris Hunt of *Mojo* magazine in 1992, he explained how he coined the term 'Northern Soul' to help staff in his record shop differentiate between different genres of black American music. His words to his staff were, "Don't waste your time playing new records out of the American chart when you've got northern people in the shop, play them these records, Northern Soul records." Northern Soul was the uptempo Motown style sound popular in northern clubs a few years prior to the opening of his Soul City shop. Dave Godin also wrote regularly for *Blues and Soul* magazine.

Interviewed in 1998 by Bill Brewster and Frank Broughton for their book 'Last Night a DJ Saved My Life', Roger sums up his time at The Twisted Wheel and explains his link to the Northern Soul scene.

"I started 'Northern Soul', but I actually find the music very limiting, because in the early days I'd play a Charlie Mingus record, then I'd play a bluebeat disc followed by a Booker T tune, then a Muddy Waters or Bo Diddley record. Gradually, there was this blanding out to one sort of sound. When I started DJing I could play what I wanted. But after three years I had to keep to the same tempo, which is what Northern Soul is."

The last record played by Roger Eagle at the Whitworth Street Twisted Wheel club on Sunday August 27th 1966 was 'Funky

Broadway' by Dyke & the Blazers. This record and its significance could almost be taken as a statement of intent by Roger, his refusal to play the predictable was what took him away from the Twisted Wheel.

Following Eagle's departure, the Whitworth Street Twisted Wheel club gathered momentum and the style of music pioneered by him became well established. Many DJ's made names for themselves at the club by playing American soul and R&B that was contemporary to the time. After many successful years the Abadi brothers finally shut the club on the 30th January 1971 with a performance from Wheel favourite Edwin Starr. The closure of the club heralded the start of one of the biggest underground musical movements ever. Other clubs such as The Golden Torch in Stoke-on-Trent, The Catacombs in Wolverhampton, and The Highland Rooms at Blackpool Mecca kept the movement going. In September 1973 the world renowned Wigan Casino opened. At the Casino it was classic and rare 1960's tunes that were played, the scene had now become retrogressive, and this is where Northern Soul really had its day, it thrived in a similar way throughout the rest of the decade and is still popular today.

Northern Soul is now a worldwide phenomenon; club nights exist all over Europe, Japan, Australia, New Zealand and the United States. Under the Northern Soul name many compilation CDs are pressed each year and the prices paid by collectors for original 1960's 45 rpm vinyl pressings may seem astonishing to the untutored. The increasing popularity of older styles of dance music could be viewed as a comment on the condition of modern popular styles of music. As Roger said in 1994, "All we are hearing now are echoes from the musical explosions of the 20th century."

Roger Eagle made a huge cultural contribution to the British musical landscape in the way he brought African-American rhythm and blues to the Mancunian public's attention. He helped inform not just Manchester's 1960s modernist generation but touring musicians from all over the UK and the world. Eagle's influence over the musical tastes of many thousands of Twisted Wheel club goers can still be felt in the North-West's love of soul, rhythm and blues and dance music in the present day. Passed down through families, through DJ's who were influenced by him and through bands whose music had been influenced by the music he played.

In the mid-1960's it would have been relatively easy for rock bands such as The Rolling Stones, The Beatles and others to suggest where their influences lay, as they had the press and media hanging on their every word, and undoubtedly this would have contributed to an awareness of African-American music that had previously been ignored. But to play this music to an audience week in/week out for three years was a positive and unprecedented achievement, especially in a country that at the time still considered itself to be white European. With Roger Eagle it wasn't even a consideration – black African-American rhythm and blues was such an integral part of rock 'n' roll and therefore modern culture that it couldn't be ignored.

5 - The Blue Note, the Staxx club and the Magic Village

Roger's first venture after The Wheel was a club called The Blue Note on Gore Street, just a couple of minutes walk from Whitworth Street. At The Blue Note Roger played a lot more records from the Stax record label, a label based in Memphis releasing soul and R&B with a more rootsy and raw style than the urban Tamla and Motown sounds coming out of Detroit. Roger stayed at The Blue Note club for about eight months before moving on to open his own club. This came about at the old Three Coins club on Fountain Street, at premises once owned by Jimmy Savile and re-named The Staxx Club in tribute to Roger's favourite Soul label. The Staxx Club logo had the same design as the Memphis record label but with an added 'X'. Apparently the club was not overly successful and quite short lived with Roger playing a mixture of ska, soul, funk and R&B but what can be said is the music he played would have been excellent and definitely more diverse than the musical road down which The Twisted Wheel was now travelling.

Roger Eagle: I was very restricted with what I could play (at The Wheel) and I thought 'I'm not getting paid enough to do this – I ain't gonna do it no more'. So I left and immediately got paid a decent wage by Debbie Fogel at The Blue Note club. I got a fiver a night for four nights, besides doing other things. I was able to play the kind of music that I liked, the range of music. Whereas the pill freaks only wanted the same dance beat – which is what makes it so boring. I was a black music fanatic and I had respect for what I was dealing with – I don't think they did.

At the Staxx club the music policy was similar, I was trying to play funk, early funk. The people that turned up were probably just people round town, pill freaks that just popped in and out. You can't look at it with hindsight, at the time it wasn't "Oh we're going to start a movement!" It was just the place to be, it was the place for the in-crowd for a while.

Brian Rae: We never used to go to the Staxx club all-nighter but we did go there on a Sunday morning after we'd been in The Wheel. We'd go down to the bogs at Piccadilly station, get changed, then go straight across to the Staxx club.

The most succesful Stax tour was the Stax/Volt European tour of 1967, being a massive fan of the roots R&B/Soul label, Roger made a point of attending a couple of the gigs when the tour hit the north of England.

Roger Eagle: The next big tour that came over really did the business, that was the Stax tour with Otis Redding, Sam & Dave, Eddie Floyd, Carla Thomas, Booker T & the MG's and The Mar-Keys. Stunning, absolutely stunning, just ripped people to pieces, and that did sell well.

I went over to see it in a bus garage in Bradford or Leeds or one of those sort of places, and there it wasn't particularly well attended, but the Manchester shows, there were two of them, and they were absolutely rammed out, absolutely fanatical, that was at The Palace. The whole balcony was moving up and down several feet. People were moving out of the way because they thought the balcony was gonna come down. It was unbelievable, unbelievable. Otis Redding was probably the greatest stage performer I've ever seen.

Mike Don moved from Edinburgh to Manchester to study at the University in 1967. Through his love of rock 'n' roll he had already come across Roger's name in relation to the *R&B Scene* magazine that Roger and his friends had put out a couple of years previously. Mike would later go on to run the underground magazine stall in the Magic Village, selling his magazines *Mole Express* and *Glass Eye*. He also sold magazines at Liverpool Stadium, as well as running the alternative bookshop Grass Roots in the centre of Manchester.

Mike Don: When I moved to Manchester to study I moved into this bedsit, the address was 14 Victoria Grove, Fallowfield. There were about 9 bedsits in this old block and I got to know the various people living in them, including a couple of fellow students who were in the Socialist society, sort of militant left wingers. From a downstairs flat I heard the strains of classic rock 'n' roll and I thought 'Who's in there?' A fellow fan? I discovered it was Roger Eagle, I actually recognised him from a picture in one of the *R&B Scene* magazines I'd managed to obtain. He was fairly distinctive, you know, about 8 foot tall. So I got to know him sort of thing and at that time he was managing Milton James. This is about '67, around the time the counter-culture thing started.

CP Lee was a member of what Roger Eagle described as Manchester's only authentic, contemporary to the time, psychedelic band; Greasy Bear. Along with Bruce Mitchell he later formed Alberto Y Los Trios Paranoias, a satirical rock group who took the rise out of anyone and everyone who took themselves even remotely seriously, especially other bands. After the band split CP went on to write his Snuff Rock Musical 'Sleak'.

CP was awarded his PhD in 1997 and has had two books published about Bob Dylan, one on Manchester's music scene called 'Shake, Rattle & Rain', and the biographical 'When We Were Thin'. He teaches Cultural Studies in the Department of Media and Performance at the University of Salford.

CP Lee: I first came across Roger Eagle when I was 16. I was in an awkward transition from being, believe it or not a 16 year-old folk fan, and I'd just seen Bob Dylan at the Free Trade Hall in 1966.

I had a girlfriend called Nina who lived in South Manchester and the house opposite always looked very intriguing. I used to see these guys in suits coming in and out of the house and there was a van and young guys with guitars and cases with a black man, a black man without a case, and also a very tall rocker with a red cardigan. Eventually I plucked up the courage to talk to these guys and the first person I spoke to was a bloke called Mike Don who lived downstairs because it was a house of flats and I found out that the big tall man, the rocker, was a guy called Roger Eagle. The black guy and the white guys were the Milton James Soul band and this was around early 1967. I would go over into the flat because Roger had an absolutely astonishing record collection and I learnt that he'd been the DJ at The Twisted Wheel club and that was very impressive to me that it was him because I realised I had heard of him. Milton James went by the by.

Roger's business was always related to taking care of, entertaining and catering for the tastes of the general public. It could also be said he had a distinct mothering side to him when it came to looking after artists – the educational as far as music was concerned, the advisory when it concerned the music industry, caring when it came to personal problems. While looking after Milton James with Laurence Selcoe, it is unlikely that that they struck any percentage management deals…

CP Lee: I think it was Roger's dream to have a hit soul band in the style of Geno Washington. He thought if you had a black American singer you could clean up in this country, Jimmy James and the Vagabonds was another one. The problem with Milton was he couldn't sing, but er… Roger never let this bother him.

Milton James was apparently from Swinton but on his press release he was 'The Boy From New York City' and he'd played the

Apollo Theatre in Harlem. His backing band also played on their own as The Gin House. From an article on the website 'Manchesterbeat' The Gin House Saxophonist, Dave Bowker recalls gigging with Milton James.

Dave Bowker: I recall faking an American accent as I introduced him onstage every night at gigs. We tried to give the impression that the whole band was from the US! It sure helped with getting to know the girls.

Bruce Mitchell is one of the finest drummers to ever come out of Manchester and for more than thirty years was a close friend to Roger Eagle, sharing a similar sense of humour and taste in both literature and music. Bruce has probably played with more bands than any other musician in Manchester, starting off his career in the 1950's and continuing into the 21st century. Playing with CP Lee in Jacko Ogg & the Head People in the 1960's, Greasy Bear and Albertos Y Los Trios Paranoias in the 1970's, he was subsequently a constant in The Durutti Column, while picking up session work along the way. Roger Eagle relates a story of seeing Bruce on his way to a gig, riding a moped, bass drum strapped to his back, the rest of his kit attached precariously to his person.

Bruce Mitchell: Around the time I first met Roger he was managing a tall thin harmonica player who was an expert on trams and Roger thought he needed a bit of a band behind him and I got roped in to play drums. I think I played one rehearsal. But, you know this guy was a lemon. All I remember is this guy was an expert on trams, vintage trams.

A little while later Roger was managing a guy called Milton James, a soul singer, he was doing it in partnership with a guy called Laurence Selcoe, a very nutty Jewish bass player. Roger at this time seemed to really enjoy firing musicians, he fired 47 musicians from the Milton James backing band.

Mike Don: At one point around this time I got word that

there was 'A Happening', a sort of hippy gathering at the old Chorlton Town Hall. So I went along and one of the people there said, "We've got this band together called Jacko Ogg and the Head People" and they gave me an address for where they were rehearsing. So I made my way there and it was basically the attic in this guy's house and there were three of them in the band. To be perfectly honest they were pretty bad version of The Jimi Hendrix Experience. Anyway I got back to Victoria Grove, met Roger and told him about this band, he was dismissive y'know? Grunts, and says, "I'm not interested". The next thing I know he's got in touch with them and he's started managing them. He changed the personnel, added Bruce Mitchell, who he already knew, that made them a bit more professional and added a bass guitarist called John Gibson. They changed their name to Greasy Bear and became the mainstay of the Manchester counter-culture hippy scene. They were pretty good.

CP Lee: I can remember a great Roger story; he was telling me that earlier in the 60's you could hire out a church hall or local council hall and you'd put up a poster saying 'Tonight, a Beat Group 2s/6d'. You didn't even have to put the name of the band on it and it would pack out because people wanted to see live music. So Roger had a big tube full of these posters that now must be worth a fortune.

He trailed Milton all over North Wales and the North-West, playing at clubs where he'd built up contacts due to the fact that Roger, as I began to learn, was an amazingly respected figure. He'd published a blues magazine (*R&B Scene*) and this was virtually unheard of at the time. I mean nowadays we'd probably refer to it as a fanzine but back then it looked really sophisticated.

Roger's love of Captain Beefheart carried on throughout his life and Captain Beefheart and the Magic Band were one of the bands that Eagle would constantly reference. When discussing Beefheart he would become very animated, Roger believed the Captain was one of the greatest artists of the twentieth century. Along with John Peel, Eagle helped to bring Beefheart to the attention of the British public, if it wasn't for them, along with fanzines such as *Zig-Zag*, it's unlikely Beefheart would have the recognition and respect he now has. From an interview with John Crumpton Roger talks here of his introduction to Beefheart.

Roger Eagle: The first time I heard Captain Beefheart was in a club I was running called The Blue Note in Manchester in 1967 or 1968. It was the Safe As Milk album and it was an import – it wasn't released at the time. I played it in the club, someone was raving about it and it just struck me that it was a very good white blues album but a bit difficult to cotton on to because it was in club conditions. It wasn't until I actually got the album and played it myself at home that it actually got to me. It struck me as being harsh and a bit jagged when I first heard it but I was running a club at the time so it was bit difficult to work out. There was something definitely different about it, there was a lot of imagery there in the lyrics, especially songs like 'Autumn's Child' or 'Electricity', they were radically different. Everybody seemed to be into peace and love and I remember people commenting at the time that it was a harsh sound.

It must have been just just before Peel started playing him because it was a brand new album at the time, it was the only thing that was available. There was possibly the A&M EP, that was very hard to find, nobody knew about it, it wasn't promoted or reviewed at the time.

Beefheart was a little more difficult to get into at first. But the strangeness of it, the difference of it was what counted. It had obviously resisted a commercial path and he was some new kind of poet. A very powerful voice and he obviously had great ideas about rhythm and instrumentation that were all his own. Ry Cooder was exactly right to guest on that first album because that was the jump from traditional blues into the Beefheartian world of fractured blues. You have to understand that in the very early days the American music business wanted a Rolling Stones, they wanted someone who could take the blues and twist them a little bit and make it popular. They didn't like what they heard because it was too difficult for them.

CP Lee: Roger was a remarkable man because he kind of adopted me musically, as I was emerging from folkiedom. My mate Mike King and I had started a, we didn't know what it was, an electric trio, which we called Jacko Ogg and the Head People. We'd originally started the band before The Magic Village and it was on Tuesday nights at a club on Gore Street called The Blue Note that they allowed us to do experiments. Jacko Ogg used to play there, with Bruce dressed in a gorilla suit and we had a rhythm guitarist called Les who was North of England bagpipe champion. Every now and then we'd say 'right get the bagpipes out' and we'd do 'Baby You're a Rich Man' by The Beatles or whatever... bombs exploding, Bruce in a gorilla suit and Dave Backhouse, who ran the lightshow, would ride his Lambretta through the crowd and Roger was DJing there.

We were the first band in Manchester to use a light show, which were in fact out of focus slides of the Blackpool illuminations with somebody's hand waved up an down in front of the lens. By 1967 we had worked out the use of glass slides with oils and revolving filters.

John Eagle is Roger's youngest brother, 10 years his junior. Here John talks about his relationship with his brother and his recollections of visiting Manchester in the 1960's. John is now a professional artist and photographer living and working in West Cork, Ireland where he spent a large part of his childhood.

John Eagle: I didn't know him at all really, I remember going up to Manchester to stay with him on Wilbraham Road. I remember he was living in a big untidy room. I can remember him using the gas cooker flame to heat this block and soften it, he said "don't tell Mum I'm doing this". That was the first time I'd seen anyone take drugs. I remember going to see a guy in The Spencer Davis Group, we had to go and wake him up, I couldn't tell you who he was. He was staying in his own place in Manchester somewhere. I remember going by taxi everywhere.

On another occasion I went to stay with him in Manchester and the woman next door, who was a Tom Jones fan, looked after me. Roger would meet me off the train at Piccadilly. I never stayed in Manchester very long, I was a youngster. You didn't dare wake him until at least 12 or 1 o'clock, I couldn't understand that as a kid.

By 1967 Roger, along with trying to find his own club, had started to appreciate the emerging rock scene, finding interesting new ideas for putting on shows, new formats and ways for artists to express themselves. This time in the sixties was a watershed for creativity and barriers were being broken down everywhere in the name of freedom and free expression. Roger would have been listening to Captain Beefheart & The Magic Band, The Pink Floyd, Cream and The Jimi Hendrix Experience, as well as music from the American West Coast such as The Grateful Dead and the emerging funk scene with artists such as James Brown and Sly & The Family Stone.

Roger Eagle: Well as a starter, for every white blues singing female ever since, Janis Joplin has been the absolute high spot of it all hasn't she? All based on the strength of, I think, one album. 'Oh Lord won't you buy me a Mercedes Benz' and 'Cry' didn't she do 'Cry'? I used to have that album. She's inspired an awful lot of women, I'll tell you that much, whether you like her or not, she was a major influence. I don't know much about her, seen bits of film of her and heard her records, and I thought she just had a voice and an attitude, she just did it, she wasn't trying to be black, she wasn't copying anybody. She was just yelling out the stuff the way she did.

Around 1967 the psychedelic drug Lysergic acid diethylamide, or LSD, was beginning to make its way onto the streets of Great Britain. A non-addictive drug known for its psychological effects, it altered thought processes, produced audio and visual hallucinatory effects and altered one's sense of time and spatial awareness. A dose smaller than a grain of salt was enough to precipitate a journey that may encompass hallucination, intense emotion and even mystical revelation.

The chemical was first synthesised in 1938 by Albert Hofmann. The first intentional ingestion of LSD was by Hofmann himself on April 19th 1943. Sandoz Laboratories in Switzerland marketed the substance as a psychiatric drug in 1947. Starting in the 1950's the CIA began a research program code named project MKULTRA which involved dispensing LSD to CIA employees, military personnel, medical practitioners, prostitutes, mentally ill patients and members of the public to study the effects of the drug, for the most part without the subject's knowledge. In the late 50's LSD was also being studied in Palo Alto, California, and offered to the public as part of research programs. This, coupled with large amounts of the drug being liberated and distributed, was how many artists, musicians and writers were first introduced to LSD.

Many active campaigners for the drug were now surfacing, this first wave of exponents saw the start of the 1960s counter-culture movement. People such as poet Allen Ginsberg, novelist and counter-culture activist Ken Kesey, writer Aldous Huxley, and, perhaps most notoriously Dr Timothy Leary whose catchphase, "Turn on, tune in, drop out" became the adopted catchphrase for the whole scene. By 1967 LSD was more easily available, it had become central to the American psychedelic subculture's notion of 'Turning on' and seeing beneath the world's veneer became central to it's manifesto.

The backlash against public use of LSD also started around the mid-sixties; its perceived damaging effects on the values of western society resulted in government action to control the availability of the drug by making any use of it illegal. It was banned in California on October 6, 1966. Other US states and the rest of the world followed. It was declared illegal in the UK after the 1971 Misuse of Drugs Act came about.

CP Lee: By this time Roger had left the Twisted Wheel and was looking for a new venue because in his own way Roger was an experimenter and he wasn't afraid of taking chances and he was aware that there was a new kind of music coming up but he wasn't sure which direction it was going to go in... But he was interested in what we were doing. He loved, believe it or not, the first Pink Floyd album, 'Piper at the Gates of Dawn', and also Roger had taken acid. Now let me set the scene.

If you smoke draw a great thing to do is sit in an armchair and listen to music, it enhances the listening pleasure, a debatable point, but one I believe in none the less. Now the same thing could be said about acid. Acid puts it into a whole new perspective. Roger was one of the first people I had met who had taken LSD and Roger had very, very specific ideas about how you should do acid; that you should do it properly in a conducive atmosphere; set and setting were important and that you should do it with a guide. So Roger, in very early 1967, offered to guide me on my first acid trip.

So the first the first thing to do is to choose the right albums to play, now there were very few back then for this sort of thing but Roger made an interesting set of selections. It was winter and it was in Withington and it was snowing. We dropped the acid around mid-day and Roger sat there smoking draw while we went up. He played gentle music at first, just sort of acoustic blues, Lightin' Hopkins and Mance Lipscomb as well, I mean a really nice cross section of blues music. Then as things got freakier Roger started playing Cannonball Adderley, Bird, Coltrane. A very strange fusion of music and then he said "Right! We're all going for a walk!" and he took us out in the snow. I think there were three or four of us and Roger paraded us round Withington. It's unbelievable now, my mind is completely blown by that when I think about it. In fact I've not thought about it for thirty odd years, I don't think. He took us into a park, and it was a completely white field of snow and I remember one of us going up to the corner and signing it – GOD. Then going back to Roger's and tailing down on the trip. So Roger was my guide on my first ever trip.

An LSD experience can be extremely frightening for the uneducated. The fact that not a lot was known about the substance in mid-60's Britain made the potential for problems even more acute. Roger would have been only too aware of this and through his thoughtful and concerned guidance CP and his companions had the best trip they could have hoped for.

CP Lee: He was very, very good because he was an incredibly kind man. I was talking to somebody in here earlier who said he used to go to the Magic Village and he said he was terrified of Roger, his height and physical presence made him very intimidating. But I have literally known this man give you the shirt off his back. I can remember when I was with Greasy Bear, which was a band that Ian Wilson, Bruce and myself had during the Magic Village period, and he would bring round boxes of groceries for us to live on, because we weren't doing that many gigs, he'd bring food round. He always made sure there was enough draw to smoke. A very kind bloke, but the ultimate kindness of Roger was his University of Music.

It's possible that Roger's experiences with LSD helped to inform his new worldview, as well as his embracing of, and participation in the social changes and counter-culture of the time. He would have seen the drug mentioned in the media and like many others would have been intrigued as to its effects. His way of looking at and experiencing the world would have changed dramatically. It's easy to imagine some sort of epiphany taking place and a plan manifesting regarding his career choice. If we say this happened around the time of The Blue Note club and came to fruition at The Magic Village we can place the timeline to 1967.

At the same time a small section of Manchester youth would have – through influence from the media, street fashions and popular music – been developing a similar set of new ideals, tastes and beliefs, so a new demographic was developing. With no real place in Manchester for this emerging scene to gather, Eagle was inspired to open his own club, a club for like-minded people – somewhere to gravitate to, the Manchester equivalent of London's UFO club or Middle Earth. Also, with an eye on the changes in social climate and consciousness happening on America's West-Coast, Eagle created a place to hang out for Mancunian outsiders, heads, poets and artists. People who were beginning to reject the regimes of religion, politics and the media and attempting to create their own futures outside the established framework

Other than DJing and a brief stint at the Kellogg's factory in Trafford Park, Roger had no recognisable work experience, so he would have been looking for something within his experience to bring to people, as well as a way of paying the rent... It was never going to be huge but saying that, Roger soon found his club and for the next two years proceeded to on put a wide and eclectic mix of music, performance and film. The rent for the place was paid to a couple called Ted and Vera Barry.

The Magic Village officially opened on 9th March 1968, with a performance from CP Lee and Bruce Mitchell's band Jacko Ogg and The Head People. Situated at No. 11 Cromford Court, a small cobbled street off Market Street, earlier in the 1960's the club was known as The Manchester Cavern and later The Jigsaw. Nothing exists of the club now as the Arndale shopping centre was built over it in the 1970s.

CP Lee: The Village was like an explosion, it was '68, '69 and petered off in about 1970. It was amazingly successful, it was always packed. Roger had great ideas, he wanted to show films there, have poets on, have Alan Prater, this old bloke who did dance and movement, the whole idea of it was that it would be an Arts centre, and then Roger realised you might as well just put bands on. You can't show a film when you've only got a five and half foot ceiling. His idea when it was open was to do this great, I don't know let's call it a psychedelic youth club and we were all devotees of Roger definitely.

Bruce Mitchell: Roger booked and managed Greasy Bear for a while until he announced to me... "That bass player, can't possibly work with him", the bass player wasn't very good, so he just went.

As you'll know he hectored on science fiction and various literatures with an inspirational summary, a review, and he would explain a book with such zeal that I used to go out and buy the book the next day and live it with him.

He always lived in horrible rents, and all he'd move in with would be a big speakered hi-fi and the records, that's all that would get there and maybe a mattress if there wasn't one there already.

Elliot Rashman: Bruce Mitchell and Roger were very, very close, Chris Lee and Roger were very, very close, I was three years younger so I was a bit starry eyed about all of them. I was Chris Lee's roadie for years.

Elliot Rashman was a Magic Village regular and would frequent the other venues where Roger would promote gigs. He became entertainments manager at Manchester University, where he met Mick Hucknall performing with his band The Frantic Elevators. Elliot later went on to manage Simply Red and helped them on the road to international success. Later, along with Andy Dodd, Mick Hucknall and Bob Harding he started the brilliant Blood & Fire reggae label which specialised in releasing classic Jamaican reggae, roots and dub recordings from the 1970's. Here Elliot explains how he first came across Roger Eagle.

Eliot Rashman: I first met Roger when I was fifteen in 1967. I used to go to the Magic Village on Saturday nights and he was the promoter, it was his club, and I was an under-age kid. At fifteen I'd already discovered acid and they used to do these over-nighters. You could stay over-night and I was obviously still living at home and you couldn't take acid at home.

It was a psychedelic dungeon the Magic Village and it was on Cromford Court, between Cannon Street and Market Street. It was right next to New Brown Street where the boutiques were, the first 60s Boutiques, it's also where 'Eighth Day' was originally, which first opened as a hippy cafe.

We'd go there, it wasn't licensed, it wasn't about alcohol, you rarely saw Roger. Roger had the office, you used to go in there because there was a cloakroom, then the office, and downstairs there was this psychedelic dungeon. I saw loads of great acts there, it was a good time to see bands because a lot of them hadn't broken and therefore you didn't have to pay lots of money. But it meant you could take a night out and trip and stay there overnight. Then in the morning you'd go down to the burger van by Victoria Station and you'd have a growler, for all I know it's still there, it used to be on the bridge... Anyway then you'd go home, 'cause it had worn off and your Mum and Dad would go "What's up with yer?" That was the first I really knew of Roger and he ran it with an iron fist, he was not particularly anti-drugs but in those days the drug squad were fascists, and they were heavy, really heavy, and he obviously tried to keep everybody from getting busted. But I have fantastic memories of the Magic Village, it was a very formative part of my life and that was for two or three years.

Dr. Stephen Hopkins was another Magic Village regular, he would later put Roger up in his father's house on Wilbraham Road in Chorlton. In the late 1970's and into the 80's Steve played keyboards with The Invisible Girls, a band formed with Martin Hannett. They played on recordings by John Cooper Clarke and Pauline Murray.

Steve Hopkins: I was a regular at the Magic Village and I sometimes did the door. Roger had this great way about him, anybody who he decided to bring into the gang he would talk them up as some sort of mythical hero in The World of Roger Eagle. There was a fella called Mike Don who had a stall in The Village that sold 'International Times'. There was also a DJ called Simon, a guy with long blonde hair. There were also the guys with the oil projector light show machines, Dave Backhouse and John Crumpton. So yes I was involved, did a bit on the door, went there many times. I remember all the crazy dancers and hippy girls. Roger only DJ'd at the Village occasionally, he left most of it to others, he concentrated on booking the bands. He had an amazing succession of bands play The Village. I remember seeing Tyrannosaurus Rex down there, I remember John Peel being there, Pink Floyd, Country Joe McDonald and Alvin Lee.

CP Lee: Periodically he'd schlepp off to the University to see somebody like Captain Beefheart and he had a guy called Simon who did the DJing at the Village so he didn't have to bother, Simon had a deal with an import record shop in Manchester so he got all the latest Californian sounds. So Roger increasingly took this back room role. However, maybe the police were hassling him.

Mike Don: He tended to call me 'The McDoon of McDoon', seeing as I was Scottish. I don't think he ever called me Mike, addressing people by name was not in his character.

Howard Fazakerley, like many sixties kids, formed a group at school, playing school dances, tennis clubs and youth clubs. His band, Lennox Avenue, played regularly at The Magic Village. Here he explains how he first came into contact with Roger Eagle.

Howard Fazakerley: My first guitar came from the guitarist in Herman's Hermits, it was a Hofner and it came with a blue and green Watkins Amp shaped like the prow of a boat and it pumped out 15 Watts of raw noise.

We originally used to go to a cellar club called The Catacombs which had bands on playing rubbish skiffle with a Christian message. We stumbled on The Magic Village by word of mouth and started to go whenever we weren't playing. Colin, our guitarist, plucked up the courage to ask Roger if we could play there and that needed courage because Roger was very big and we were small and young. We expected him to ask us to come in and play for him before he let us on his stage, but he did something a little smarter than that. He said we were playing next Thursday, a night when they usually just played records and the place was dead. If I remember right we didn't get paid but the promise was if we were ok he would book us again after money was discussed.

So Roger liked us and we played there regularly usually on Friday nights for the next 18 months. We sometimes did support work on Saturday nights. One of the other bands was Bruce Mitchell's Bluesline and the most bizarre sight was seeing Bruce arriving at the club with his drums strapped to a Honda 50.

Colin, our guitarist, became friendly with Roger and it was with him I went to Roger's flat in Fallowfield and the only thing I can remember of it was his stereo system, which was truly Jamaican in size many years before such things existed and his television. Each time his telly stopped working he would buy another and stick it on top of the old one. Memory dims but I'd say they were at least five high.

Mike Don: It opened a lot of the time, the major acts usually played on a Saturday night at the all-nighter. Occasionally you'd get a big name act on a Friday or a Sunday if that was the only date they could fit in. They tried opening throughout the week but they couldn't get enough people in to make it pay. It was always an all-nighter on a Saturday, it started at 7pm on a Saturday and went on until 7am on the Sunday. It was 200 capacity but sometimes they didn't make 200. It was set up as a kind of Manchester equivalent to London's UFO club but I would say there was more emphasis on the music and less on the counter-culture thing.

Brian Jackson: I had, by this time, left government employment and was working as a bus driver. I noticed that this club was running, I kept seeing the adverts but because I was working I couldn't always get there. At this time another guy joined the bus company called Steve Watts, or Sergio as he was known. He was a conductor and he would work with me and we deliberately elected to do late shifts for two reasons; one, they were easy to get and two, other drivers would gladly not do a late shift so that they could go out and have a drink and get back by midnight. Our idea of going out was to find a club that was open all-night and the Magic Village was exactly that club. We went along and checked it out and sure enough it was Roger Eagle. I thought 'oh my god it's him!' I don't think he recognised me straight away, he reluctantly did later but chose to take no notice of me.

I was a semi-regular at the Magic Village, Roger was running it and his girlfriend at the time was Patsy Robinson, whom I'd met earlier. Penny Henry was also a very good friend of Roger's at this time. Roger spent a lot of time at Penny's flat.

Penny Henry was another long-term friend of Rogers. Arriving in Manchester in 1968 to attend art school, Penny became one of the founder members of the Eighth Day Cafe, as well as working at Manchester University and later The Hacienda club. Here she speaks about her memories of Roger Eagle at the time of the Magic Village.

Penny Henry: When I first met Roger it was with a friend called Emily, she said "Lets go down to The Magic Village" and he was there. That's where I got to know him. He was always very friendly, I think he always really liked me and I liked him. My biggest memory of Roger was of him giving me a shoulder ride around the Magic Village which was hilariously funny.

I used to go to Piccadilly Records when Barry Ancill ran it and there was a girl who worked there called Patsy and Roger was going out with her at that time. He talked to me a lot about stuff – I think Patsy really broke his heart. They were engaged and I think she ran off with somebody else and I don't think Roger met or found anybody else after Patsy. I don't think he found anybody who was quite like her and I think he was quite lonely for most of his adult life. My abiding memory of him is that he felt really cheated that he'd lost the woman he loved.

Roger Eagle: The Captain Beefheart song 'Autumn's Child' is one of those records that really moves me, it reminds me of a girl I used to know a million years ago. It has an other worldly quality to it, a timeless quality. You can't dance to it, you can tap your foot to it but the tempo changes. It has something very special.

Allan Frost: I remember Chris Lee with frizzy hair, I think the first time I saw his band was at Shotton Town Hall and then when Roger was working at The Blue Note. I saw him at The Village all the time. He was certainly one of founding figures of the Manchester hippy movement, although he was not much more than a schoolboy at the time.

Allan Frost first met Roger while working for CND. He went on to work at the Magic Village, eventually taking it over in the final months after Roger had left. Allan would go on to be Roger's personal chauffeur for the next 20 odd years, probably attending most of the gigs Roger promoted in and around the North-West from 1968 to the early 90's. Allan sadly passed away in 2006.

Allan Frost: The guy who actually owned the building was called Ted Barry, he's dead now, he died penniless in a derelict farmhouse, I believe, up in West Yorkshire, somewhere that way. I think by then his wife would have left him, she was Jewish, her name was Vera. In the early days of The Village she would run the door. Ted Barry owned clubs throughout Manchester, a place called the Silver Moon and another one next to The Magic Village that I can't remember the name of. Roger chose the bands, he'd do all the booking and everything, and Vera would sit on the door taking money, that's all she did. Ted was a hard bastard; he used to charge a lot of money for the rent of the place. Roger was a good guy, he bought in a lot of the hippy sort of bands, bands like The Nice, Country Joe and the Fish, that sort of thing. He wasn't doing much DJing, he did very little DJing. There was Paul and there was Simon, the two DJ's. It used to be quite a popular little place you know the DJ box. The Village set out was, at one end there was an empty room where nothing was done, nobody went there. Then there was an archway that housed a jukebox with a lot of great records on it, adjacent to this was a room which the jukebox faced into. In fact imagine this room as one line of small rooms. After that was the coffee bar area, no alcohol was served there.

Nicky Crewe got to know Roger through attending The Magic Village and The Liverpool Stadium, she also worked at The Eighth Day Cafe and food co-operative which was then on New Brown Street, very close to the Magic Village premises.

Nicky Crewe: I went to The Magic Village when I could. I had some quite intense periods of time there. Then I'd be whisked back to boarding school and wouldn't be able to go, I'd say it was over a period of maybe only a year. I saw a lot of good bands there. I seem to remember seeing Sonny Terry and Brownie McGhee there I'm sure. I sometimes wonder whether I imagined it because everything is so kind of heightened when you are that age, there was so much going on for me. I was sort of like the baby of the group of people I hung around with. Cathy Hopkins was in our group and Michelle who married Dimitri from Leroy & the Kools. Michelle and I were the youngsters and we were getting to know people who were in their 20's and possibly in their 30's who were very serious about their music.

Bruce Mitchell: The Magic Village was next to the Cromford Club in Cromford Court and Roger had that place boiling, it was right in the middle of the psychedelic era and it was a very good all-nighter.

Penny Henry: I remember Bruce Mitchell at The Magic Village handing out instruments so that everybody could play along. I remember that vividly.

Stan Hoffman: He had a little club in Manchester called The Magic Village, I played there loads of times. We had lots of different names, musicians like Bruce Mitchell, Jeff Walters, Dave Cakebread and Tosh Ryan sometimes – Tosh was a very good alto player. They all lived together on Didsbury Park with Archie McNabb who was a black conga drummer from Jamaica.

Val Randall was another Magic Village regular who went on to become a lifelong friend to Roger, here she explains how difficult it was travelling into Manchester from the country to visit a late night club as a teenager and also how she first met Roger.

Val Randall: I was into, shall we say, alternative music when I was seventeen in 1968, a friend and I were doing our A Levels and also working in the Market Cafe in Nelson on Saturdays. We'd heard of The Magic Village. We both came from quite strict upbringings, one wasn't allowed to go dashing off all around the country, plus we didn't have a car. So we finally got our parents to agree to us going to Manchester on the understanding we got the last bus back. The last bus back to Nelson was at ten to eleven... and there he was, he frightened me to death, I mean I'm 6 foot, I thought who on earth is this man? After that we went a few more times and he said "You should be staying!" you know how he issued orders?

Elliot Rashman: John Mayall's Bluesbreakers would play regularly at The Magic Village because they were a touring band. It was after Clapton but Peter Green was the guitarist, the first time was Peter Green, the second, third and fourth Mick Taylor. He had the best horn section in the country; jazzers like Dick Heckstall-Smith and Larry Beckett, just the best English jazz players and he could put bands together, so right away at the the age of fifteen I was introduced to real players. It's the first time I heard 'Clapton is God' because they were an obscure band, we're not talking about a hit band here. The only people that would have known about John Mayall would have been the bluesers.

As well as putting on well known acts such The Pink Floyd, Joe Cocker, The Nice and Fairport Convention, Roger was saying "Well if there's a new Beatles or Stones around here, this is the perfect place for them to make themselves known and work up their act". British bands such Elmer Gantry's Velvet Opera, The Edgar Broughton band, Jethro Tull, The Third Ear band, Glass Menagerie, The Groundhogs and The Deviants also played the Magic Village.

Elliot Rashman: I also saw Jethro Tull there, who were a local band from Blackpool and because it was such a tiny little place and it was 2 o'clock in the morning, they'd do two sets. There'd be a lot of banter with the audience, I distinctly remember Ian Anderson saying "I'm gonna make a fucking fortune standing on one leg playing the flute," it was meant as a joke but that's kind of what he did. I saw people like Tom Rush there, I saw Tom Paxton there, a lot of those American folkies were already going out of fashion.

Roger Eagle: John Peel was certainly responsible for introducing this country to Captain Beefheart.

Elliot Rashman: Roger was also instrumental in getting Beefheart recognised in this country, him and Peel introduced Beefheart properly. He was convinced Beefheart was unique, years before anyone else realised. To him Trout Mask Replica was possibly the greatest album made by a white man. So Beefheart was a big player in Roger's universe.

Roger Eagle: Then I got Beefheart's Troutmask Replica on import, probably the first copy to come into the UK. I played it quite a bit before it began to get to me. I remember thinking it's going to take a while. But that is his masterwork, I think there just wasn't anybody else like him at all. He was definitely off to one side of the mainstream. I found it difficult to reconcile that with the fact that he was on a Warner Brothers label, I thought that very strange.

CP Lee: Then of course you've got the Captain Beefheart connection which begins around the late sixties. Beefheart is like a perfect assimilation of Howlin' Wolf, Lightnin' Hopkins, John Coltrane; a wonderful synthesis of all these sounds and Roger fell in love with Beefheart really, so that became a major part of your education. As soon as an album came out you'd rush straight over to Roger's, bang it on the turntable and there you go.

Another was Ritchie Havens, he was crazy about Ritchie Havens. Ritchie Havens did a double album on Frank Zappa's label, I think in '68, and I think it had 'Strawberry Fields' on it, and 'Just like a Woman', it was a gatefold sleeve, very fizzydelic inside. He'd play that again and again and again as the ultimate crossover of black and white fusion. Ritchie Havens, a black man playing white composer's music.

Roger tried to get me into Muddy Waters' 'Electric Mud', it took me years to get into it, I couldn't get it, no matter what, despite repeated listening. Again and again he'd be "Right! Sit down! Listen!" Another of his favourites from this time were Creedence Clearwater Revival, he was absolutely stone crazy for

John Fogerty. He used to say about them "This was bringing it all back home" because you'd had the psychedelic improvisations of '67, you've got Soft Machine emerging, Pink Floyd, people like that, and Roger would say, "they've had a go at it, but now it's moving into other areas."

Val Randall: After I'd been to the Magic Village three or four times, he used to ring me up at home and he used to play music over the phone for two hours at a stretch, stuff like Beefheart which I'd never heard. My Mother would come in and say "Are you still on that phone?" I'd be sitting there with the phone glued to my ear, my ear hurt at the end of it.

Brian Rae: I DJ'd at the Magic Village in about 1969, I did it twice but Roger wasn't there on those nights.

Steve Hopkins: He tuned into John Peel's 'Perfumed Garden' show before anyone else, as soon as the American west coast psychedelic thing started happening he was bringing it over here. He put on Elmer Gantry's Velvet Opera, Clear Light, Country Joe, he loved Country Joe. He loved Peter Green's Fleetwood Mac, Creedence Clearwater Revival, Jefferson Airplane. The Grateful Dead were one of his favourites.

The 'Folk revival' of the early 60's would, in 1968, have been on it's last legs, or at least following Bob Dylan's lead and turning 'electric'. Mainstream pop bands were trying their hand at psychedelia but the bands that Roger Eagle booked to play at The Magic Village would have been representing the transition between British psychedelia and the emergence of progressive rock. Something like 'Acid Folk' or 'Psychedelic Folk' or the 'Acid Underground' perhaps – quite English in essence but definitely on nodding terms with the American West-Coast scene of The Doors, Jefferson Airplane, Love, Buffalo Springfield, Big Brother and the Holding Company and The Grateful Dead.

Brian Jackson: The stage at the Magic Village was like a plinth, no more than a couple of feet above the floor. You could just sit on the edge of it but that was unwise because somebody had painted it with what appeared to be never dry paint, if anyone walked across the stage you could hear their feet as they walked over the sticky paint. Many an unwary person in their latest Levi's sat down feeling weary and ended up sat in paint; it was a dive, it wouldn't have been half the fun if it wasn't. My problem was it was usually midnight or 1am before I could get there and I'd usually miss the first set and couldn't find out who the band was because they'd not been announced properly, either that or there'd been a change. What I can say is a good time was had by all.

I actually met Elliot Rashman and his cousin Joe here for the first time, we became inseparable and we're still friends to this day.

Val Randall: With The Village being a cellar club, the walls used to run with water, it also had a low ceiling and moss growing on the walls, the toilets were awful.

Allan Frost: I remember round about this time Roger got slung out of his flat because he couldn't afford the rent. His flat was down Withington Road, me and Dave Backhouse had to go down there and collect his gear, at least what we could carry; records, magazines, books all sorts. He moved in to The Magic Village then, he'd got his bed in the office. He was always short of money when it came to the landlord, never short of money when it came to Ted Barry. If he upset Ted Barry, Ted Barry would just shut the club, just like that. So he would always pay the club rent. But with his living accommodation he would often get into trouble with his landlords. In one of his flats near Chorlton, he was laying on his bed one evening, and Dave Backhouse is sat there, Roger says to him, "Get off your arse and go and get me a hooker", so Dave says "Ok" and he went off down the Moss to some club and he said to some guy there "I want a hooker", the guy said

"Meet me round the back in five minutes", so Dave went round the back and was met by half a dozen black guys, who jumped on him, took his money and beat him up – he was a bit gullible.

*

David Bowie played the Manchester Free Trade Hall on Saturday 22nd February 1969 as support to Tyrannosaurus Rex. The Magic Village was somewhere touring musicians would check out when playing in town. John Constantine, who worked in the cloakroom and behind the coffee bar, remembered hanging David's coat up and charging him sixpence...

John Constantine: I recall Bowie playing an acoustic set to about thirty people in the bar, just for the fun of it, and as a warm up for his concert at The Free Trade Hall the following night. It was fantastic.

Allan Frost: Yeah, Roger was away doing a gig, I think it was possibly in Bolton or somewhere like that, he used to put on occasional gigs at places like the Houldsworth Hall which was on Deansgate. So this night I'm sat on the door there taking money as I used to when he was away and this geezer comes strolling up, "Hiya, I'm the roadie for David Bowie" and I said "Oh, very good, nice to meet you". He says, "We're in the motor outside, David was wondering if it was ok if he came in and played a set for you for nothing," I said "Are we talking about the same David Bowie?"

He'd just done a gig in town and they just wanted to chill a bit, so they came in. Not far from the jukebox there was a set of fire escape stairs and he just got his acoustic guitar and went and sat on the stairs. He didn't introduce himself or anything, he just started playing. a lot of folky stuff. Some people at that time saw him as bit of a traitor to the hippy cause because he'd gone pop. There was a guy called Russ for instance, he had blonde hair and looked just like Brian Jones, he really disliked Bowie, we'd spoken about him before and he actually went over and listened to him and gave him a try. He came over to me afterwards and said, "That guy is wonderful!"

After he'd finished playing I went over and had a long chat with him, standing next to the jukebox talking about the records that were on there, all sorts of things. I embarrassed him slightly by putting one of his records on. When it came on he said, "Oh my God no!" I said "What's the matter?" he said "People are gonna think I put the record on!" I just said "Don't worry," we got on well, he was a nice guy.

Elliot Rashman: Roger had this military bearing that was weird, he had a look of almost a Second World War RAF pilot, you could imagine him with a waxed moustache and everything, he was a big man, imposing, and I was terrified of him, until I got to know him and then I realised he had one love in life and that was music.

Roger would say, "Look! Listen to this!" and you'd think "Shit he's gonna hit me!" When I was 16-17 that's what it looked like he was gonna do. He was rude, you thought it was rude, because as a kid you didn't meet adults like that. It was said with such authority it might as well have been the police. So you went, "I'll listen to it, ok", "NOW!" So he gave us all this weird collective unconscious.

Roger's main inspiration came from his desire to musically educate those in his social circle. If someone was open and genuinely interested in Roger's ideas on music, he seemed to delight in passing on what he had learned and experienced. This seems to have stemmed from his three years of DJing at the Twisted Wheel, that and the fact that a lot of the music he found interesting was never played on the radio and couldn't be read about in magazines. The amount of stories and background information he'd amassed was already enormous. Although the accepted standard for the DJ was to talk over the microphone to introduce the songs, Roger didn't really do that, he preferred to let the music speak for itself. His way of informing you about music involved a one-on-one personal education. The way he'd describe a song was in the same way a child might; sheer joy, belief and an almost painful calling to play the tunes to others – having experienced some kind of religious reverie that had to be passed on – so that others could experience these tunes and their magical powers. Every track would have a story, right down to the minutiae. Every story told with a fanatic's passion, an understanding of every musician on the record, the producer of the song, and personal details of the artist and their relativity to the story of rock 'n' roll.

Val Randall: He also, as everyone else has said, had this spontaneous generosity and kindness. I can remember I'd broken up with the love of my life in every sense and I was beside myself. I got in at about one in the morning, I hadn't been drinking and I couldn't think of anything else to do so I just rang him, and of course he was still out at the club. I thought Jesus, when he gets back he'll be furious. At 3 o'clock in the morning he rang me, and he stayed on the phone until he was satisfied I was ok.

Steve Hopkins: He lived in a flat in East Didsbury for a while with a family of academics, a Jewish family. I think they were called Mestel. There were three or four teenage girls and the father was a professor. It was there I took LSD for the second or third time. I was still living with my parents so it would be late 60's. I must have met him before Bruce brought him round but I didn't know him that well. We ended up in his flat, a gang of us, all tripping. He was really entertaining. It put him on the spot really, all of us turning up and saying "Sorry Roger, we're all tripping, we've got nowhere to go." So he had to let us in.

CP Lee: Do you know the great story about Captain Beefheart playing Southport Floral Hall in 1968? Roger and I are there to see him and it's like everything is set up but there's no band and the promoter knows Roger and he's like, "Where are they, where are they?" and Roger's like "I'm off" and we go outside the venue and we see a van with these really weird looking people inside. We wander up to them and the promoter knocks on the window and Beefheart winds the window down, the promoter says "Are you Captain Beefheart and the Magic Band?" he says "Yes!", the promoter says, "Well are you going to play?", Beefheart says "Just checking the vibe" and with that they all trooped out and did the gig.

Brian Smith: I never went to The Magic Village at night, I went in a couple of lunchtimes, I hadn't seen Roger for years. It was closed. I saw him on Market Street, he dragged me in to see his jukebox. I was working in Manchester at the time on Blackfriars Street, I just happened to be walking up Market Street and Roger's coming the other way and I hear, "Ah Smith!", I hadn't seen him for four or five years, "Ah Smith, you must come down and see this jukebox", I got dragged down into the Magic Village and they had this jukebox with some amazing stuff on it. I went in there a couple of times when he said he was going to be there.

Martin Eagle: Mum went up to visit Roger when he was running The Magic Village, she stayed upstairs on the door taking the money. She was showing a bit of her own mother there. Her mother was Irish and she liked to go to the races and have a bit of a flutter, mum rather liked a similar sort of thing.

Doreen Allen was a friend to Roger Eagle for nearly thirty years, working at the various venues he promoted, including The Liverpool Stadium and Eric's; taking care of catering, looking after the bands, doing secretarial work and generally taking care of tasks Roger couldn't do. On more than one occasion Doreen helped Roger to find living accommodation. Doreen has also promoted bands and ran the 'Planet X' club night in Liverpool.

Doreen Allen: I used to put on bands in a pub called O'Conner's Tavern in Liverpool. Roger was managing Greasy Bear, I'd booked them for a gig and Roger came over from Manchester with them. Roger was loosely managing them I think, or he had something to do with them. I don't know if he'd just gone along for the ride or what, that was 1969 or 70, that was my first meeting with him. I was putting bands on there for about two years; heavy rock type bands that sort of stuff, that's how I got into promoting really. Most of the bands that played for me in O'Conner's were from Manchester, I used to have Stackwaddy on, they were on John Peel's Dandelion label. Another band was Gravy Train, I was quite involved in all that scene before The Stadium.

Brian Jackson: I must have gone to The Village a couple of dozen times maybe more. I saw a variety of bands, some of them fairly local. I saw the Pink Fairies and Pink Floyd on the same night. I think Roger had double-booked or the word Pink had confused somebody. One of the best gigs I saw there was the incredible Liverpool Scene with Roger McGough, Adrian Henry and the crew.

Bob Harding Did CP tell you about his Roger wind-up when Roger was running the Magic Village? You'd have to ask CP about this, he can do the accent and stuff. He really had Roger going, Roger really thought he was speaking to John Lennon. CP made out that he was looking for somewhere to do some shows and apparently Roger was going, "And what's your bag now John?" and CP went, "Er . . paper bag". After the phone call finished Roger was like floating, and something comes up and Roger went, "Don't talk to me now, I've just spoken to... Lennon." You'll have to speak to CP if you want the full story.

Mike Don: At that time you still had registered legal heroin addicts and there was this one guy whose name I can't remember who used to go to The Village. One night he made arrangements with the DJ at the time – possibly Mike Marshall – to play the Velvet Underground's 'Heroin', got a blue spotlight pointed at the stage and proceeded to shoot up on the stage. Roger was absolutely livid and threw the guy out, this guy couldn't understand why Roger was so upset, he said, "But it's legal for me!"

Allan Frost: Mike Don was one of the real characters from The Magic Village, a Scottish guy, blind as a bat, wouldn't wear glasses or anything, I think he thought they'd make him look like a dork. He used to have a stall at The Village selling underground books and newspapers such as *International Times* and also a local Manchester underground paper called *Glass Eye*. One time Bruce Mitchell turned up in his Mini-van, he jumped out and everyone's going "What's happening?" because he's got a wood-saw in his hand. So we all went down the stairs to see what Bruce was up to with the saw, he had a mischievous look on his face. He went up to Mike Don and said, "Will you put your stall in the middle of the room please?"

Mike Don said "Why?"

Bruce said, "Roger's instructions, will you clear a space please?"

Mike said, "Why?"

With that he said, "Roger's asked me to cut the stall in half", he got the saw and started to saw it in half, it was so funny, just Bruce Mitchell being crazy, he was younger then, but he was still old, he must be ninety if he's a day.

Brian Jackson: I don't remember the place being raided. There may have been the odd undercover snooping for all I know. It's almost like they left him alone, it's almost like it was too far ahead for them to know what was going on. My recollection of The Magic Village was that it was a safe refuge for psychedelic people, an atmosphere where there were no fights or bad vibes and people made friends which lasted for many years.

CP Lee: The Wheel and The Village were basically the only two places allowed to function and it was so that they (the Police) could say, "Ha, of course we let them do what they want to do". But also I had been in the office when the fire brigade had come in to do an inspection and they got a bottle of Johnny Walker Black Label whisky each, shook hands and on their merry way. Now the drug squad as well, they never raided there, they might wait outside and they had their ideas who was dealing. Even The Wheel got raided, but as far as I'm aware The Village never got raided, so Roger must have been paying the right people there.

At The Magic Village, Roger would have been part of the scene – the gang. Ripping off the kids, being a 'Bread Head' or 'Selling out to the man' would have been complete anathema to him. This attitude was probably one he carried throughout his life, also the fact that he never claimed Social Security benefits meant he had no safety net, so he had to keep moving. Although the ideology and thinking behind The Magic Village would have been very important, it's probable that Roger struggled to make much money. The fact that he was still only 26 when The Village was at its height would possibly have meant his outlook and business nous was informed by his contemporaries, the people he socialised with. Also, the high rent he had to stump up to Ted Barry, along with the fact that the club had no alcohol license and ultimately wasn't big enough to make much of a profit, must have held him back. His imminent move to The Liverpool Stadium seems to bear this out, he'd learned the ropes, done his promoting apprenticeship and now the notion of making a profit would seem to have been, next to the music, his apparent motivation.

Allan Frost: When Roger decided to pack in the club, he had a talk with me and said, "Do you think you could do it? Do you think you could run the place because I'm getting out." I said, "Yeah" so we went and had a word with Ted Barry, and Ted taught me something that night that I've never forgotten.

Ted said, after we'd had a good long discussion,"Can you do the job?",

I said "I think so".

He says "I don't want somebody who thinks so, I want somebody who knows so."

So I said, "Ok, I can do the job."

He said, "That's good enough for me."

From then on if I know I'm good enough to do a job I say I can do it, not 'I think I can do it' because that gives people the wrong impression.

When I took over The Magic Village from Roger I was paying £70 a week rent, and I found out later, a lot later, that Ted Barry didn't own the building and £70 a week in the late Sixties was a lot of money. Then there was the hassle we got from the Drug Squad, namely Brian Hill. He had me in his office a couple of times, threatening me with jail if I didn't kick all the druggies out, and you can't, and he kept sending these people down there, all plain clothes stuff, they weren't dressed like hippies or anything, they were dressed in suits and things.

The moment they drew up at the door you knew who it was, the word went round straight away. But one of the Drug Squad guys, I can't remember his name, quite a nice guy, at that time he would have been about 25 years old, always wore colourful ties, well he couldn't find any shop that stocked this record that he wanted. So he got one of the hippy girls from The Village to go and buy it for him. He paid her obviously, it was 'Suzanne' by Leonard Cohen. But you'd also have people like Ted Exley, he was a Sergeant on the Drug Squad, he used to drive about in battered cars pissed out of his head and that's how his boss Brian Hill died. At Christmas one year he was driving around north Manchester, visiting various clubs and pubs, got pissed and crashed into a lamp post on his way back to his office and was killed. Ted Exley though, if he said white was black, white was black.

Steve Hopkins: He was beaten down and very worried about Ted Barry, the gangster who owned The Magic Village premises. Roger was always telling us this, I never knew quite whether to believe him or not, but he seemed genuinely afraid of this guy.

CP Lee: He was probably under a lot of pressure and nobody in Manchester ever thanks you for anything, periodically they'll set you up and then piss all over you if you've got too big for your boots.

Mike Don: I think the last gig at The Magic Village was January 3rd 1970.

The significance of The Magic Village was that in the two short years that it was running Roger Eagle helped set up a space for like minded individuals to congregate; a family of artists, musicians and creative people that would form the basis of Manchester's music and arts community for many years to come. Roger wanted people to be entertained, educated, enthralled, mystified, thrilled but above all safe.

6 - Liverpool Stadium

Roger's decision to change from putting bands on at The Magic Village in Manchester to booking and promoting at the much larger Liverpool Stadium could have been for just one reason or a combination of many. It was established in the previous chapter that his payable rent at The Magic Village was becoming difficult to find, there was also the constant threat of eviction from owner Ted Barry. If this was the case it would seem logical for Roger to have moved on to something prospectively bigger and better. If this is taken into consideration and tied in with the virtual closing down of the whole of the Manchester coffee bar and club scene by Chief Constable J.A. Mckay and the subsequent Act of Parliament, then one can begin to understand Roger's move.

Elliot Rashman: The next I knew he was at The Liverpool Stadium, which I have less memory of, I saw Captain Beefheart there, blah, blah, blah.

Having spent two years travelling through North Africa, Europe and India, Geoff Davis returned to Liverpool to work for a carpet manufacturer running a showroom on Church Street in the centre of Liverpool. After being offered the job of area manager in another part of the country, Geoff decided to do the thing that was closest to his heart and open a record shop. The first Probe record shop opened in early January 1971 on Clarence Street off Mount Pleasant in Liverpool. Later, another branch operated in the Whitechapel area of Liverpool in a hippy emporium called 'Silly Billies'. Later still, in 1976, Probe relocated to Button Street, just yards from the Eric's club that was later opened by Roger and Ken Testi on Mathew Street.

Geoff Davis: I thought if I open this shop I'm going to be getting far less money but it's what I want to do. It started to interest me, the idea of having a dream record shop, the sort of record shop I'd always wanted to go into and find everything that was my taste. So we, Annie my ex-wife and I, decided to do that. There was nothing else like it in London, there was nothing else like it in Britain, it was the first weird or out-and-out head record shop in Britain.

Within a fortnight of opening this familiar looking figure came in and he came over, I'd seen him around town, he came in to put posters up for The Stadium, we became friends socially right away. Roger would often spend time at the shop, he was another mouthy bugger. Well we would take the piss out of each other, Roger preferred that style I think. He liked Liverpool, he liked the scouse character, the cheek.

CP Lee: By 1970 Roger's disillusioned with it, he's moved on, wants to try something else. The next thing we hear is, he's got this boxing arena in Liverpool called The Liverpool Stadium and this has got to be 1970-71 and we get booked to support Cat Stevens. Greasy Bear are supporting Cat Stevens and I've never been there and I get there and I can't believe it! There's a boxing ring in the middle and it stinks of liniment and embrocation. So we play this gig and I can't believe it. Roger has been a genius, absolutely fantastic.

So now he can afford to book big people, like Captain Beefheart, who could never have played The Village because it was too small, so he's got Mott the Hoople, he's got all these massive acts, and once again Roger is remarkably successful.

Geoff Davis: The Stadium was this massive boxing arena and the bands played where the ring was. The sound was not great, but

I've heard worse. Roger would say stuff like, "We've got Steve Miller on you know, I expect to see you there" stuff like that. So anything that appealed to me I'd go. I wasn't somebody who'd go every week like some people. Some bands that he'd put on I just didn't like. The likes of Uriah Heep or these prog rock bands. But I did go to an awful lot because he was often putting very good stuff on.

Doreen Allen: Roger started putting bands on at the Stadium in 1970 and he asked me to work down there. So I was there right at the start sorting out the catering and anything else that Roger wanted me to sort out. It was brilliant at the Stadium, I'd say I went to every show. It probably wasn't a good venue for the bands to play I wouldn't think because the sound was awful and it was freezing cold, the bands would have hypothermia just doing their sound check. I remember Status Quo doing their sound check and they were freezing, so I said "Come on, we'll play hide'n'seek" it was great for playing hide'n'seek in the Stadium, loads of places to hide.

Steve Hardstaff was another very close friend of Roger's, sharing a similar taste in music and humour. A well known Liverpool artist and graphic designer Steve has a very distinctive style that incorporates early rock 'n' roll, blues and R&B icons into apocalyptic scenes with various backdrops. He has served as senior lecturer in art history and museum studies at Liverpool's John Moores University, and has had a book of his work called 'Cover Art' published by the University of Chicago Press.

Steve Hardstaff: It would have been at the Stadium when I first met Roger, it was when he first started putting gigs on there. I only ever knew him in Liverpool, I never knew him in Manchester. At the time he was travelling from Manchester to do the shows, at the same time he would have been getting friendly with Geoff Davis and various other people on the Liverpool music scene.

He always called me by my surname, he never called me Steve except when it was one-to-one. He was into wit and irony, Monty Python, The Goons, particularly Peter Sellers, Lord Buckley. It would have been partly from public school. He was a rebel wasn't he? A bit of an outcast from his academic family, even though he loved his Mum, he was gutted when she died.

In the Summer of 1971 Steve Hopkins was a University student whose father (the writer Billy Hopkins) had a huge house on Wilbraham Road in Chorlton, Manchester. Steve, much to his father's dismay, decided to drop out of University after a year and was given the job of letting the house out as flats while his parents moved to Africa. In Steve's words, it rapidly turned into a sort of commune.

Steve Hopkins: There were six bedrooms, two very big living rooms and three cellars. Virtually every one of those rooms was occupied by students, wannabes and various other people. I think it was Bruce Mitchell who brought Roger round and said "Can you help Roger he's short of somewhere to live?".

I knew him at The Village, he'd made a good impression but the house was full, there was just this one room down in the basement. I lived in the basement in a reasonably decked out room, but this other was a tiny little space, which was basically a coal hole. I said to him "There's this space here, if you're willing to wait two days I can clean it up." I was a bit hesitant to charge, I think I said, "How about a fiver a month or something?", which was probably cheeky anyway. So I swept it out, put some kind of lino down, at which point it was like a prison cell, you had enough room for a bed and enough room to do press-ups by the bed.

At this stage he'd not bought his great monophonic sound system, with the great big speaker, as well as his stacks of LP's, which even at this stage would have filled a wardrobe or two. His sound system had just one speaker and it had a big sticker on it that said 'Back To Mono', it was wood, maybe walnut, it was massive. He was really insistent that it had to be mono for a lot of stuff, later on he got stereo gear. He'd say, "This is recorded in mono, it sounds best in mono". So he moved in and he said "That's all I need, as long as I've got somewhere to store my records safely and somewhere to sleep."

He must have stayed for a few months. Sometimes you'd go round to his room and knock on his door and he'd look at you and go "No, I don't wanna see anyone right now... oh go on then, come in, have you heard this?" and out would come the packet of Kools.

One of his personal things was playing 'Patience', he'd spend a lot of time in his flat with a pack of cards and his menthol fags. He'd do that when he had nervous energy to expend. If he had people round he'd play 'Scrabble', he was proud of the fact his mother edited the Oxford Literary Guides to Britain and Ireland. He also liked to play 'Risk', which was a different game with Roger. It became really serious, y'know, world domination, that was what he intended. I suspect he had the same drive and make-up as many people that became successful entrepreneurs.

Bruce Mitchell: When Roger was promoting at the Stadium the gigs used to finish at eleven and once he'd cashed up and done everything, he'd go back, and I'd usually be there with him, driving him back sometimes, whatever. He was living on Wilbraham Road in a place Steve Hopkins' dad owned. He knew Roger well and Roger lived in his basement next to the central heating boiler.

He'd get in at twelve or one o'clock and have a through the night game of Risk, it was a kind of popular board game made by the same people as Monopoly, it's about having armies and attacking and Roger liked this and a load of us would go round and he'd have the music going, the game going, and you know the basement would be packed.

There were two extremes to Roger, if his gig had done well that night he was insufferable, he'd be so full of himself, he'd go (adopts brilliant impersonation), "Of course, er, what you're doing's wrong Mitchell!"

He was like that, he was pompous but if he lost money on a gig, he was marvellous, he'd be talking about how rubbish he was, it was like, "Some promoters do this, and do that, I do this!"

His way of explaining things was so comical, it was a pleasure to be in his company. I just lived down the road, and my wife would hate it when she knew there was a Stadium gig coming up because she knew I'd be out all night.

The records would be put on in this way.

"Ok Mitchell, the greatest rock 'n' roll record ever made, what is it?"

He'd put something on, and you'd get eight bars, by which time he'd lost interest.

"Ok, now listen to this",

He'd whip that one off.

"Ok Mitchell this is the best such and such".

It was like some sort of funny quiz and then he'd go off into a description of a book he'd read, his enthusiasm for stuff was so infectious.

Allan Frost: I used to work with Roger at the Stadium all the time, I don't know how he would have got there if I hadn't give him a lift, squeezing him into my mini-van. The main thing I'd do would be to stay with the bands during the day. I'd go and sit up in the hotel with them, making sure they got to the gig on time, that sort of thing. I remember at the Led Zeppelin gig having a big argument with one of their roadies where we were screaming about shotguns and things at each other and Peter Grant was around, I'm just glad I didn't start shouting at him, nice guy in his own way.

Pete Fulwell was at the time of the Liverpool Stadium working as a Graphic Designer, he later went on to run the Liverpool club Eric's after Ken Testi and Roger Eagle had opened it. Here Pete explains how he first came across Roger when Led Zeppelin played the Stadium on the 29th November 1971.

Pete Fulwell: I first met Roger when he was promoting at the Stadium. Led Zeppelin were on and I'd gone there to meet Peter Grant, their manager. I considered myself to be working in the music business, graphic design, which is another story but through a roundabout route I'd got to meet Mr Grant. He was a character, I won't hear a word said against him, he was so helpful to me, a lovely man, heavy on the record companies and the industry but outside of that he was a really nice guy, dead helpful. So I'd gone to the Stadium to meet him. The memory of what Roger looked like then grows very dim, he was just somebody who was running the venue where I was going to meet somebody. It wasn't until much later, 1976, that we started to get very close.

Geoff Davis: What Roger and I both shared was that we were both strong characters, what I mean is you put yourself over in quite a forthright manner. We got on very well, our musical tastes would sometimes coincide and often not. Roger was not into classical music, whereas I've always been into it. Roger was not one of those people with massively catholic tastes, his range was more from R&B, rock 'n' roll and reggae. Some people will get into one groove and they're there with it for life, Roger would turn people onto music and all that. Don't get me wrong, I'm not saying he'd go off reggae or he'd go off R&B. But he'd find another thing, he'd find another aspect, it's all an interconnecting thing of rhythm based music.

In 1972 Bruce Mitchell, along with Tosh Ryan and Victor Brox, helped set up the co-operative 'Music Force' to help musicians find work. Run by musicians it involved an agency and gig promotion service, eventually it went on to encompass many aspects of the music business including graphic design, fly-posting, equipment hire, transport, record production and releases. It was set up in the main as a reaction to the London based music scene and the dearth of opportunities for Manchester musicians to make any headway in the bleak period of the early 70's. Later involved in 'Music Force' was Martin Hannett, who went on to form Rabid Records with Tosh Ryan and later still went on to produce, to huge acclaim, the studio work of Joy Division, among many others.

Bruce Mitchell: At the start of the Stadium Roger was nearly always a percentage promoter, that means if it's your venue and someone wants to put a big act in, well I don't want to take the risk, I'll just take ten percent off the top. But if there was an act that was important to Roger, he had to take the risk, he always promoted at his own risk. Captain Beefheart & the Magic Band, that would've been important. Do you know the size of the acts that played at the Stadium? Some of the world's biggest acts played there! Led Zeppelin played there, when Black Sabbath broke they played there, Traffic played there. Mott the Hoople played there, he did the tour where they had Max Wall opening. I did a record with him years later.

Allan Frost: The artist who got the most stick at the Stadium was Max Wall, he was on with Mott the Hoople and the whole thing was presented as some sort of rock 'n' roll circus, and he's telling jokes and they weren't appropriate for the crowd. So some guy threw an empty beer can on to the stage and somebody else threw a can and he threw them back at the audience, so they totally bombarded him with cans, he wasn't happy.

Bruce Mitchell: When he (Roger) was creeping and he had a big party of people with him he'd go, "Mitchell, Mitchell, tell 'em what Max Wall said to yer". Max Wall was marvellous company. He played at the Stadium and some of the crowd were throwing cans and backstage some girls went up to him to apologise and he said, "No no, don't worry about it... The only sadness is they were all empty." The band liked to have dinner after the show and they always liked Max to be there because he was such great company, telling stories, and Ian Hunter from the band said, "I'm so upset at the behaviour of those people, shouting at you while you were doing your act," and Max said, "If my agent had seen that he'd have turned in his quicklime."

Max was marvellous company. On that particular tour they had a circus act and Max was on just before Mott the Hoople, when Ian Hunter came on stage just after that incident he really gave 'em some grief.

Allan Frost: When Chuck Berry played his equipment wouldn't work and he got all upset and annoyed and walked off. There was nothing he could do, he had no sound stuff with him.

Slade were well loved at the Stadium, all the people that were working for Roger had to get down in front of the stage and stop people getting on stage, they attracted a kind football crowd, they were tearing up rows of seats this particular night and throwing them at us. It was alright, it was a buzz, it was part of what was happening. I read on the sleeve notes of one their albums that they wrote 'Cum On Feel the Noize' about the Stadium, the noise from the crowd was so loud it felt like the whole place was vibrating.

Steve Hopkins: I worked at the Stadium and knocked about there, saw the various acts that Roger promoted, Chuck Berry was a stalwart of Roger's and was guaranteed to get a crowd. Roger liked him but he also said, "No, he's a complete bastard he won't go on until he's got the money in his hand." I remember Argent playing there, David Bowie, Led Zeppelin, Beefheart, Sha Na Na and Commander Cody & the Lost Planet Airmen.

Geoff Davis: Once I got used to going to the Stadium on a regular basis I saw some great stuff there. I remember Roger put Chuck Berry on and it didn't do well. This was just before he had his second stage of popularity with that terrible 'My Ding a Ling'. Roger came up to me just before Chuck Berry was due on, there was only a couple of hundred people there if that, and he said "Have you got any money with you?" I had money in my back pocket from the shop. He said "Chuck Berry wants £3000 cash before he'll go on, and I haven't got it." So I go up there, backstage, and there's Chuck Berry sitting on the stairs with some real scrubber of a woman, probably an amateur prostitute, and he won't go on until he's got this money. So Roger gets all the money from the till, I go up and give him what I've got, a couple of hundred something like that and we just about managed to scrape enough money to pay Chuck, who then went on. He lost money that night of course. Roger, as with a lot of gigs, lost a lot of money. The thing with Chuck Berry then; very rarely if ever were you going to get a good show. He was very rarely interested and he'd get a local band to back him. He wouldn't rehearse or he'd just do one quick run through on the day, the band even did the solos right. He couldn't give a fuck, he played for about 40 minutes, you'd have seen a better tribute band, musically it was very disappointing.

Norman Killon became one of the resident DJ's at Eric's club in 1976, here he explains how he first met Roger Eagle.

Norman Killon: When Probe was in 'Silly Billies' Roger would come in to buy his records, I was also DJ on a hospital radio at the time. Whenever he was putting the big acts on at the Stadium I'd ask Roger if it was ok to do an interview, I spoke to Canned Heat, Chuck Berry whoever, that's how I got to know Roger.

Geoff Davis: We were one of the stalls in there (Silly Billies), we eventually ended up, because other people kept dropping out, having the whole basement area. That was in Whitechapel, right in the centre of town.

Steve Hardstaff: Before I met Roger I was a partner with

Pete Fulwell in a design studio called Modula Design.

Pete Fulwell: When I left University I had three mates and we decided it would be a good idea to run a club. It was all quite naive, how do we get the money? Tell you what, we'll each do our own thing, this was in '71-72, and we said we'll get together in three or four years time.

One guy set up a printing and typesetting firm, one guy decided he'd set up a lightshow, a tour lightshow. That was the first one to fall; it was such a fashion based thing that within twelve months it had gone out of fashion. He ended up going to work for the BBC in drama and being very successful. The other guy was a promoter, he was actually a rival of Roger's, because at that time theirs was the only gig in town and Roger had a deal with the owners of the Stadium, that any gig that was put on there he had to promote, or co-promote, they had to go through him.

I decided to do design, I didn't know a lot about it, but I knew a lot of people who were illustrators and most of them were mates. So I set up a design firm and started doing that and we'd all use each other, you know you'd use the printer to set up the posters and so on.

The design firm did ok but in the meantime Phil Davies, the guy who went into promoting, had died of a brain tumour, it's a shame because he was a lovely guy. He'd done a few things round Liverpool and he very quickly got connected with Rikki Farr who hosted the Isle of Wight Festivals, along with the Foulk brothers who promoted them in the late 60's, early 70's. They were based in London and still active four or five years later. Phil bought us in to do the design, we did stuff like the NME Poll winners concerts, that's how I got to know Peter Grant.

Led Zeppelin did a gig at the university and we were a bit short of cash at the time, so I went to see the social secretary and I asked him if we could do some Zeppelin posters and sell them to the queue. He said you'd better talk to the manager and have you got his number? Yeah. So I phoned from there and he answered the phone. He said, "well yeah, I've got to approve the design, and if I say ok I get 10%". So we did the design and because it was before faxes I had to Red Star this stuff to him. We actually struggled to pay for the courier to get permission to do the poster. Anyway he said "yeah, come and see me after the gig I'll be up with the band". So we did our selling, then went to see him afterwards, played it absolutely straight and cashed up y'know. He said, "When you're next in London you come and see me" and he started giving us work and he introduced us to the design departments of all the major record companies and at the time they were massive and you know, once you get an introduction from him, you're in.

Allan Frost: I went to everything that was ever on at the Stadium. I think the funniest one for me was when I was up in the St. George's hotel over St. John's precinct with The Sweet, they were pop but they rocked. The kids loved them and we were over there and we got to know each other quite well. Anyway the time came for them to do the gig, so we all got in their limo and the chauffeur drove us over to the Stadium. We all jumped out of the limo and headed for the back door, which led behind the pay desk, and Roger was stood there, Billy Bennett, Dave Backhouse and about half a dozen other guys mainly from Liverpool, Roger shouted "Link arms, link arms!" there were hundreds of girls, just swarming trying to get over the top of him to get to the band. Anyway we're running from the limo to the stage door, we got to the stage door and something drew my attention away. I looked back and I thought a girl had broken through, I couldn't think how she'd done it, but this girl was going in the entrance after the band. So I dived on this he/she, hauls him out, and I'm about to throw him back in the crowd, he looked round and I thought "Oh shit!" I think it was Steve Priest, I threw him back in the doorway.

Doreen Allen: Another memory is of The New York Dolls and Lou Reed, when Lou Reed refused to play with them. I remember because I was still working in a normal job at the time as a secretary in an office around the corner. It was midweek, I'm sure it was a Thursday or something. I'd come from work and I was just going through the big doors to get into the Stadium and The New York Dolls were walking out. They looked bloody gorgeous, they held the door open for me, and I said to Roger, "Where are they going?" and he said "Lou Reed's refused to play with them", I was in such a mood. But God got Lou Reed back because in the middle of his set all the electricity went. I think The New York Dolls must have cursed him again, I think there were only 2 or 300 hundred people in the audience.

Allan Frost: The New York Dolls turned up to play there on the same night as Lou Reed, they were double booked. Lou Reed's manager said to Roger, "You've got to have one or the other and Lou Reed ain't gonna play on the same stage as The Dolls", so Roger said to The Dolls 'Good night', and they'd even got their make-up on by then.

Nicky Crewe: Martin Hannett lived in that house on Wilbraham Road when we were there and the portrayal of Martin in films such as 'Twenty-four Hour Party People' I don't really get. Martin was different then, he had a sort of gaucheness really in social situations, I wouldn't say Roger was gauche but he wasn't accessible. If you liked the things he liked it meant you had common ground and that was great. I would say that because we were into the music that he liked, he got on with us. I would say definitely my musical education was influenced by him.

Ken Testi road managed the Liverpool band Deaf School until he teamed up with Roger Eagle and Pete Fulwell and opened Eric's club on Mathew Street in 1976.

Ken Testi: I first met Roger when he was doing the Liverpool

Stadium, I'd been aware of him for a while, he was actually the sole promoter at the Liverpool Stadium for years. Anything that came into Liverpool, the Stadium was the only place of any capacity at the time that could take a rock 'n' roll show even though it was a horrible venue.

It was built out of corrugated tin and the place was a boxing stadium. They could only use one half of it because the stage went across the boxing ring. It was well before the days of graphic equalisers and the din in there was terrible. It was like trying to do a gig in a biscuit tin; it was horrible, it really was poor. But none the less it was the only venue Liverpool had. Roger had nailed the agent down on it, so anything that came in had to go through Roger, so he was in a nice position there.

To put concerts on and publicise events, Roger would have had to use booking agents and printing workshops. There happened to be both of these in a building on Renshaw Street.

As Social Secretary at Liverpool University in 1965 Alan Cottam first experienced the booking of live bands. In 1968 he set up his own business booking acts for the Liverpool student circuit. He later branched out into promotions and alongside Roger Eagle co-promoted many acts at the Liverpool Stadium.

Alan Cottam: Roger had the promoting rights for the music at the Liverpool Stadium, Mickey Duff was the boxing promoter. The Stadium was owned by John Moores who started the Littlewoods Pools company.

At that stage I was handling quite a few bands and Roger would book some of the bands that would appear there through me and my agency. I leased a building on Renshaw Street, took one of the floors and opened an office which was called Scaffascope. At the time I was the main booker at Liverpool University. Pete Fulwell had a printing business and they were on the top floor of the same building as my company, they did a lot of posters for me for the concerts.

In the mid-1970's John Watkins worked with Alan Cottam and was instrumental in helping Roger move from Manchester to Liverpool, he also worked with Roger's future business partner Pete Fulwell.

John Watkins: I first met Roger in Alan Cottam's agency. Alan ran an entertainments agency in Renshaw Street in Liverpool. He ran the agency from there with a guy called Phil Davies, it was an agency that worked for bands, it wasn't cabaret work. My girlfriend worked for this agency, and I was a designer and I used to work upstairs for a design group called 'Modula' or 'Paper Tiger' with Pete Fulwell.

When I left 'Modula' or 'Paper Tiger', I did freelance work for Alan Cottam and also for Roger. Roger and Alan Cottam worked together, they almost went into partnership, but it wasn't a full partnership, because when Alan Cottam went bankrupt Roger didn't get touched on that. I'd be given the job of designing the posters for the Stadium, then they'd hire a car for me and I'd go round and flypost and collect the tickets. So I'd be driving down to Wolverhampton to put posters up, I'd go up to Preston, parts of Manchester, Warrington, Sheffield all over. Because the Stadium held about 4000 they could also split it down, because it was a boxing venue and in the round, so they would only use one side of the stage. So for most of the gigs it was 2000 capacity. They also put on a couple of gigs at the Liverpool Empire, I remember going to see The Pretty Things there and Roger gave me free tickets.

Alan Cottam: I opened the agency to book acts into student venues because there was no-one else doing it at the time. So from there I went to promote at a student union place called the Mountford Hall, I did quite a lot of name acts such as The Who and Bob Marley.

Roger and I worked very closely on the Liverpool Stadium and I actually promoted acts there, I did Led Zeppelin and various others. After that we collaborated quite a bit on different ventures.

The Stadium was a barn of a place and of course it was all set up for boxing. The stage was the boxing ring. We did experiments and did a few in the round, Led Zeppelin was one of them. In fact when they played it was one of their first gigs as Led Zeppelin.

Mike Don: At that time Roger tended to sort of move into a flat, not pay the rent and before they threw him out he'd move in somewhere else. He tended to move fairly often. I lost contact with him after he moved over to Liverpool on a permanent basis, for most of the time when the Stadium was going he was still based in Manchester.

Steve Hardstaff: I suppose the next contact I had with Roger was when he started coming in the old Probe Shop on Clarence Street. I worked there as a Saturday boy, I was still teaching at art college but I worked at Probe so I could indulge my ghastly avarice in terms of collecting vinyl.

Steve Hopkins: I've got a wealth of memories about him, one in particular he had some business down in London, he was going there to deal with promoters or record companies, and he took me and someone else with him. We went round various record company headquarters trying to blag LP's and posters. Roger was also inquiring about up and coming bands. We came back via Oxford, where his brother Martin, the astronomer, lived. Roger of course didn't tell us we were going to see his brother, it was more like "Ok Hopkins, you've passed the test, I think you can go on to phase two now, I'm gonna show you the rings of Saturn! Right! Are you ready for this? Hang on we better pull over and spliff up."

We turned up at his mother's house and Martin was a rather shy and retiring character. Roger got him to get the telescope out and show us the rings of Saturn. Then we came back by a very long route, he suddenly had a yen to go back via Wales, we had to go right round the coast of Wales. He wanted to promote at Bangor University.

We had quite a few good road trips and of course it was made good by the sort of madness, it wasn't quite 'Fear and Loathing in Las Vegas', but it was getting that way.

Bruce Mitchell: Roger's mother was fantastic, brilliant. She stayed with me a couple of times. We stayed down there as well, she had this big house down in Oxford and she lived there on her own, sometimes Martin lived there, sometimes John stayed there.

If Roger had a group going through, that was where they would lodge, and we stopped there once with Greasy Bear. It was important at that time with rock bands to have Hell's Angels as your roadies, part of the image y'know, and one of the ones with us was called Animal, a six footer and a proper animal, he used to grunt at people, carry equipment in, punch people on the way out. So we're all there and we get taken into this elegant lounge and Dorothy says "I've made tea" and there's these horrible musicians and this elegant woman pushing this big tea trolley, and there's Animal, and she says "Tea Animal?" and "Animal, more cake?" She was a proper upper class woman and she would treat everybody the same. Every now and again you'd get a spin of what she was like, "Roger, I've got the plumber coming in the morning, now stay in your room if you would, remember the last time you were here, you frightened the electrician?" There was a telescope in the back garden, because Martin was an astronomer, he was an astronomer and John was a fork lift driver.

John Watkins: I really liked Roger because Roger was into music. He managed to keep the Stadium going so he must have had business sense. He believed in it, he wanted to put those bands on, his enthusiasm for that was brilliant, he wanted to help and influence the bands he worked with. I also feel that with his love and belief in the music he was never going to make any money, but he always survived, if one thing didn't work he'd bounce off and disappear.

Geoff Davis: Mike Don was sometimes Roger's lift, Roger would use his connections, he'd sometimes come in the shop with Mike Don and he'd go back to Manchester with him. Mike had the Grassroots bookshop in Manchester in the 70's and 80's.

Mike Don: When we went to the Stadium it was Allan Frost or Dave Backhouse driving, we used to travel over there in the afternoon and travel back at night.

Penny Henry: When Roger put gigs on at the Liverpool Stadium I went to see Captain Beefheart. I remember his wife sitting on stage knitting. I also remember going to meet Arthur Lee, Roger knew I was bats about the band Love. When Roger put Love on at the Stadium he took me backstage to meet Arthur Lee - I took him a pot plant as a gift and he started screaming at me "What the fuck have you brought this for!?" I was really scared and I hid behind Roger. Roger actually said he never forgave him for doing that to me. He knew I was really into his music, it was just a gesture, I didn't really think it through.

From the days of The Blue Note club and The Magic Village when he first became exposed to the music of Captain Beefheart & The Magic Band it would have been very important for Roger and his mates to check out any gig that Beefheart was to do in the North of England, any vinyl release would have been anticipated with trepidation. From the interview with John Crumpton Roger tells of promoting Captain Beefheart.

Roger Eagle: I was a club promoter then I became a concert promoter, I booked Beefheart three times and I promoted two of the concerts, Mel Bush booked the third.

I quite simply did a deal with the agency. They say 'Captain Beefheat's coming over, do you want a date?' and you say 'Yes' and you argue briefly over the money, then you do the deal. I remember the first time I saw a Beefheart contract, it had page after page of lighting clauses. I remember one light he wanted was 'Bastard Amber' and he wanted a 'Super trooper hollow spot', that in those days could only be got from the continent. We just had to say no, we couldn't do it. I think that was Beefheart being deliberately difficult, a Beefheart show was not about lights. There's no point in going on about that stupid nonsense about hiring very expensive lighting equipment, it just added to the whole cost with no particular effect.

"You only have so much say when you're a promoter, you're there to service the act, to sell tickets and to make sure the act gets paid. A promoter is not particularly important. With Beefheart I would have held out for proper sound checks with a proper rig, with people who could actually manage the guy and talk to him, and say 'Listen, just do as you're told, then we'll get a good sound.' You've got to do that with him, because Beefheart is an extreme individual, and I don't suppose he listens.

From around 1973 Roger became reasonably well acquainted with Beefheart himself, or to give the man his proper title Don Van Vliet. Roger put Captain Beefheart & the Magic Band on at the Liverpool Stadium three times during the time he promoted gigs there, on one occasion actually joining the tour and travelling on the band's bus. Roger would later go on to claim Don was telepathic, the fact that Don won all Roger's money playing cards on the bus makes Roger's claim seem slightly naive but it wouldn't be the first time people who knew Don had made this claim. His particular way of working with musicians engendered an extremely close and personal relationship, the musician having to bring Don's visions to life. Basically the musicians were taught by Don how to play, thus having to de-learn anything they'd learned beforehand. As well as this Don also exercised an unusual amount of mental control over the musicians he worked with, even in social situations, being able to second-guess them in most situations.

Roger Eagle: I travelled with him (Captain Beefheart) quite a bit. I played cards with him once on a coach coming back from Bradford through Rochdale. I lost £13 to him playing Black Jack. He is not a good man to play cards with I can tell you that much. He'd ask you what card you wanted, and he'd give you one off, then he'd deal himself the right card and take your money.

Geoff Davis: Of course Beefheart played three times at the Stadium, it was just amazing, absolutely amazing and Roger invited me to come down for the sound check, and I met Beefheart. I didn't know a lot about him but he was everything you read about, in the sense that he's off his head. They were in a huddle; Beefheart, Zoot Horn Rollo and one or two others, quite close to the stage, and I thought I'll get a bit closer, have a closer look, and as I was walking past Beefheart beckoned to me,

He says "Hi!"

And I said, "Hello, alright."

He says, "I know you."

I said, "Oh, I don't think we've met actually."

He says, "I know you."

I said, "Well well well you know me eh?"

He says, "Yeah, you don't put out the light."

And I said, "Well I can't really argue with that."

He says, "You don't go out."

And I said, "Well what can I say?"

He says, "Don't go out!"

I thought you know, what could he mean? I thought about this a lot, I talked to other people and they said "Oh he saw something in you!" I don't know, then we spoke about Howlin' Wolf, we spoke about trees, how we have to talk to them and cherish them, all this sort of stuff. There was nothing general at all.

Nicky Crewe: Roger took Cathy Hopkins and I on tour with Captain Beefheart. I remember going over to the Stadium to see Captain Beefheart. Cathy and I went, and Dimitri and some of the others as well. After that gig Roger, Cathy and I seemed to go to quite a lot of tour dates. We ended up travelling on the bus with Captain Beefheart and the Magic Band. For many years Cathy had a drawing that Don had done for her, I think she gave it to Steve her brother. Don was a man with a lot of presence I have to say, he and Roger were great friends, they had a huge amount in common. In some ways it was a presence they must have recognised in one another I think.

What happened to me was I had a bit of a fling with the road manager, maybe it's unfair to call it that, he was a lovely man called Bill Shumo.

John Watkins: I think going on tour with Captain Beefheart really did something for him. He went on tour for a week on the bus, they'd get stoned and talk and of course this English guy knew a lot about American blues and what was going on in the States, and I think they sort of clicked, so Beefheart took him on the tour bus with him. I think if he had problems with his confidence that really gave him stronger confidence, because Beefheart was an artist he really believed in, and because he wasn't just a musician, he was a painter as well.

Nicky Crewe: I sometimes joke that when Cathy and I went on tour with Captain Beefheart maybe it did Roger's image some good but that certainly isn't why he took us, he took us because we loved the music. Cathy was very good with Roger because she was very light hearted with him. People could be quite intimidated by him, Cathy's lightheartedness made him more accessible to me.

Roger Eagle: The English audiences recognised a towering talent in Beefheart, and they were prepared to put up with the sound. They saw through it and said "This man is special" because they understood it without prejudice. They didn't have those commercial filters, which it seems Americans in general need. Otherwise the greatest American music of all-time – the blues, well jazz and blues, but particularly blues went virtually unnoticed for fifty years, it was hardly ever played on mainstream radio at all.

The fact that a lot of the music Roger considered relevant was never played on most UK and US radio stations gave him reason to look on it as special, relevant and important enough to make sure it was kept alive. Add that to the fact that pop and rock weeklies would also only cover the popular artists of the time. These are the main reasons he was so evangelical about certain artists, he felt that many of them hadn't received the recognition they deserved. Only people such as Eagle and John Peel had the courage to actually attempt to do something about what they considered to be a huge oversight.

Alan Cottam: The Stadium was a great gig providing you got a lot of people in. If your tickets didn't sell and you only got 7 or 800 in a 5,000 capacity venue it was poor. The acoustics weren't the best but in that era they were all so loud it didn't really matter. I don't think anybody could hear what was going on. The bands seemed to love it because they kept going back – Rod Stewart being one, he loved the place, he seemed to play twice a year with the various bands he played with. It was a bit rough and ready, the dressing rooms left a bit to be desired because of course they were designed for boxers. It became one of 'the' venues, there weren't many places like, all the big arenas were just being built. It was kind of in between your Liverpool Empire or Manchester Apollo and Wembley Arena. Bands would use the place as a stepping stone. We put Queen on there and the next thing you knew they were playing football stadiums. It was a hippy venue I suppose, there'd be someone selling joss sticks and posters, Geoff Davis would have a stall from Probe Records, it was a bit of an event really, we'd put at least three acts on. There was no bar there, it wasn't licensed, we always used to nip in a pub opposite and all the bands would go in there too before the gig.

Steve Hopkins: When I was employed at the Liverpool Stadium I had a specific role, after they'd done the flyposting he'd always make sure a certain number of posters were left over. They were well produced, big colour things, and he'd give me the job of selling them in the foyer. I was also gofer for the various artists that performed there.

Val Randall: I only went to the Stadium once and when I got to Liverpool from Birmingham where I was staying I thought where the hell am I? So I asked a policeman, he said "You're going to the Stadium? Do you know Roger Eagle?" I said "Yes, I'm going there to meet him." He said, "Well that's disgusting, I thought he was more of a gentleman, he should be escorting you to a place like this, I'll take you, come with me." So we get to the pub where we're supposed to meet him and he says, "Roger! You deserted this young lady, you want your hand slapping." Roger said, "Oh Val can look after herself." He was a good policeman, I thought "God! Does everybody know this man?" And of course they did didn't they?

Nicky Crewe: I went to the Liverpool Stadium and saw Sha Na Na. Then I met up with Dimitri and that crowd and they were in a band. That was Leroy and the Kools and I was one of the backing singers. Allan Frost did a bit of roadie work for us, through knowing that lot I ended of being a part of the band Drivin' Rock and Roger was our manager. I think we did really well, the girls all had day jobs. I'd done a term at university and hated it, so I'd come back to live in the North of England. I ended up living at Wilbraham Road in the same house that Roger had lived in the cellar. A girl called Ann O'Malley had just gone to Israel and they said "You can have Ann's room". They also said you can have Ann's place in the band. But I did already know them, it's not quite as weird as it sounds. So then I met up with Roger and Allan and everyone again. Roger spent a lot of time round at Wilbraham Road.

CP Lee: Sha Na Na played the Stadium, they were a greasers band from the States who played Woodstock. They were doing a UK tour and one night they were at Southport Floral Hall, the next night they were playing the Stadium, the next night they were playing Blackpool. Roger and I followed them round. We were driven by a friend of ours called Neville, we started with them on the Friday in Liverpool. At that time they were Roger's favourite group because they were doing 'Get a Job' they were doing all the rock 'n' roll favourites like 'At the Hop' by Danny & the Juniors and they had an amazing stage show. A wonderful stage show, three guys up front, everybody dancing in unison, it was a joy. You can see them on the Woodstock movie, they blew Woodstock apart. Everybody wanted bluesey jams or whatever and here's these blokes who sweat because they work, it even knocked the Woodstock people back. But Roger and I stayed with them for three days in the North-West, going from gig to gig in this car, it was quite a weekend that was.

When Eric's club started in 1976, Will Sergeant and Ian McCulloch became regulars, they later went on to form Echo and the Bunnymen who played their first gigs in the club. Here Will describes his first live gig experiences at Liverpool Stadium.

Will Sergeant: I used to go to the Stadium, my first gig was Slade supported by Status Quo there. I saw everybody there, I saw the Pink Fairies there and the sound was terrible. I used to go and watch Alex Harvey there, his was my favourite band at the time, I saw Bad Company's first gig there. Doreen worked there and she used to do these soups and 'Nudgers', which were like buns with cheese in them.

Mark Thomas: The first time I saw Roger was when I was 13 or 14 at Liverpool Stadium, I went to a lot of gigs there. Roger was a pretty formidable kind of guy. At the Stadium they had bootleg stalls in the foyer and some people used to rob them and say put it under their great coat and disappear. Obviously the stall holders complained to Roger and I once saw him walk down the entire front row of the Stadium before the support act had started, just taking LP's off people and giving them a clip round the head and everybody took it you know? You didn't mess, he didn't like hammer them, he just gave them a clip round the head, that was the first time I saw him. He always wore red and black, had a fairly fierce looking face, a big black moustache, he looked a bit like he was from another world.

Roger's hair was also grown out to almost an afro style, the well kept moustache giving him a slight resemblance to the actor Tom Selleck.

Allan Frost: In St. John's precinct in Liverpool there was a ticket agency, I can't remember what it was called. This place sold tickets for the Stadium but it was also other places like the Philharmonic. I used to have to go up there and collect large sums of money, I say large, they were large sums of money then, like £3000 or whatever, which would go almost straight away to one of the bands. I'd just stick it in my jacket and walk through Liverpool, I didn't think about it, I just did it. Mrs. Kaye was a little white haired old lady who ran the ticket agency in the precinct, until one day she ran off with all the money. Nobody suspected a thing, it just didn't open up the next week. Roger found that funny for quite a long time actually. I don't think she got caught, I don't know, I hope not. A sweet little old lady, with a white curly perm.

Bob Harding was also a member of Albertos Y Los Trios Paranoias and The Mothmen. The Mothmen released two albums, the title of the first 'Pay Attention' was a tribute to Roger Eagle. He later went on to work for the management team who looked after Simply Red, then along with Elliot Rashman ran the Blood & Fire reggae label in Manchester. Here Bob talks about his earliest recollections of Roger.

Bob Harding: I can't absolutely remember the first time I met Roger, it must have been in the mid 70's when I was in the Albertos. Roger promoted a lot of gigs for us and that's got to be when I first met him, we played the Stadium quite a few times. Of course he was always putting on stuff such as Captain Beefheart and we'd go over from Manchester and watch stuff like that. In fact Roger still owes us some money from one of those Stadium shows, only about £20, you'd probably only get about £30 for a support spot there in those days. We just did it for the crack.

He started giving me tapes. You know about Roger and his tapes, fantastic, what an education you know? Apart from the fact he was a really nice guy. What I remember about Roger is that he was this guy on a mission to spread this music to everybody. He exposed me to so much stuff I didn't know. With jazz, blues and R&B, I knew the genres but particular records I'd never heard before. The only one I couldn't get was rockabilly, he liked rockabilly a lot then. He'd say, "Listen to this, this is some really dark rockabilly" and I'd say "But Roger it sounds like all the rest of the rockabilly you've played me." That's the one area I didn't get.

John Watkins: At the time Roger was still living in Manchester. It's true that his bed was held up with all those *R&B Scene* magazines. I went to his place in Manchester. He fancied my girlfriend. that's what got us over there, we got invited over because we had a car, he lived in Percy Street, behind the cathedral. He was quite morose in some ways although he was talking and playing music, I said to him kind of out of the blue "Come on mate, come over to Liverpool." I could see he was quite lonely and he did and we were quite happy that he did. Also because of what Alan Cottam was doing and what Phil Davies was doing he was into that, he listened to me. This was all innocent stuff, there was no plan or anything. So I said come to Liverpool, and he came and lived with us in Greenheys Road, this was before he got the place on Sefton Park. So the record collection was in my basement.

Doreen Allen: He lived at an old coach house in Sefton Park, I got him that place, I was always his estate agent.

Geoff Davis: Roger would often stay up at Buckingham Avenue with us, because a lot of the time when he was working in Liverpool he was still living in Manchester, so I was one of the places or maybe the main place where he would stay over. Then he moved to Liverpool, on the other side of Sefton Park to me. It was on Livingstone Drive, in a little cottage in the grounds of a big house. You walked up this little drive and it was like an adjunct to the main house, perhaps originally occupied by a gardener or member of staff who worked at the house. Roger would wreck anywhere he went, you tried not to go to the toilet there, going to the toilet was not an issue. He would always do his own cooking when he was down on his arse, there would be records, tapes, magazines and stuff all over the place, not a care for decoration, penniless as we might know it.

Steve Hardstaff: I remember when he first moved to Liverpool he lived in a cottage on Sefton Park. I was doing the odd little piece of artwork for him then, it would have been in the days of *The Last Trumpet*. Roger started it and coerced me into doing it. You know what Roger was like, he'd bully you, which was terrific, that was a good thing about him, he bullied you into listening to music. We worked together on *The Last Trumpet* at the cottage.

We kind of discovered reggae concurrently, this was about the same time as the pre-release singles were coming into Probe from Jamaica. When we started to get interested in them Roger was also a promoter getting free reggae vinyl from the early independent British companies. We'd keep the vocal stuff but we'd chuck the dub albums away. When I say chuck away, we were passing them on without listening to them. We thought they were just boring instrumentals. When I say dub albums, it was very early, it would have been 'Version' albums.

Anyway to cut a long story short, one day at the cottage at Sefton Park I can't remember the artist but we played this record and of course we'd smoked some very strong black probably and it was a revelation.

He said "Stephen, you've got to listen to this, now!"

I'm going, "What the fuck is it?"

He says, "It's another one of those instrumentals."

Of course he put it on and it blew us away. From then on we were both more interested in the engineers, the producer and the dub than the vocal. I remember very distinctly sitting round there at that cottage and him playing the album that started it off. I don't think it would have been a Jamaican album. It was possibly one of those dodgy London pressings. Probably done by Jamaicans over here. Roger and I were both into ska and bluebeat before we were into reggae. At that time white folk weren't really buying reggae stuff, it was a bit scary going into a black record shop.

In an interview broadcast on Radio Merseyside in 1977, Roger Eagle spoke about the early 1970's music scene.

"In the early seventies, there was rock, and lots of it. Some of it was good and some of it was bad, some of it was interesting but it was getting more and more pompous; over-extended solos and all that kind of nonsense. It was getting boring. I was getting worried at the beginning of 1976 because the only music I was really interested in was Jamaican music."

The Last Trumpet was a free magazine/fanzine set up by Roger Eagle and Steve Hardstaff to cover parts of the music business that trade weeklies such as *Melody Maker*, *Sounds* and *New Musical*

Express chose not to feature. Set up towards the end of the Liverpool Stadium and distributed to sympathetic venues, shops and cafes across Liverpool, it was an attempt to inform the public about local gigs and music that was either marginalised or ignored by the national music press. It featured record reviews by Roger, art by Steve with contributions from many others. As an example, below is part of an article entitled 'This is Reggae Music' written by Roger.

"The cymbals hiss like snakes on the summer lawns of Kingston. This morning, as we were finishing this issue of The Trumpet, a big box of reggae trundled in through the door. These records I'm going to mention are the ones which stood out on first hearing. Starting with 'Black Star Liner' by Fred Locks on Grounation GRO 2032. The rhythm is heavy and the vocals have an urgency which caught my attention as I blundered about in the early morning trying to get the day started. Great for dancing and blundering. Secondly an album by King Tubby - King Tubby the Dub Master presents The Roots of Dub which is the past master of this highly distinctive Jamaican music at his best. The electronic skills of an engineer working with musicians Family Man Barrett and Carlton Davis, to name only two, is indeed an experience. If you are not aware yet of Dub, maybe you could give this album a listen. It is absolutely ideal for parties.

"To my mind it is impossible to separate this music from dancing and as the US soul thing begins to get just a little too much, a fresh and happy music like this could well start to sell heavily to those whose social lives revolve round the dance floor. If you heard the Big Youth album mentioned in our second issue, you might well associate his music with U. Roy, who is I think, Big Youth's musical inspiration. U. Roy has a single out on Grounation GRO 2010 called 'Jump for Joy'. Heavy duty Dub on the B side, which I prefer, called 'Heavy Duty Festival', a fine sound indeed, with the perfectly sympathetic mixture of recording technique and raw rhythm. Again, a perfect party record. A quick mention here for the Cimarons, who have 'Tradition' out on Vulcan 1005, flipped with their reggae version of the Fatback Band's 'Wicki Wacki'. The Cimarons are

one of the acts who are working out from Vulcan Records. They have been most keen to promote their music in the North-West, and if you can offer their artists work, I'm sure they'd be most co-operative with publicity material.

"Doubtless other shops will be stocking reggae and dub in the near future, but for the time being I have found that the most helpful are: The Soul and Reggae Shack in Granby St., Probe Records and Silly Billies and Virgin Records."

This article is significant in that it shows another example of Eagle's quest to turn people on to music they may not normally have given the time of day to.

Geoff Davis: Because of his love of reggae he would encourage me to get these Jamaican imports in, stuff that was pressed in Jamaica during the week, sometimes very rough pressings, and we'd have them in Liverpool on Friday. The vinyl would go to this place called Black Wax in Birmingham who specialised in Jamaican imports, we were the only place in this area that sold them, a lot would go to London and Birmingham. Black Wax bringing these imports in was a new thing at the time. The artists were not big names in reggae at the time, but they were subsequently, Joe Gibbs productions, all sorts of names, Yabby U, Big Youth. At that time Virgin caught on to reggae pretty quickly with their Frontline label, that was a little later, it was more '74/ 75. Often the studio was the most important thing, that's what the black youth in Liverpool were interested in; the studio, the engineer followed by the producer and even latterly the vocalist. It was the sound they were after.

So Roger would be there waiting for this delivery van to turn up on a Friday. It would turn up to the shop on Clarence Street and Roger would be suggesting and telling us what to get, as well as the stuff I already knew, practically helping himself really, I don't mean stealing anything, he'd just take over. The bloke had a small van, so we'd be at the back outside picking stuff out, but he was always there first. They'd queue in the shop practically to get this stuff, so he'd be made up with these.

Steve Hardstaff: Probe was one of the first shops, certainly in Liverpool, to get Jamaican pre-releases, my memory is a bit hazy, but Roger would come in and bully them out of me. He'd say, "Stephen, give me these reggae pre-releases and I'll tape them and bring them back", and I'd say, "Fuckin' 'ell Rog, it's more than me life's worth!" Anyway I wanted to do it myself, we used to fight over the pre-releases.

Geoff Davis: There wasn't necessarily a big market for reggae and dub in Liverpool, but in a way it was what the shop had always done. We'd not always done reggae, but we'd stocked reggae since we'd opened, it was just a case of what you could get hold of then. The shop was always like a broad specialist shop that started off as a head shop or head record shop, whatever you want to call it on the ground it was all alternative music, whether it was black music or American rock, we sold world music in 1971. I'd be dipping in and out of all these things, so there was probably no other shop like it.

Bob Harding: When I think back it was definitely Roger that turned me on to reggae. As I said he used to give us all these tapes, not all reggae, and we had these tapes in the Albertos' van, we had a VW microbus for years, and this particular tape had probably been lying in the glove compartment for a couple of months and one day one us decided to put it on, and I thought "what the fuck is this?" I'd never heard dub before and there was one particular track that stood out and hooked me into it, that was 'Great Stone' the dub of the tune by Prince Alla. Little did I know that 15 years later we'd be releasing that track on the Blood & Fire label.

John Watkins: He turned me onto a lot of bands I'd never heard, especially soul bands that I didn't know anything about. I was well into blues but I didn't know the soul bands that were coming out of America. It was bands in the style of the Average White Band he was into. The area in Liverpool I was living in was a black area, Liverpool 8. That was good for us and good for him, it helped him move across from Manchester to Liverpool. I knew The Chants, they were the first black harmony band in England, they played when The Beatles were called The Silver Beatles and some of them went on to form The Real Thing, they came out of that whole area of Liverpool.

Geoff Davis: Also Roger was a big Grateful Dead fan, we went down to see them at Alexander Palace in London. We drove from there to his mum's outside Oxford, I met his mum and we went for lunch with her at a pub by the river the following day. We also went to Blenheim Palace after that. That was with Roger, Steve Hardstaff and myself.

On September 9th, 10th and 11th 1974, The Grateful Dead played 3 nights at London's Alexander Palace.

John Watkins: Another thing that Roger picked up on, especially when they opened Eric's, was that a lot of the local Liverpool bands were helped by Alan Cottam, bands such as Deaf School and Amsterdam Lil and when Roger came over from Manchester he introduced Manchester bands to Alan such as Greasy Bear. When I left Liverpool, Roger was just getting to know Pete Fulwell.

Alan Cottam: At that time I was looking after some Liverpool bands such as Supercharge with Albie Donnelly, Deaf School and Amsterdam Lil.

Martin Dempsey was a member of various Liverpool bands including, Albert Dock, Yachts, Pink Military, It's Immaterial and also the Mel-O-Tones.

Martin Dempsey: As far as I know I got to know him (Roger) through Steve Hardstaff, the Deaf School connection, the Stadium and me doing bits of fly-posting for them.

Alan Cottam: I knew Roger very well, he was always a very amenable guy. Roger had his finger in quite a few pies. Roger, Geoff Davis and myself all used to kind of work alongside each other. It was like we crossed over and had good mutual contacts with places like The Everyman theatre, we were well connected with the arts in general you know? My role was more with the pop/rock side of things. It was a thriving scene at the time.

Pete Fulwell: I was similar to Roger really, in the sense that we weren't social in the way most people are. Both of us were social, but it was kind of on our own ground, because the work we were doing was social, it meant meeting lots of people. But on a personal level we're both quite solitary characters, we didn't bump into each other in pubs and clubs downtown because neither of us would have been there. Our agendas converged if you like.

In 1975 Bernie Connor was just another schoolboy intrigued by the life and bustle of the centre of Liverpool. His interest in music was enhanced when he started going to gigs at the Liverpool Stadium with his elder brother. His teenage musical years were further enhanced by the advent of Eric's and working in Geoff Davis' Probe records shop. His knowledge and love of music was inspired by Roger Eagle's musical education system. Bernie is a great DJ and has his own Internet radio show.

Bernie Connor: I saw loads of things at the Stadium; the first Stadium gig I went to was when I was 12. I went to see Mott The Hoople with me brother. I recall going to the Stadium to see Thin Lizzy. I remember this mad bloke just shouting at the punters. Probe used to have this satellite shop in Whitechapel in Liverpool in 'Silly Billies' which was a clothes shop that Norman Killon used to run and I'd see this bloke knockin' around there, and I'd seen him up in Clarence Street. I didn't know who these people were, I just knew Geoff to talk to because Geoff was running the shop.

In the Spring of 1975 Don Van Vliet (Captain Beefheart) found himself without a record deal. His old school friend, Frank Zappa, offered to put up the money to record a new album, this album came to be known as the 'Bat Chain Puller' album. Zappa was also to be executive producer on the album. In the end Zappa decided to let Don produce the album himself, he would just check on the progress from time to time. The group rehearsed the songs for three weeks, then went into the studio, the album was recorded in four days at Paramount Studios in Los Angeles.

Around mid 1976 Don Van Vliet sent Roger Eagle a parcel containing several sets of recordings including a reel of quarter inch tape in a box labelled "Apes Ma" as well as various cassettes and writings on various bits of paper. A rough sketch of a gorilla was taped to the lid of the quarter-inch tape box, obviously drawn by Don himself. Don requested that Roger hold these tapes in England as they were early or demo versions of the 'Bat Chain Puller' album.

By November 1976 Virgin records, the company expected to release the album, had held the tapes for 3 months, with no release date set. To compound the frustration Don Van Vliet must have felt at having recorded an album comparable to his best work held back, stories of the master tape that was sent to Virgin being copied and widely distributed as a bootleg began to circulate. Add to that stories of Zappa's falling out with business partner Herb Cohen, and stories put out by Don of various 'Signed pieces of paper' and the attendant complications, the album was doomed.

In 1978 Don put together a new Magic Band and re-recorded many of the tracks off 'Bat Chain Puller'. The new album was named 'Shiny Beast' (Bat Chain Puller) and was released in the US in late 1978 by Warner Brothers, the UK release coming slightly later.

Suffice to say the original 'Bat Chain Puller' album has still not been released, it resides in the 'Zappa Family trust' vaults.

CP Lee: In 1968 I first saw Beefheart at Manchester University, at the end of the gig I went backstage and Beefheart gave me his Harmonica. Now ten years later I'm in New York in a rehearsal studio. Also in the rehearsal studios are Captain Beefheart & the Magic Band, Earth, Wind & Fire and the Albertos. We were in the canteen refectory coffee bar and there's Don, and I go "Hi Don, I don't suppose you remember me."

He says, "Of course I do, how's the harmonica?" and we spent about an hour talking about Roger.

He said, "I had a falling out with Roger". Roger smoked Kools cigarettes because Beefheart smoked Kools. Beefheart said, "I've fallen out with Roger because he tried to rob me."

I said, "No, that's impossible",

By the end of the conversation he said, "Give Roger my love, he's an amazing man".

Geoff Davis: Me and Roger would often go and see bands in Manchester. Roger, Hardstaff and myself saw Bob Marley at Belle Vue, quite early on - fantastic. By this time he must have been living in Liverpool so I'd be the transport as well, if something good was coming up in Manchester and it wasn't going to Liverpool we'd go and see it in Manchester, Little Feat for instance.

Ken Testi: Subsequently I was tour managing a band called Deaf School, they came out of Liverpool art college in 1974 and because they were the only band in Liverpool that had an audience, from a promoter's point of view, they were the only band worth booking. That's how the band came to Roger's attention. So the band started doing a few shows with Roger here and there. He'd known for some time that the Stadium was going to go, so he was trying to do club gigs, just testing the water or trying to find a parachute I think.

*

Roger Eagle and John Lee Hooker in the Brazennose Street Twisted Wheel office and (below) with Roger Fairhurst - Photos: Brian Smith

Roger with Muddy Waters and Roger Fairhurst

Roger Eagle, Neil Carter & Muddy Waters - Photos: Brian Smith

From left Dave Waggett, unknown, Chuck Berry, Neil Carter front and Roger.

From second left, Roger Fairhurst, Dave Waggett, Memphis Slim & Roger
Photos: Brian Smith

Roger and friends at the Brazennose Street Twisted Wheel, c 1964.

Roger Eagle with 'The Hand' and friends at the Twisted Wheel
Photos: Brian Smith

*Roger Eagle with Dave Waggett and photographer Brian Smith on right,
Brazennose Street, Twisted Wheel. c 1964.*

*Roger with Millie Small c 1964
Photos courtesy of Brian Smith*

Roger with Rudi Pompili from Bill Haley's Comets - photo Brian Smith

Roger with Otis Spann. - photo Brian Smith

Roger clowning behind the DJ booth bike wheels with Screaming Jay Hawkins.

Screaming Jay Hawkins sparks up with Roger Eagle behind the Twisted Wheel turntables.
Photos courtesy of Brian Smith

It is impossible to write an account of the North-West music scene of the 1970's and 80's without mentioning Anthony H. Wilson. He graduated from Jesus College Cambridge and in 1973 began work at Granada TV studios, firstly as an anchorman and local news reporter. He progressed to getting his own local news and music programme called 'So It Goes'. Under pretty much the same format 'So It Goes' mutated into 'What's On'. Over the next 35 years Wilson became something of a household name in North-West England appearing in many different guises on TV and radio. In 2002 he changed his name from Tony back to Anthony. He founded Factory Records in 1978 and in 1982, along with members of the band New Order, opened the legendary Hacienda club in Manchester. He worked hard to elevate the city of Manchester's profile and his influence and work in and around the Manchester music and entertainment scene has been huge. Tony contracted renal cancer and died of a heart attack on 10th August 2007.

Anthony H. Wilson: When I came back to Manchester in mid '73 to work at Granada I found the job wonderful but the social life that went with the job not. I'd had three years at university and two years in London of sex and drugs and rock 'n' roll, so I wanted to continue that life. I suppose I found my entrance to that life three miles south of Manchester in a place called Didsbury. It was really through the Albertos. I became friendly with C.P. Lee in particular, and the others in that crowd, and I probably met Roger through them, I probably met him when the Albertos played at some point. All I can say is he was a gentle giant, sort of rather tall, rather big, quite serious.

Jayne Casey has become one of the luminaries of Liverpool culture, an appropriate representative of the city and it's deep cultural heritage. Her early life was marred by the early death of her mother and being raised by an alcoholic father, eventually leaving home at 14 and later spending time in a succession of children's homes. After working in a hair salon in St. John's precinct, she came into contact with characters such as Pete and Lynne Burns and Holly Johnson. Later she started her own vintage clothing store on Mathew Street, she also went on to front three seminal Liverpool bands, Big in Japan, Pink Military Stand Alone and Pink Industry. In 1992 she co-founded the Liverpool club Cream and also became Director of Performing Arts at The Bluecoat. More recently Jayne opened the Liverpool biennial celebrations and was co-creative director of the European Capital of Culture Festival in 2008.

Jayne Casey: I used to have a little vintage clothes shop on Mathew Street in a building called the 'Liverpool School of Dream Drama and Pun'. It was run by some artists, I had the downstairs and it was called Aunt Twackies. I was already friends with Pete Burns, Holly and Paul. We were already a posse, this was before punk and everybody used to be really aggressive towards us. So we had this posse, but I also had this following of interested people who just used to turn up at Aunt Twackies everyday to kind of stare, a lot of gay boys.

Bernie Connor: I went to school in town, I went to Campion, up London Road way. At dinner times I was always fascinated by the town, I grew up in Speke which is miles away from town – town for me was a big deal.

Somebody told me there was this place in Mathew Street where The Cavern used to be, it was where Deaf School rehearsed and this was Aunt Twackies. It was this weird art centre, clothes shop, hippy drop in sort of place and Deaf School used to rehearse there on a Thursday and you could just go in. Along with the smell of patchouli and joss sticks and these strange people, people I would never ever encounter in my day to day life in Speke. It was obviously some kind of hippy thing left over from the 60's and The Cavern you know. This was before Eric's opened.

The Stadium was still going then and Roger had done this

magazine called *The Last Trumpet*. Him and Steve Hardstaff did it together and I'd read them. Then I saw him handing out these magazines in Virgin in St. John's Precinct. He was carrying them round in a bag and putting them on the counter. He had this revolting lumber jacket on, his clothes sense was bad for a man who had such impeccable taste in music.

Bill Drummond studied at Liverpool art college, he worked at The Everyman Theatre in Liverpool and he also worked at Eric's as handyman/carpenter. He later went on to form the Liverpool based band Big In Japan. He managed The Teardrop Explodes and later Echo & The Bunnymen. In the 1980's he went on to form with Jimmy Cauty the extremely successful situationist rockers the KLF who in 1991 were the biggest selling singles act in the world. After famously quitting the music business in 1992 he is now a widely published and successful author, amongst many other things.

Bill Drummond: I saw the red shirt first. I was standing outside the Liverpool Stadium waiting to see Dr. Feelgood and Roogalator, everyone in the queue was scared of this guy, he seemed to tower over us, everyone was like "Will he let us in?" I can't remember any security it was just Roger, just him with his persona, with his imposing presence. That was like no other gig I'd been to anywhere else. Not because of the band, it was the fact that it was in a boxing stadium. I'd never been there before, the fact that the band played on the boxing ring and the rest of the place is cordoned off. But he was just in control, or as much as you could be.

The sound at the Stadium was terrible but seeing Dr. Feelgood there, it added to Dr Feelgood, it added to their starkness, their kind of monochrome feel. If it was a band with subtleties I imagine it would have been terrible.

In the same way that skiffle heralded the advent of rock 'n' roll, the mid-70's pub rock scene set in motion the punk explosion. 1974–76 saw the emergence of pub rock in the UK, ultimately a reaction to the pomp and overblown styles of the progressive rock scene. Bands such as Eddie and the Hot Rods, Dr Feelgood and Roogalator were starting to appear at the Stadium. These bands plied their trade in smaller London venues and the fact that they were starting to tour the country signifies a general interest in a back to basics rock music ethic. Something Roger Eagle would certainly have taken into consideration while putting together his plans for Eric's.

Ken Testi: Deaf School also did a few gigs with Roger in a place called The Metro. We also did a support slot at the Stadium for him as well. That was a show he wasn't pulling many tickets for and he thought Deaf School could pull some local interest.

Bernie Connor: I also went to the last gig at the Stadium which was Eddie & The Hot Rods and Ultravox, I saw Lizzy there in '76, I saw Gong.

Will Sergeant: When Thin Lizzy played at The Stadium apparently a girl got raped round the back or somewhere in the vicinity. It got closed down after that, I think they were looking for a reason to close it down anyway. All the freaks of Liverpool used to turn up there, it was a proper 'Withnail and I' scene at the time.

METRO

Bill Drummond: After the Stadium he had a club called The Metro, and it was to be rhythm and blues. I think it was Roger and Al Peters. It was a cellar club, this was before punk had kicked in, at the end of the Stadium. It didn't last that long and it didn't have a vibe. The Metro was the name of the club but it may not have been the name of the night. It may have been 'Rhythm and Blues

& Beyond' it would be 'Boom Boom Out Go The Lights' and straight into Beefheart with some rhythm and blues in between.

Doreen Allen: Roger did a club called The Metro before Eric's. Pete and Ken weren't involved. It was a basement club, Deaf School used to play there, it was going for 6 or 7 months. It was on a street down by the office area of Liverpool, it was off Victoria Street way. That was really good, there's a picture on one of Deaf School's albums taken in The Metro.

Ken Testi: I'd been on the road for a couple of years with Deaf School at this point, it's about 1976 now, and the Stadium had about half a dozen gigs left. I came off the road with Deaf School and I was looking for something to do. I helped Roger out with the last half dozen gigs at the Stadium and we were talking up the idea of doing a club.

7 - Eric's

Bernie Connor: I got to know Roger through Probe really, through Geoff, I worked in Probe from when I was very young. I was a Saturday boy; me and Pete Wylie, although Pete worked there before me. It was great while it happened I'm proud to say, even if it only touched my life in the briefest way, it would have made a profound difference. However it touched my life in a huge way, I spent all my youth either in Probe or in Eric's; fuck school, what's that for? It doesn't make sense.

Roger had such a deep influence on the way I look at music. Out of all the younger ones who worked in Probe and went to Eric's he knew I was interested, I listened to the music. He turned me on to John Coltrane and Captain Beefheart.

Geoff Davis: We opened the big Probe shop in '76 and it was Roger that encouraged me to get down into town. We went to look at this building, he said, "Look there's this building going here off Mathew Street, on Button Street," he said he'd take an office there, which he did. Then he said, "Come on now Geoffrey get up off your arse, you've got to expand here a bit, you can't be stuck up there all your life on Clarence Street." So it was things like that with Roger.

Any scene needs a leader, a seer, a sage, a knowledgeable, hep, trustworthy scholar. Someone who's done their homework, someone who lives and breathes music, someone who, according to Pete Fulwell who co-ran Eric's with Roger and Ken Testi, studied the weekly music press in the same way a professional gambler studies racing form. Someone with a grasp of and hunger for music, someone whose main motivation was to educate people about the 20th century's finest popular music. Eagle's move from promoting at the huge Liverpool Stadium to running a small capacity club in the heart of Liverpool came at a fortuitous time as far as the national zeitgeist was concerned. Both Fulwell and Eagle never set out to create a punk and new wave club but that is exactly what they did. Putting on gigs by all the notable bands from the British and US punk and new wave scenes, as well as many other gigs from genres as diverse as jazz, cajun, folk, country, reggae, early electro-pop and blues.

Ken Testi: The whole reason for calling it Eric's was because it was a piss take of Anabelle's or Sinatra's and that kind of generic thing. It was male, it was anglo-saxon.

Pete Fulwell: So Peter Grant had given us this work and by then I was ready to do this club, but the others weren't. I ended up in the spring and summer of '76 hanging out with Roger. He had this kind of flat, well it was a coach house associated with a big house by Sefton Park. It was in a bit of a state and there was a third guy involved, Ken Testi, he was Deaf School's road manager, and the three of us were talking about this club. Roger's perception of it fitted in perfectly with mine and that was a club for people that don't normally go to clubs. The idea was there are lots of people out there who love music but aren't part of clubland, it was disco then. We wanted to get people in who weren't part of that, didn't want to be part of that, but did want to see good music in a club setting. So we set this thing up, in the meantime I still had my firm.

The first few gigs were actually session nights, a night at an existing club, the first Eric's sessions. The club was in Mathew Street but it was a different club, it was next door. The club's name was Gatsby's and that's where the first few gigs happened. During that time I sold the business and used the money from that for the deposit on the club that we moved into. It would be very fashionable now; it was pure 70's, the publicity material included people in flares and big lapels, it was called the 'Revolution' disco and there were big papier mache motifs of Che Guevara and The Beatles, a weird mixture. Needless to say we weren't going to have a rock club with all that stuff in. So we stripped it all out, painted it all black, the woodwork red and off we went.

The only one of us who had any idea about what we were doing was Roger, he knew how to book bands, because that's what he'd done. Ken had some background with people that were running bars, so it was, "Ok, you take care of the bar." My background was marketing and publicity so I did that.

Ken Testi: Well, in Mathew Street there is a building that has it's frontage on Victoria Street, it's called the Fruit Exchange. There was a guy called Roy Adams who owned the original Cavern Club which is across the road. The council purchased the building on a compulsory repossession order to sink the airshaft for the underground railway. Roy Adams used the compensation he received to buy the premises across the road, which he called 'The New Cavern'. The New Cavern was on 2 floors, a ground floor and a basement, it didn't work. So he split it into 2 clubs. The basement club was accessed via Mathew Street, the ground floor club via Victoria Street. We did the first few shows in the Victoria Street club and because we didn't want Eric's punters walking through a door that said 'Gatsby's', we opened a fire escape door on Mathew Street, stuck a board outside with Eric's on, which I painted, and that was the entrance.

Jayne Casey: At the time Liverpool was in the throws of Militant, the docks were still running, and they all went out en masse on a Friday night and we were their sport. It was a laugh but it got a bit hairy and a bit heavy at times but we were good at getting away from it. But then Eric's opened in that environment, and it was like "Oh my god we've got a home", it was amazing.

Bill Drummond: I had my workshop underneath Aunt Twackies, which was Jayne Casey's clothes shop in the Liverpool School of Music, in fact everyone had different stalls. On the floor above there was a cafe, the floor below was my workshop. Roger would go into Aunt Twackies and he'd see a scene. Aunt Twackies was where I got to know Jayne Casey. Holly and Paul Rutherford would be dodgin' school and hangin' out, Jayne Casey's place was somewhere these young gay boys could hang out, they had their mother figure, they'd be making cups of tea and stuff.

Roger knew instinctively to get them on side. If you're gonna have a club, where is the youth movement? It's those ones there that are wearing the purple or lime green socks, they were too young for the Bowie/Roxy thing. These are the tastemakers, these are the people that are really frowned upon right now but they'll be the ones that create the scene. That's what he did that was right.

Jayne Casey: Anyway one day I was in the shop and this really big man came bounding in and he said, "I'm opening a club on Saturday, I want you and all your posse to come, here's the tickets, you've got to come," and he bounded out again. For us it was like we couldn't get into clubs, we used to spend our Saturday nights going round having a laugh, getting knocked back from clubs, that was our highlight, the amount of stress we could cause for the doormen. So for us it was a really unusual occurrence for somebody to want us to go to their club, so it stuck out you know? He came back the next day and brought a poster to put up and he was just haranguing me, "You gotta come to my club, you gotta come, you gotta come, you gotta bring all your friends." So I went, actually we all went to the opening night, and that was sort of the beginnings of it.

Ken Testi: We were the first and only people ever to put a queue out of Mathew Street, round to Victoria Street, back into North John Road then back into Mathew Street. The Beatles never did that. That was for The Runaways, it was all male at that show.

Bill Drummond: I remember the queue for one of the first nights at Eric's, it was for The Runaways, I remember seeing it because I was working across the road and thinking 'What's this for?' It must have been just rock lads thinking 'Ooh chicks in a band!' because no one was a fan of The Runaways.

Norman Killon: I remember the queue going round into Victoria Street. The Runaways were on before the Pistols and The Stranglers, the Pistols and The Stranglers were on upstairs at what was 'Gatsby's'. Deaf School also played there. There wasn't many people there for the Pistols, less than a hundred. Probably more for The Stranglers because at that point they were more popular because they sounded like The Doors.

As Ken Testi and Pete Fulwell have explained, the first few gigs at Eric's were session nights under the Eric's banner, at a club on Mathew Street originally called Gatsby's, upstairs from where Eric's ended up. There is no doubt whatsoever that the Sex Pistols played there on October 15th 1976. Roger would have been aware of their presence due to the fact that by this time they had not only appeared in the national music press on several occasions but had also appeared on TV in the North-West. Their appearance on Tony Wilson's 'So It Goes' just happened to be their first TV appearance. They had also played in Manchester twice at the Lesser Free Trade Hall. These two shows galvanised the Manchester music scene, it's safe to say that more than thirty years after the fact, their influence is still being felt.

Paul Morley: Perhaps Liverpool in some ways was slow to get going because they didn't have the Sex Pistols visit twice. The closest the Pistols got was Chester, some time in the Autumn of 1976.

Because of writer Paul Morley's statement from an article published in *The Guardian* on May 21st 2006 titled 'A Northern Soul' and Wilson's following assertion that the Sex Pistols didn't play at Eric's, the questions that were put to Wilson have been left in the narrative.

Bill Sykes: I remember Roger telling me he put the Sex Pistols on at Eric's before the Bill Grundy incident.

Anthony H Wilson: No he fucking didn't!

Bill Sykes: That's what he told me.

Anthony H Wilson: No, that's a complete lie, absolute total lie, not at all, it's actually the reverse of that. Absolutely not, the Pistols did not play. The Pistols did not come back to the North-West after July 20th, the second Manchester gig in '76. That's why Liverpool was so far behind Manchester. I always think that what Richard Boon and Howard Devoto did bringing the Pistols to Manchester on June 4th, was the same thing as the Germans putting Lenin into a cattle cart and sending the train into Russia. They sent this spark, this firebrand, into Russia to fuck up the Russians, which of course it did, it caused a revolution and the rest of it. Similarly bringing the Pistols to Manchester. The point is the Pistols did not get to Liverpool.

These are the confirmed gigs The Sex Pistols played in the North-West after July 20th 1976. Historically it's important the record be set straight.

13th September 1976: Quaintways, Chester
15th September 1976: Lodestar, Ribchester, Blackburn
14th October 1976: Mr Digby's, Birkenhead
15th October 1976: Eric's, Liverpool
9th December 1976: Electric Circus, Manchester
19th December 1976: Electric Circus, Manchester

It probably may not have been the best idea discussing anything to do with Liverpool with Tony, as we shall see it seems he got a little mixed up with his account.

Bill Sykes: Didn't they play the Electric Circus?

Anthony H Wilson: No. Oh, yes they did, that's what I'm saying, until the November 'Anarchy Tour', the whole point about the November 'Anarchy Tour' is, it was the time that it was taking off all around the country, and that was four weeks after Grundy.

Wilson always insisted that the two Sex Pistols gigs in 1976 galvanised the Manchester music scene of the late 70's. Asserting that because the band didn't play Liverpool the city didn't experience the profound repercussions that Manchester did. This is, of course, completely untrue. As Bill Drummond reveals, when the Pistols played Eric's on October 15th 1976, they just weren't that good at that particular gig. And as Pete Wylie later states, the show that kick-started the Liverpool punk scene of the later 70's was the May 5th 1977 gig by the Clash.

Ken Testi: I booked the Pistols for Eric's and that took place upstairs in what was Gatsby's. We got a band called Albert Dock to support them, I didn't enjoy it, they were trying to live up to this persona they were developing. Not friendly. With the music there was a dynamic there but it was early days for them. The attitude of the people around them wasn't constructive in any way plus the horror of walking into the dressing room after they'd left and finding it ankle deep in broken glass. It wasn't a pleasant gig.

Bill Drummond: The only time Roger put the Pistols on there were probably only fifty people there and they were shit anyway. Paul Morley curated a CD called 'North By North-West', he also wrote the sleeve notes and he made out the Pistols never played Liverpool, they only played Manchester. The reason they didn't have any influence was because they were shit that night. If they'd been great they would have had an influence. About ten of us went along, and having seen them we went "Ok, so that's London" and they were shit.

Pete Wylie: At Eric's, year zero was May 5th 1977, The Clash. Everyone who made a great record in the next ten years from Liverpool was there that night. Bill Drummond, The Bunnymen, Budgie from Siouxsie & the Banshees, Ian Broudie from The Lightning Seeds, obviously Holly and Paul and Pete Burns and Jayne Casey, we were all there. We were a Clash town from that point on.

Henry Priestman played in the bands Albert Dock and Yachts in the early stages of Eric's history. He formed the band It's Immaterial with former members of Yachts and had chart success with 'Driving Away From Home' in the 1980's. In 1987 he was part of the Liverpool band the Christians who had several chart hits on the Island Record label.

Henry Priestman: I went to the first three gigs at Eric's and I was also in a band called Albert Dock, we supported The Sex Pistols when they played at Eric's. The Pistols went on first and played in what was 'Gatsby's' originally, we went on after them and played downstairs. It seemed cathartic at the time, we were ripping pictures of the Beatles off the walls. It had been called The New Cavern and The Revolution but it still had pictures of The Beatles, they were faces in relief, big faces.

Albert Dock became Yachts when Eric's had started properly, we used to rehearse there, I don't know why Roger and Ken let us, we used to leave our gear set up on the stage and take it off if there was a gig on.

Martin Dempsey: When we supported The Sex Pistols at Eric's we got a poster printed ourselves, Eric's had their own poster but we thought we'd do our own, so we went to this printers and knocked a crap little poster up. We played on the third night supporting The Sex Pistols and at that time we were called Albert

Dock. The full name was Albert Dock and the Cod Warriors featuring the Fishfingerettes but when we played support to The Sex Pistols we just put it down as Albert Dock so we could get it on a poster really. It was a weird set up at the club when it first opened, the headline band played upstairs and the support played downstairs later on, it was the wrong way round, the support band was on last. We had a couple of pints with them in The Grapes round the corner, the band were quite chatty but Lydon was just kind of aloof. We'd played a few pub gigs and art college parties, we used to borrow Deaf School's gear and rehearse in a room at the art college.

Bob Bellis was the drummer in both 'Albert Dock' and the 'Yachts', he later went on to share a run down flat with Roger Eagle in the Toxteth area.

Bob Bellis: Kevin Ward, who was part of Deaf School, took me round to meet Roger when he lived in this little kind of porter's lodge on the edge of Sefton Park, it was a one-up one-down kind of thing. When we got there Roger had just got hold of the first vinyl pressing to come into the country from the Jamaica Sunsplash festival. Of course we had a couple of recreational cigarettes and he put this record on and blew us all away you know? Obviously we'd never heard anything like that before, it was the first time, it was incredible.

At the time we called ourselves Albert Dock and the Cod Warriors and Roger put us on at The She Club, this was just before Eric's opened. We supported the Pistols at their gig at Eric's under the name Albert Dock and they hid in their dressing room because they thought all these northerners were going to beat them up for publicity. It turns out they were they were really nice fellas, you know? Then Eric's kicked in proper, Albert Dock fell to bits and we became The Yachts and Roger put us on there a few times. He put us on there when Elvis first played, that's how we got involved with Jake Riviera and Stiff records.

Jayne Casey: So then I formed a relationship with Roger because I had a shop opposite, I became part of Roger's structure, also because I was at the centre of this unusual scene that Roger was keen to get in the club. That's why I had a different relationship to him than the other musicians did, because they got to know him as time went on, but I knew him from the beginning because I was part of his promotional structure. I was really the only younger person from that scene who became friends with him, I'd go back to his flat after the club and things.

Steve Hardstaff: I didn't do much work for Eric's really. There was no work to be done because all of the gigs Roger put on came with posters. The main publicity for Eric's was the leaflets, the gig listings and Roger did those himself. I think I did the odd one or two what could be referred to as flyers nowadays, they would have been A4. My main collaboration pre-Eric's was *The Last Trumpet*.

Norman Killon: At the first four Eric's gigs Roger was DJ, but he realised that he wouldn't be able to stay behind the turntables because he'd got all this other stuff to do. So I said, "I'll do it for nothing" which I did for a long time, I got a drink.

Martin Dempsey: Roger had been to one of the parties we'd done at the art college to see us play. I was DJing, playing soul and blues and he liked some of the stuff I was playing and he said, "Do you want to bring some of your records down and do an hour at the club sometime?" so I used to do a regular Thursday night slot. Thursday night was a good night, it was basically a night for up and coming and unheard of bands. Roger would wheel and deal to get anybody to play for next to nothing if he could, he'd put like three or four bands on in one night, it was great to be involved, but a lot of it happened for very little money.

The Illuminatus Trilogy, written by Robert Anton Wilson, was performed for the first time on stage at 'The Science Fiction

159

Theatre of Liverpool', 18 Mathew Street, Liverpool 2 on 23rd November 1976, encompassing three twelve hour performances. Directed by Ken Campbell and including many soon to be celebrated performers, such as David Rappaport and Bill Nighy, it has become known as a pivotal point in Liverpool stage history.

Jayne Casey: Roger encouraged me to get a band together. Above the building that I was in a theatre director had turned up called Ken Campbell and he had the rights to put on the first stage production of a trilogy of books called 'The Illuminati', a really famous trilogy of books by Robert Anton Wilson. Bill Drummond was the set designer, Ian Broudie was the guitarist in the band in the play and Ken wanted me to be the singer, but I would never sing, but I was acting in it. So in that scenario I became friends with Ian and Bill. Ken Campbell always used to say, "She should sing, she should sing". So when 'The Illuminati' finished Bill formed a band and asked me to be in it, and then Roger took us on from there. So Big In Japan came out of The Illuminati, which is the weirdest starting point.

Ken Testi: After a couple of weeks of doing shows upstairs we showed Roy Adams how to fill a building, we really did. Roy Adams was impressed with our performance and he was so desperate to offload these premises. He made us a generous offer on the basement, we said "Well we've no chance of raising a mortgage," he said, "Don't worry, I'll guarantee the mortgage, all you've got to do is make the payments and I've sold it." It was at that point that we bought Pete Fulwell in.

After the gig at Eric's in October '76, plus the attendant publicity following the Bill Grundy incident, the prospect of having The Sex Pistols on again at Eric's would have been compelling to Roger and Ken which is why, when they were offered the Pistols again for what would have been the 'Anarchy in the UK Tour', they didn't hesitate in re-booking them. As can be seen on the posters from the time, initially they were booked to play at Liverpool Stadium on Saturday 11th December 1976 but due to the controversy and outrage surrounding the Bill Grundy incident just days before, a change of the gig venue to Eric's was suggested.

Ken Testi: Then they were back with the big tour. The leader of Liverpool City Council at the time was Sir Trevor Jones who was a Liberal. At the time Radio Merseyside interviewed me for something, it was one of these interviews where you don't actually get to speak to the opposition. They interview you, interview the other person and then cut it together. Basically I put my point and he put his point and the line he went out on was, "Not in my town!" He had no concept of what was happening really, he was just another riding the media wave that the Bill Grundy episode had precipitated. As a result I got a call from Pete Fulwell the following day saying, "Look I've just had a call from Roy Adams and he wants to see us in his office right now." So I pulled some clothes on and got down to his office about 10 o'clock. He was ashen faced, he'd had two very senior policemen visit him wearing a lot of braid and leaving him under no illusion that if the show went ahead the premises would have considerable difficulty re-obtaining it's license. So we had to pull the gig.

Anthony H Wilson: I had already planned to spend a day with a film crew with them in Manchester, and my producer cancelled my film crew from a phone box at Hebden Bridge railway station at 8 o'clock in the morning after reading a leader in *The Times* saying these people are dangerous. I arrived with my film crew at 8:30, it was too late then, I couldn't do it. I was absolutely outraged, I had a furious row.

On the Thursday I had this music program called 'What's On' and on this Thursday a phone call came through to me at Granada and it's Roger. "Tony, just to let you know, I know you were going to put the Pistols concert on 'What's On' this weekend, unfortunately I had a visit yesterday afternoon from Merseyside police, they said if I allow this dangerous group to appear at Eric's on Friday night, I will not have my license renewed in the Spring."

Ken Testi: I know that McLaren has said since that they wanted all the gigs pulled but at the time we had a growing fan base that was really looking forward to that show. We'd sold a substantial number of tickets on the strength of it and it was quite a severe blow to us. Not the first and not the last.

Anthony H Wilson: So then I got this phone call from Roger and I go "Oh for fuck's sake Roger that's terrible but I quite understand, if you're going to lose your license you've got no choice." I got so angry about it, the next morning, Friday morning, I wrote my script for the next night's program and had someone from the graphics department change the logo for the program to 'What's Off'. There was a thirty-second spiel about The Sex Pistols at Eric's, blah blah blah, and then at 2 in the afternoon I was called into my boss's office and told, "This attack on Merseyside police, this is out, you can't mention it in the program." I said, "This is my program, this is about me, and that's what it's about, blah blah blah". I was completely obnoxious, threw a fit, had hysterics, shouted a bit. But they said, "No, it's out tonight, and it's your choice, you can either do it without this in the program or you can walk out of the building now." So I took the decision to be professional and do the program without it. Later when I came out of the studio I said, "Fuck you all, I'm gone."

I remember going to Ireland that weekend and spending a long three day weekend somewhere on the West coast, walking up and down the beach. Then when I got back on the Tuesday I was called into Plowright's office (David Plowright, programme controller and joint Managing Director of Granada TV). Plowright sat me down and said, "You can leave, we'd rather keep you but if you are going to stay in this fucking company we pay your wages, and we can tell you what to do, that's how life works. If you wanna do what you want, start your own TV station." So I learnt my lesson, if someone's paying your salary you do what you're told. So I stayed at Granada and signed an extra clause in my contract saying I will do whatever you fucking tell me.

So a second Liverpool gig for the Sex Pistols never came about but the reaction they engendered countrywide, across all class and cultural barriers, seems rather quaint now, a complete overreaction to a phenomenon that was essentially pop music. The band were considered by the government of the time, our moral guardians, to be a serious threat to the stability of the nation, and the sanity of its youth.

Doreen Allen: I worked in the office at the back of Probe and I worked with Ken Testi at the very beginning of Eric's. But then they got the actual lease on Eric's and we had our own office then. Roger would come into Eric's every morning for his post and his records, I used to open up at about 10 or 11 o'clock. I used to work in the office in the day time you see, I used to do the badges and the memberships.

Norman Killon: The early part of the week was like local bands, it was like having a rehearsal in front of people. I did quite a lot of the big nights, The Clash and other stuff. It was difficult for me and it was difficult for the punters. He wanted to have an identity for the club and he was still getting the old Revolution club punters coming in, the hard rock end of it. There were no punk records available, there were a few reggae records, what are you gonna play? I made the mistake of playing some hard rock once, kind of Family and Free, and Roger came over and said "No stop, don't play any of that stuff!", he would have been happy if I'd played 60's R&B. So I got the idea that that wasn't what you play, you've got to find another way and ignore the people coming up to you saying "Stop playing this crap!" which they did. They'd come up and ask for Led Zep and Free or whatever, so it took a while for it to gain it's specific identity for itself. Not long after that the records started to come out.

Martin Dempsey: Yeah I got on well with Roger, I used to do a bit of painting and repairing furniture and stuff at the club. I used to chauffeur him about now and again because he didn't drive. Steve Hardstaff and Roger were very good mates and Steve was one of my best mates. The thing I remember best about Roger is of going round to his flat when he lived on Faulkner Street and he had all these extremely wonderful records all over the place in a terrible state of disrepair. There was a cat running round so there'd be cat hair everywhere and he used to make these big fry ups and he'd have a huge frying pan full of stuff, horrible, but that was his thing these massive fry ups. It can't have done him a lot of good in the long run. We used to go round at lunch times, have a couple of spliffs and listen to a few of his tunes. He was always trying to get stuff off Steve, Steve was working part time in Probe as well as teaching at the art college. So Steve would order stuff for Roger and drop them round. Steve would never lend Roger records, they used to get mashed up.

THE ERIC'S JUKEBOX

The jukebox as a club focal point was there in The Magic Village and possibly had its roots much earlier, in fact Roger's love of the jukebox as a teaching tool must have had it's roots in his formative teenage years when rock 'n' roll was first making waves in the UK.

Bernie Connor: We helped bring the jukebox into the club, it was on scaffold planks, we got it down the stairs. It was me, Kevin Connolly and Alan Jones. Roger disappeared upstairs, did his usual Ali Bongo mumbo jumbo thing. We filled it full of records and the first record we played was 'Goin' to a Gogo' by Smokey Robinson & the Miracles. I remember being shit-faced one night standing by the jukebox and when 'Goin' to a Gogo' came on he leaned over and said "Listen to when the guitar and bass come in", and he was absolutely right. If I hear that record now I just wanna hear the intro over and over again. It's possibly the greatest intro to a record ever.

Pete Fulwell: That was Roger's soul, that's what that was. Roger's attitude to music and putting shows on wasn't 'Let's entertain people' it was to educate people. He was an educator, I've never met anyone like him. He had a real passion for certain kinds of music, it was his mission in life to make people understand that music. For some people it would be the wrong kind of music, you'd hear doors slamming in their heads. Whereas with other people it was exactly what they needed, and wanted, he could make them flower. He had an encyclopaedic knowledge and collection as well. The jukebox tended towards his rockabilly type stuff, it was older stuff. It was a teaching machine that's what it was and very precious to his heart, it was really important to him and to a lot of people. The punks would be going "Oh The Damned aren't on it", you'd get all that. They hadn't been 'Rogered' as it were. He'd often stand by the jukebox and give the talk if necessary. He'd bring the whole thing to life, I don't know anyone who worked with him or knew him who wasn't touched by that. If anything that's what I remember him most for, the passion and the wanting to educate people.

Martin Dempsey: As soon as Eric's started you had the jukebox in the corner which was fucking wonderful, you just had to listen and Roger's whole thing was 'You must hear this! You must hear this!' It influenced everyone, however subliminally, what it did was take away from that historical Liverpool thing, as if the message was 'Anybody can do this, just do what you want to do, however you're going to do it'. Consequently the scene spawned all these different kinds of bands, doing their own versions of what they wanted to do and the underlying thing was they all wanted to play at this club or they wanted to hang out there, be there. Because if you were accepted by Roger you were obviously cool, you know what I mean? One of his major strengths was that he made stuff accessible, that you otherwise wouldn't have got to hear, stuff you wouldn't have heard from John Peel, you couldn't afford to miss what he was putting on, even if you'd never heard of them.

Mick Hucknall: The jukebox in Eric's just summed Roger up - you'd have 'Anarchy in UK' next to 'A Night in Tunisia' by Charlie Parker. That eclectic thing had a huge effect on my attitude toward the music I make, cos I don't make one type of music - they classify it as 'soul music' but we have reggae tunes and jazz tunes. I've always been into the sweeter side of music.

As Pete Fulwell states, they knew quite early on that Eric's wasn't going to work and against sensible business acumen they decided to run with it. With Eagle's open booking policy they were able to put on not only the best up and coming bands from the punk and new wave era but also many up and coming local bands, who were able to play their debut gigs and later carve out careers on an international stage.

Pete Fulwell: We did all kinds of forecasts before we started, based on assumptions of how many people we'd do on average coming down to the club, what they would spend at the bar, what we'd gross, what we'd net on the door, stuff like that. I'm a bit of a numbers person, the most numerate out of the three of us, so I'd do that bit and three months in we have a meeting, we look at the picture and clear as day it's doomed. Financially it's got no chance. It was clear that all the assumptions we had made were wrong. It was also clear what we would have to do to fix it and we consciously decided 'Fuck it, no', if we have to do those things we're not actually doing what we wanna do. The game is keep it flying as long as possible, but you know it's going to crash.

Speaking about the early days at Eric's, Roger sums up the essence of what became a vibrant scene.

Roger Eagle: Well it was all new then. There wasn't real rivalry as there is now. It was all now and exciting and the little factions didn't exist. You could put a number of groups on and be sure of a good response. As time passed, people became more selective and with the factions; punks, skins, mods etc., people tended to stop coming when it wasn't their 'brand' of music. I used to book groups because I liked them. I like giving a chance to undiscovered groups but I also had to turn down a lot of groups and at one stage there were 200 bands on the waiting list who wanted to be given the chance to appear at Eric's.

In an article that appeared in the weekly music paper the *Melody Maker* from October 8th 1977, Roger was interviewed by Ian Birch about the Liverpool music scene and Eric's club. The article was entitled 'Mersey, The Beat Goes On'. Here Roger explains the importance of a club as opposed to a venue.

"Clubs to me are much more important to the scheme of things, because concerts are a one off; you either have a good time and go home, or you don't have a good time and go home. If you're part of a club, you're part of a family and this club is run as a club, it's not an opportunist thing where we take the money and run. We're very keen on membership and the strongest discipline we have here is to deprive people of their membership, that hurts and people respect that.

In the same interview Roger talked about the City of Liverpool living in the shadow of The Beatles and how it affected the city's musical future. With local bands from the time such as The Yachts, The Spitfire Boys, Big in Japan, Berlin, The Destroyers, The Accelerators and Those Naughty Lumps all creating their own following in the area having been given a common platform to launch their music; Roger and the Eric's team were helping to revitalise a very important aspect of the city's cultural heritage.

"I think there was a lack of self-confidence in Liverpool, and it's coming back strongly now, it'll be fairly unstoppable once the momentum gets moving. It isn't really a lack of self-confidence, it's more like all the best people left the city, like The Beatles. They didn't stay here and re-invest in Liverpool, open recording studios, a restaurant whatever, they just left, and I think people got very depressed about that and thought the talent had gone.

Geoff Davis: There were so many nights that stick out in a way.

Norman Killon: There were a lot of duff nights as well.

Geoff Davis: The Only Ones played on a Sunday night, they were just fantastic and there was hardly anybody there, Link Wray was fantastic.

Norman Killon: He was on with Robert Gordon.

Geoff Davis: Eric's has this reputation for just being a punk club, but it wasn't, they had on people like John Martyn and Stanley Clarke.

Norman Killon: Then you'd get zydeco bands, you know Queen Ida and Rockin' Dopsie.

ERIC'S MATINEE

Pete Fulwell: There was a thing on local radio about live music in Liverpool with a phone-in that I was listening to and there was a procession of 14 and 15 year olds phoning in and saying "What's going on? We love the music, we buy the records of these bands but we can't go and see them at Eric's because they won't let us in." Because it was licensed and they had to be 18 or over they were saying "Why isn't there something for us?" And I thought

'Fuckin' right!" and I said to Roger, "What's the possibility of when you book the bands, getting them to do a matinee first?" The bands will get more money, we'll open it with soft drinks for the matinee and open the bar later.

Jayne Casey: Roger sort of adopted me, I'd only been out of a children's home a year. I'd left a children's home a year earlier with a bin bag full of clothes and a lifetime of abuse. That little bald headed girl was the real McCoy, that was the most fucked up little girl you've ever met in your life and Roger really recognised that and gave me a level of protection in a way. He allowed me to be myself, he didn't try to change me, he encouraged the dysfunction, it made him laugh, it amused him. But he also understood that there was nowhere else for me to be at that moment in time. He gave me the space and the stage on which to express all this nuttiness. He tried to help me and make me see things that I couldn't see sometimes. But he never said, "Oh you're nuts, you've gotta get your act together", he was great.

Bill Drummond: I'd been working as a carpenter designing and building stage sets at the Everyman theatre. When I started doing Big In Japan I became Eric's handyman. I'd build walls, do carpentry, do the bar. I also did get-ins, security, Roger wanted to take me on in the office, I don't know why. I was 23, 24 at that time, everybody else was 18, 19, 20 in general.

Here Bill Drummond explains the origins of Big in Japan, who were almost a reverse supergroup. In subsequent years the various members of the band have racked up 8 UK No 1 singles and 35 Top 30 chart singles. As well as 2 UK No 1 albums and 13 top 30 chart albums between them.

Bill Drummond: I knew Clive Langer from the band Deaf School, he was a year below me at Art College, I got to know him when I came back to Liverpool and I was working at The Everyman Theatre. Deaf School played a show at The Everyman, I got to know Clive through other members of the band.

So I'm with Phil the singer from Deaf School, Bob Wooler, who'd DJ'd at The Cavern, and Clive in The Grapes pub on Mathew Street, half past seven, 5th May 1977. Clive was off to America the next day with Deaf School and he's telling me we've got to form a band. Their second album was about to come out but he realised even at that point that Deaf School are not going to happen, they're kind of yesterday's thing. So Clive was wanting out and wanting to be part of this whole new energy. He was wanting us three to form a band and they were talking about me being in Deaf School but that was stupid, that would never have worked. Clive said, "You start being a band, write some songs, rehearse and when I get back from America I'll join." We went to Eric's that night, saw The Clash and next day we started being this band without a name.

From the *Melody Maker* interview, October 1977 with Ian Birch, Roger Eagle explains some of his ideas for Big in Japan and his concept of what could be possible for the future of clubs and the way people perceive music.

"The idea behind Big in Japan is not necessarily to make a lot of records or do a lot of concerts but to appear in different parts of the world, this is my own concept, taking it on a couple of years from punk and dub. One of my great ambitions is to have a club in major cities around the world and fly people around the chain, dropping people off and picking people up. The idea is to do dreadful damage to people's concepts of music in different parts of the world."

Bill Drummond: By the time Deaf School get back we've done a couple of gigs with three or four songs. Then, I went away with my wife for a holiday in early August, and Roger, the bastard, gets the band into a studio to record a single while I'm away. A song I had written, or co-written, we'd already got Jayne Casey in to be the singer. They got Clive in to play the guitar. So while I'm away not only did Elvis die, I came back to find the band had recorded a single. Roger was like "What? How come this has happened?" I'm like, "It serves me right for going on holiday." But the pisser is I had all these ideas of what that song should sound like. All these production ideas and all these different things, and it's this teeny weeny little thing and it's nothing like I wanted it to be. I had this epic, Phil Spectorish thing in mind. A month doesn't go by without me thinking how that song should have been produced. That's well over 30 years ago. The B-Side was by the Yachts, under the name 'Chuddy Nuddies', that was Martin Dempsey, the Yachts were signed at that time.

We didn't do many gigs under that line-up, in the first line-up there were just three of us. Then we got Jayne in to be the singer, then we got Ian Broudie in to be second guitarist. Stunning. I knew Ian when he was 15/16 and still at school. I was working on a stage set for something and he'd been bought in to do the music and I just thought "What? This spotty little kid?" He was just fantastic.

Jayne Casey: So Roger sort of adopted me, he really looked after me, he'd take me home and feed me goat curry and just throw loads of records on. He'd throw loads of records on and he'd go, "This is Studio One, listen to that bass, listen to the horns." He'd never listen to a song all the way through and the next time he'd put it on he'd go "Who did those horns?" so yeah he gave me a proper musical education.

Bill Drummond: The thing Roger put on before Eric's at The Metro, 'R&B and Beyond', it was Al Peters and all the old guys who'd been around for ages, that wasn't gonna work, he knew he had to get them in to make it the place to be. He'd let us in for nothing, I was in Big In Japan, then I was working there building the walls, doing the bars and painting it. If you had a choice of asking Holly Johnson, Paul Rutherford or me to build you a wall, you're gonna ask me.

From the *Melody Maker* interview again, Roger talks about the optimism and creativity that was in the air in 1977, also how he thought it would be looked back upon.

"I'm hoping that in 10-20 years time people will look back and not just see The Beatles. They'll see now as a very fertile breeding ground. Liverpudlians are probably the last to realise it and I only hope that this time more of the money stays in Liverpool. In fact I know it will. People are beginning to compete again and it's really good."

Bill Drummond: I'm not sure how Roger came to manage us. He would just say "Bill, you've got a show in Rhyl" or whatever and he'd just tell us £60 or £80. He'd look at me because I was the one with the driving license, I'd have to hire a van and get everything together, he'd do nothing other than get the gig. I don't know if he made any money, it wasn't as if we'd have to hand over any commission. Maybe there was a year contract. He did try and get record company interest, he was in a good position to because lots of companies were hanging around thinking this is gonna take over the world. He was in a good position, we were either shit or he wasn't a good manager. He never tried to give us direction, he'd try and get you to listen to dub. Pete Fulwell had more of that kind of influence; he has a real political agenda about things. Pete would say to us "This is what you should be doing, this is what it's about." You would never get that from Roger, there was an aura about him that wasn't threatening, but almost foreboding.

Jayne Casey: Pete Fulwell used to run the office, answering the phone, taking gigs and things. What Roger did was give us a stage, and from there everything followed. So everything came through Eric's, he was involved on a day to day level. Big In Japan used to rehearse in Eric's everyday, so yeah he was involved but Pete was the administrator so to speak. Big In Japan wasn't a band that needed its hand holding, there were quite a few together people in it. Roger threw in creative things by encouraging us.

Doreen Allen: Roger was brilliant with contracts, he'd give it to me and say, "Rip the rider up!" I'd say, "But Roger," he'd say, "Rip the rider up!" Then he'd say "No we don't need to have four people to help bring in the equipment, no, no, no!" But you see Roger was never there when the bands arrived, soft bugger here was though. So when the bands arrived they'd say, "Where's the humpers to bring in the equipment ?" And I'd have to say, "Erm, erm there aren't any." So I'd get on the phone then to Roger, he'd say phone Dave C, he'd be there with just 10 minutes notice, the band would be sat there refusing to move any equipment. That was typical Roger.

Bernie Connor: I was too young to go to Eric's from the get-go, I went from '77 onwards. I was fifteen. From '78 onwards I was in there all the time. Me and my mate Kevin Connolly used to do the odd jobs in there, we decorated the place and what have you.

REGGAE NIGHTS AT ERIC'S

The reggae and dub influence at Eric's had nothing to do with Johnny Rotten, the Clash or the Slits – although their patronage must have helped later, there was no Don Letts, nor was there a Notting Hill Carnival as a reference point. It was purely and simply Roger Eagle, his record collection and his determination to drench the Eric's crowd in what he believed was the best music around.

Bill Drummond: One of the things Roger and I could get on about was R&B. I didn't like dub, I didn't smoke dope, but I loved reggae, I liked the songs more. I wasn't into the construction of the reggae producer, but I think that was because I wasn't interested in smoking dope and because that was Roger's thing, that style of music makes more sense.

Geoff Davis: Roger would put reggae bands on. Remember Black Slate, they had a hit, he'd have them on as much as he could, he'd have them on supporting bigger bands and on their own. I've lost count of the reggae bands I saw there, I'd like to know about that.

Steve Hardstaff: After a gig by Jamaican reggae band The Gladiators who were on a Virgin Records tour, Roger and I were sat up in the office. Pete wasn't there and Ken wasn't there. We'd both watched the gig and it was great. Anyway Prince Tony Robinson, who was managing the band, came into the office and pulled out what I think was a Magnum and just demanded money from Roger. The band had already been paid and apparently he did it at most gigs, whether it was a dummy gun or not I don't know. I think Roger gave him some money, I just kind of blanched, because we were binned as well, stoned you know.

Bill Drummond: Enough people must have told you about the bands he put on at Eric's, especially the reggae bands, they would cost a fucking fortune, and they'd be so difficult. I look back and think, well of course they were. They're coming over from Jamaica and they're thinking "Ok, we're gonna take you for everything we can". Roger would pay a fortune for these bands to come over and they would just take advantage of the situation. I know that can be justified though because Roger loved the music and respected those guys so much and nobody would turn up at the gigs but for me being into jazz and folk, he'd bring that element into the club as well, Bert Jansch would play, there'd be a Peter Hamill solo gig with guitar, which was great for me. If you were an out-of-town punk who'd bought into the whole punk thing, you wouldn't have wanted to know about Bert Jansch and Hamill or some of the jazz stuff.

Jayne Casey: I think more importantly Roger taught me a lot of great philosophy, I don't know whose quote it is but he used to use the term "It's as important as life itself" and for a seventeen year-old to learn that term about culture is quite profound. His point was it's not something you're just doing or making, it's not some consumer product, this is as important as life itself. Your engagement with culture, the culture that you're involved with, that you're participating in and contributing to - this isn't a game. This is the most important thing you'll ever find in life, this is life. This has empowered me, it's given me an edge, people know I have a deep commitment to what I do.

Another thing Roger taught me was always go to the source, you've got to get to the source of it, this is a lesson I've tried to pass on to my son. The most influential things become a part of you, it becomes your way. It's like; don't fuck about, this is culture, this is everything, this can change lives. So he gave a lot of depth to me, and that is what I'm eternally grateful for. He's such an important dude, it wasn't a game, he wasn't just a club promoter, he was the source. He was like a teacher, he was there to teach those people.

Pete Fulwell: Roger would educate some of the up and coming bands. He would have them round at his flat and with some of them it wasn't relevant to them or they didn't want to see it, or they wanted to know more about something else. And it wouldn't have been what Roger wanted to tell them, and because Roger had a curriculum and if that didn't fit what you needed, tough shit! He'd try to persuade you that it did, "But no Roger, it's the wrong genre, I wanna hear more about this other stuff." Harrumph! Rubbish that!

Bernie Connor: To me Roger would be like, "This is somebody you should meet." Roger used to do that all the time, that was one of his things, "Bernie, Bernie, Bernie, this man here is Richard Boon, he manages the Buzzcocks, talk to him." That was I think his public school breeding that did that. I think with us being shy working class types who knew our place, I'm talking about myself and my mates, we just stand around at the back and sort of wait for people to introduce themselves. Roger was "Come here! You should be meeting these people. These people will change your life!" He was absolutely right on most occasions.

He dragged us into the office once and said "Listen to this!" It was a cassette demo of The Pop Group, I'd never heard The Pop Group but I'd read about them in the *NME*. It was a cassette demo and he was absolutely right about that. He liked it because it was like Cecil Taylor.

Student and Eric's regular Julian Cope got his first band together at Eric's. Along with Ian McCulloch and Pete Wylie he formed his first band, The Crucial Three, the band didn't progress beyond rehearsal. Cope also participated in two other short lived bands The Nova Mob with Wylie and A Shallow Madness with McCulloch. The initial ideas eventually became reality when all three formed what would become successful chart acts, The Teardrop Explodes, Echo & the Bunnymen and Wah! Heat. From his book 'Head On' Julian describes his first impressions of Roger.

"Eric's was a basement, a real basement with bass that climbed round the walls. That first night they played 'Great Stone' by King Tubby and I hung out by the DJ. I didn't speak right away as he was transfixed, a guy about 38 with old, old clothes and a moustache. Right after King Tubby came 'Tail Dragger' by Howlin' Wolf, then 'Roadrunner', then 'Ask the Angels' by Patti Smith. Finally I plucked up courage to talk to the DJ. He was Roger Eagle. He ran the club. He had been born only for music and I couldn't tell whether he liked or hated me. But he talked to me and that was enough."

Pete Fulwell: I met his mum once. Roger was very proud of his mum and to be honest when I met his mum he made more sense as well, they were more similar than they looked. They were coming from the same place in different ways; an upper-middle class Oxbridge background, so an intellectual environment is what he grew up in.

When asked by Ian Birch in the *Melody Maker* in October 1977 if he felt that the new upsurge in local talent was more than just a locally supported aspiration built around a handful of groups, Roger answered like this.

"Yeah definitely, but I'm a bit disappointed in a lot of the local groups in that they are just identikit punks. What we're doing is getting a white group and a black group together and we're merging. We're going to do a 12 inch dub from Liverpool 8 and downtown. It's still at a very embryonic stage but there'll be three black singers and a white and black rhythm section. We'll probably do an old Burning Spear tune 'Rockers Time' and do a nine minute dub of it, now that to me is interesting."

Pete Fulwell: This is how the whole thing with Tony [Wilson] happened, we put one out first of all on a band called Big In Japan, on the B side was a band who'd already signed to Stiff called Yachts. So they called themselves the 'Chuddy Nuddies', we wanted them to do a pop-dub thing, y'know mix pop with dub, because they were kind of poppy anyway. We did one with Mick Hucknall's Frantic Elevators, we also did one with Holly Johnson, who went on to Frankie Goes to Hollywood.

I was quite into bands that weren't big at that time, there were a few I wanted to put records out on. Roger and I had an agreement that we'd only do them on Eric's if we both wanted them on it. He didn't want some of the stuff I wanted so I set another label up called 'Inevitable', Pete Burns was one of them, so was Pete Wylie.

So anyway quite early on, the club is in serious trouble, we're living hand to mouth on cash flow and we've got these bands coming to us saying "Will you put a record out on us?" one of them was Orchestral Manoeuvres in the Dark and there were others. We knew they were right, but we didn't have the money to do it.

Roger was also involved in booking bands at the Factory nights at the Russell Club in Manchester. He also worked with

Dougie James, who along with Alan Wise was booking the acts at Rafters in Manchester as far back as 1977. Here Dougie explains some of his working connections to Roger.

Dougie James: When I was working at Fagins with the 'Soul Train' I went downstairs and spoke to the owner John Bagnall and told him, "I'm gonna turn this into a punk venue" and I did. I was the first to bring punk into the city centre. We had Elvis Costello, Siouxsie & the Banshees, Dire Straits.

Roger and I booked the bands together, he booked them for Liverpool, I booked them for Manchester and we got them cheaper. If we'd got them from London we'd have two gigs for them to play, the first would be Liverpool, the second would be Manchester.

Alan Wise: Roger was very knowledgeable about music, he wasn't so much a promoter, he put on music he liked, when he put on music he didn't like he did it reluctantly. In the end he had to put on the same pop music and indie music dross as the rest of us did.

Alan Wise worked alongside Dougie James at Rafters and also promoted bands in Manchester in the late 70's and early 80's at the same time as Roger was booking bands at Eric's in Liverpool.

Alan Wise: When Roger was doing Eric's we ran a club in Manchester called Rafters, we had various acts we used to work with and manage. We were part of a cartel that used to promote in various towns and we became friends with him.

This story from the Manchester District Music Archive explains a little more of Manchester's then equivalent club to Eric's.

Steve McGarr: I used to produce all the in-house promo posters for Rafters. I would buy a huge roll of yellow Dayglo paper and do these giant posters, probably three to five feet in length. The lettering was all hand drawn in black with various shades of red and green, in a kind of graffiti style. Dougie James was the promoter and each week he'd give me a list of names of the upcoming bands and I'd do a separate poster for each one. Rob Gretton was the house DJ, so he was working there and I'd be hanging out two or three times a week. That's where Rob first saw Warsaw, if I recall correctly, before the name change to Joy Division. I can remember wandering upstairs many times into Fagins. Dougie James and the Soul Train played there a lot – I can recall seeing Tony Wilson get up on stage with Dougie one night – and you'd find Ray Teret or Sad Cafe in there having a drink.

Bob Bellis: Roger lived in my flat at the end of Aigburth Road for a couple of years which was kind of amusing. You'd come home from Eric's and you'd have The Damned there and a bunch of Swiss punks sat in the corner. The place was a big old gothic type house, the rooms in it were thirty foot square, long corridors, a massive great place. I got on really well with Roger because I used to take the piss out of him because of his size and his kind of dour demeanour, he used to like it. I didn't take any shit off him and we'd have a laugh about it.

For a little while Roger and I shared the same girlfriend, only I didn't realise. We had this telephone line in the flat, he'd taken the phone into his room, and I needed to use it because the band were about to go on tour, I needed to check about getting picked up and stuff. Anyway he was in his room with this person and he wouldn't let me have the phone. So the other guy who shared the flat with us, 'Stretch' Barton who was 6ft 6 and about as large as a bit of string, just happened to have a Land Rover differential there, so he smashed his door in to get the phone. This was around the time we realised we were seeing the same person. That was quite fun.

TONY WILSON'S ERIC'S OBSESSION

It's well known that Tony Wilson would tell anyone at any opportune or even inopportune moment, that he was responsible for putting The Sex Pistols on TV for the first time – although he didn't get them at his club. While working for Granada, Tony's idea for Factory Records was nurtured and pretty much hi-jacked from ideas learned from Pete Fulwell, Roger Eagle, Ken Testi and the scene at Eric's club on Mathew Street, Liverpool.

What Tony did for Manchester was incredible; bringing business, investment and enterprise to the city, taking the focus away from the capital – all helped by the annual 'In The City' seminar, which he chaired. His priorities however were completely different to those of Roger Eagle. Aside from the fact that Tony was an established face on regional TV station Granada, Roger didn't have the same urge for self-promotion as Tony did, therefore he never became the household name that Tony did – it wasn't something he was interested in. Roger's behind-the-scenes nurturing of local talent and one-on-one guidance to anyone interested in the roots of modern music was what drove him on. His whole reason for being was the music not the kudos. Certainly not the big art statement.

Ken Testi: Let me say first of all that Tony Wilson was of enormous assistance to us when we started because he had a little slot on Granada Reports which as you know is the teatime show, it was a 5 or 10 minute slot, once a week. We fed him details of the shows, and it was a surprise and a delight that they not only picked up on it but they stayed with it. We were able to rely on Wilson's enthusiasm to bring a few people in and that was very good for us. We were enormously grateful to him for that, make no mistake and Tony would come over to the club, and of course he was a bit of a celeb because he was on telly.

He liked what we were doing enormously and as time went by he opened his own venue in Hulme which was called The Factory. But he had very few music business connections. He saw what we were doing and he wanted to repeat it in Manchester.

So we booked the bands for him and that worked very well for us because we were getting an act for two nights there was a marginal saving which meant we could do three shows, two on Saturday at Eric's, and the Friday at The Factory. We were already a key venue on the touring circuit this just reinforced that.

Pete Fulwell: We always had a fantastic relationship with Tony, really good, he was amazingly supportive in the early stages. Working at Granada, it wouldn't have happened the way it did without him. He really was supportive and he fancied doing some gigs over in Manchester. So the way we did it was we booked them and we promoted the night together and Tony fronted it. This was at The Russell Club in Hulme and the sessions were called 'The Factory'. Some bands wouldn't come out of London unless it was at least a couple of gigs, so it meant we could get more bands out, they'd play Eric's one night, Factory the other, that was how it worked.

Steve Hardstaff: Roger used to get me to DJ the odd gig he didn't want to do. One in particular was at The Russell Club in Manchester by the reggae band Culture. I was the only white guy in the place, and I had this trunk full of Roger's records and pre-release twelves, all Jamaican stuff. The Manchester Rastas, who weren't really Rastas of course because they would have been nice to me if they were, were getting very heavy and trying to nick this stuff. I got saved by the band in the end who took me on the bus and got me so binned that I couldn't get back to Liverpool. I was too ill, I'd never smoked Jamaican weed before, I thought I had but I hadn't. I woke up on the tour bus in the morning, I refused anymore hospitality except for cups of tea and legged it back to Liverpool. Then I had to try and explain it away to my missus.

Bill Drummond: Big In Japan had a bigger following in Manchester than Liverpool, that was to do with Roger making those things happen. We could go and play Rafters and pack it out, we'd pack it out more than if they got, say, Generation X.

Roger also had a relationship with Tony Wilson, so through that Tony knew we were a big draw, so when The Factory in Hulme opened we played at one of the first gigs that were put on there. There's a poster with the number FAC1, Big In Japan are on that, it was us and A Certain Ratio.

Ken Testi: So a little later Wilson's moved on, he's got 'So It Goes' and he elects to film 50% of the film footage he does at Eric's. We did Nick Lowe, Dave Edmunds, Ian Dury & the Blockheads, Ultravox, Costello and this further enhances our reputation. Because we've got substantial TV exposure we're enjoying our relationship with Tony Wilson enormously. It was a two-way street, he was getting something off us he couldn't get anywhere else.

Bob Bellis: In that flat on Aigburth Road Tony Wilson and his mob from Manchester used to come over regularly. They'd go to Eric's, then after the gig they'd end up at the flat, in effect picking Roger's brains. This is before Factory kicked off and he definitely got a lot of his ideas off Roger. Obviously I'd be sat round with them, getting stoned, listening to music, whatever, and Wilson was definitely ringing every bit of information out of him that he could. I think they understood each other – put it that way. It's kind of annoying that with all that 'Twenty-four Hour Party People' nonsense, Roger's not even mentioned on the sidelines, you'd think that he would be.

Steve Hardstaff: Wilson certainly used to buy all his records in Probe because I used to serve him. He used to come in and say "What should I be buying?" I used to say "Well there's these Jamaican pre-releases and this rockabilly shit, you gotta listen to that, and there's this punk shit, you gotta listen to that." He came in on a weekly basis, for a time anyway.

ERIC'S FACTORY – JULY 1978
LIVERPOOL – MANCHESTER EP

Anthony H Wilson: I suppose the main bit of the story for me was Roger phoning me up on my home phone in Charlesworth and saying: "Tony, you know we had a record label last year called Eric's that the 'Big In Japan' single was on?"

"Yes, Roger"

"Pete and I are going to re-start it, and we'd like you to be head of A&R."

This is something like July of '78, and I was incredibly flattered, great, you know?

So I say, "When do you want to do this?"

He says, "When can you get over to Liverpool?"

"Well I'm working, so Sunday" and it was a Sunday afternoon. Already in the phone conversation he said he knew I was managing The Durutti Column and he also knew I was friends with Rob Gretton and that we'd put Joy Division on at The Russell club. We talked about doing a Liverpool-Manchester collaboration. That evening, as fate would have it, I took LSD, I was round at Chris Joyce's house, who was the then drummer with The Durutti Column, and I began obsessing with this copy of Santana's Abraxas which was from the Far East, done in tissue paper and plastic sealed.

So the next day I drive over to Liverpool and already I'm thinking, I'm imagining how you could do this. Well if there's four bands, I'm beginning to imagine the Factory Sampler. So I got to Liverpool and went down to the basement office about 3 o'clock on a Sunday afternoon and sat down. I turned up that afternoon with Roger to put out a record that would get my group The Durutti Column signed and would get my mate Rob's group signed. Roger wasn't behind the wall, he knew that the secret to this release was having Joy Division, because already the buzz was there for Joy Division.

So we had two Liverpool bands and two Manchester bands and after about an hour Roger says "We'll do a twelve inch single with two tracks on each side, one track each". I said "Let's do a double seven inch, a double seven inch EP, so there's eight tracks." It would be the first commercial double seven inch since The Beatles 'Magical Mystery Tour'. For whatever reason Roger had got stuck on the idea of a twelve inch single, and I'd got stuck on this double seven inch in this weird plastic packaging. So we argued for about half an hour, not bad temperedly, and I said "Listen I'll have to think about this."

Pete Fulwell: So I actually set up a meeting with Tony, we went over to Manchester. I said why don't we form, rather than what was becoming common, a city-based label, why don't we form a two city label? Why don't we do a label that is Liverpool and Manchester? A label that has got, as was then, Manchester's cool and Liverpool's pop sensibility. The reaction was Yeah! Tony had some ideas for packaging and stuff and we were gonna call it 'Eric's Factory', because the two gigs we were putting on were at Eric's and The Factory.

We did all the sums, spoke to Rough Trade, it was going to be Joy Division heading up the Manchester E.P. and Orchestral Manoeuvres heading up the Liverpool one. We discussed with Rough Trade how many Joy Division would sell, let's say 10 000, did the sums, got the spread sheets, went through all that at the meeting. Tony was buzzing about this new packaging he'd come across on a trip to Japan. So he was really up for the box that the stuff went in, and rightly, the way the thing was presented was really important, that was where his head was. Then it all went quiet.

Ken Testi: We'd done early records with Big In Japan and others and it was good, it was exciting stuff. But we decided a label from Liverpool might not be able to take on the London labels, or one from Manchester might not achieve critical mass. But there was a greater chance of it working if there was a North-West label that had a foot in both Liverpool and Manchester. That label was to be 'Eric's Factory', the first release was going to be an EP with contributions from OMD and Joy Division. Pete produced a super business plan with it and it was that business plan Tony disappeared with to set up Factory Records. We never saw him again.

Anthony H Wilson: I remember getting back and by that point they'd built the M62. You used to have to go down the East Lancs Road but by the late 70's you had the M62 and I remember passing Huyton and the beginning of the motorway there and suddenly going 'Fuck it!' I wanna do a double seven inch, we'll do it ourselves. If Roger can bring a fucking record out we can bring a record out and having driven down the motorway west and being flattered at being asked to be Eric's new A&R man, I drove back thinking "Fuck it, we'll do it ourselves!" I went straight to Erasmus' flat (Alan Erasmus, then manager of The Durutti Column) in West Didsbury and said, "Alan I've had a nice meeting with Roger but they want to do a twelve inch single and I want to do a double seven, why don't we do it ourselves?"

So the origin of Factory records is a falling out over the format of this Manchester/Liverpool collaboration, who knows, if Roger hadn't rung me at home saying will you do it, I might have been just a TV presenter.

Pete Fulwell: The next thing that happened was it came out, and it was on Factory, though if you look at FAC2 they didn't take the 'Eric's Factory' logo off, so there are some collectors items there, I noticed that when I saw it, it still had the fucking logo on there.

Ken Testi: I'm told Wilson changed all the artwork. The artwork had 'Eric's Factory' on it. The only bit he forgot to change was the actual label imprint. I believe the first 500 pressings still had 'Eric's Factory' on them.

Brian Smith: There was an interview of Tony Wilson's from that time that they put out live, when he was working for Granada. They were broadcasting live from Eric's, the studio had announced it, something like "Over to Tony at Eric's". But just at the instant that Tony was going to talk to him, Roger decided he wasn't going to talk as a protest for something or other. So he just sat there imperious with his fag on. I think he had the big sheepskin jacket on, I don't think he wore anything else, he just sat there with his legs crossed puffing away. Wilson fired a couple of questions at him and he just totally ignored him. So he had nothing.

Jayne Casey: I think with what happened with Tony Wilson and the record wasn't great malice, it was just one of those things that happens. But having said that Tony never really gave Roger and the whole Eric's thing it's due, which he should have done. Because of the fact that The Factory and The Hacienda wouldn't have been there without Eric's and in the same way Cream wouldn't have existed without The Hacienda. At Eric's, Tony Wilson was mesmerised by the whole scene.

The Factory Sampler released in December 1978 on the Factory Records label (FAC2), featuring The Durutti Column, John Dowie, Cabaret Voltaire and Joy Division. Today a copy of one of the initial 5,000 pressed of the gatefold 2 x 7" singles will command upwards of £200.

Bernie Connor: I used to work in the cloakroom at Eric's when I was 16 and I remember one night I had to get some change, so I went over to the office, knocked on door, "Come in!" So I goes in there and there's a copy of 'East Of The River Nile' by Augustus Pablo on the desk with this piece of hash about 3 or 4 Ounces, with hindsight it was some sort of blonde Afghani and it just smelled awesome.

I opened the door and there were all these people in there;

Roger, Tony Wilson, Martin Hannett and Bruce Mitchell and I'm like "Oh fuck!" and they're all stoned and they're looking at me you know? I just focussed on a piece of paper and I've never forgotten it, a piece of foolscap paper pinned to the office wall and written on it, very, very badly were the words 'Everything Is Temporary'. I just stood looking at it while Roger sorted the change out for me.

As Pete Fulwell and Ken Testi both state, Tony Wilson initially helped out significantly with promoting and publicising Eric's and the bands it was putting on. He spent many hours at Eric's filming performances for his 'What's On' TV programme. Perhaps not common knowledge is the fact Wilson spent many evenings socialising with Roger Eagle, learning how Eric's was run, the school of thought behind it and why it worked. In other words receiving specialised Eagle music tuition, something that Tony would almost certainly have been loathe to admit.

A little known fact about Roger Eagle is that he booked many of the bands for Tony Wilson's Factory club nights. The Factory was situated on Royce Road in the Hulme area of Manchester, later known as the PSV club, then known as The Russell Club. The Factory became the showcase venue for the early Factory Records roster of bands. The idea to open the Factory night in the first place had been inspired by Eric's, Tony had seen the potential Eric's had and with this in mind Tony co-opted Roger's talents to start his own venue. Although the Eric's/Factory collaboration was a natural progression from the Factory club, what became of it could be seen as a snub to the trust and friendship shown by Eagle and Fulwell.

Ultimately, the way Wilson used their ideas and ran with them meant that they had been taken in by someone they thought they could trust. The business connection was at best rather tenuous and there is no law against the theft of ideas, it's the nature of capitalism, the law of the jungle. This kind of treatment must have made its mark on Eagle, for without Eagle's influence, Wilson's Factory empire might never have happened.

Manchester's musical legacy of the late 1970's, 80's and 90's is rich and deep, with Tony Wilson being generally regarded as a major force and influence but it would seem that Roger Eagle has been almost written out of the story of the North-West's musical heritage in favour of numerous books about The Beatles and different aspects of The Factory Records story; both lucrative and self-perpetuating sectors of the music industry in their own right.

Will Sergeant: He was scary Roger, to me and the band. I was 19 when I first started going to Eric's, he was kind of like this weird enigma. He'd swan around with his moustache, he was tall and a bit scary, I didn't really have many conversations with him. As a spotty little punk rocker he wasn't the sort of bloke I'd go up and speak to.

Mark Thomas: In 1978 I was playing in a punk band up in North Wales and I thought I'd chance my arm and I phoned up Eric's to try and speak to him and get a gig. He was surprisingly open and we ended up playing there. It was very funny, he said there won't be any money, I said, "We're coming from Wales, couldn't you sort us something?" Stony silence. Yeah fiver, that was it. It was a good crack, we played with The Teardrop Explodes and Orchestral Manoeuvres in the Dark. The band was called The Inadequates, there was quite a few in and about 20 came with us. We didn't go down very well.

The Inadequates gig mentioned by Mark Thomas was on November 23rd 1978.

Steve Hopkins: I drove Roger over to Liverpool on more than one occasion when he was doing Eric's. We went over to do a couple of gigs there and I also played at one gig there, which was some mad thing that Tosh Ryan had set up with Rabid Records.

I was a musician as well, I played keyboards and I got involved with Martin Hannett, I did quite a lot of work with Martin. I hung about Rabid Records, I wasn't involved in Jilted John's single but I did work on the album. I also worked on the John Cooper-Clarke albums with The Invisible Girls.

Mike Badger was another Eric's regular influenced by the creative watershed of Eric's and the cultural changes the punk movement brought about. He was involved with a band called Neuklon which, among others, featured a young Lee Mavers. Mike was also a member of the first incarnation of Liverpool band The La's. Mike has also been involved with the Liverpool label Viper, along with artist Steve Hardstaff and musician Paul Hemmings.

Mike Badger: The first time I saw him would have been in Probe and generally around, he was an unforgettable guy. I started going to Eric's when I was about 16, towards the end of '78, so I'd missed all the '77 stuff like The Clash, The Stranglers and The Ramones because I was too young to get in. When I started going I was too young but they kind of turned a blind eye. But I did go to a lot of gigs there and I'm very grateful to Roger for that; I saw The Undertones, The Cure, The Damned, Joy Division, The Pretenders, Madness and loads of reggae. I've always thought of Eric's as the place where the misfits fitted in. It wasn't a punk club as such, it was much bigger than that, punk narrows it down too much. It happened simultaneously, I mean I saw Alexis Korner down there, it was filmed for Granada TV, Roger put Sonny Terry and Brownie McGhee on. With him being that much older, his knowledge of music went back that much further.

Eventually Roger to me was a fixture round town, like Geoff Davis in Probe. If you could get enough money together and you'd not spent it on records you'd go to Eric's, you wouldn't even know who was going to be on and you probably wouldn't have heard of them before, it could have been anyone – you know?

Stan Hoffman: I did play at Eric's once, I played one of those Rock Against Racism gigs there and Chris Gill, who was our guitarist, turned up in a Nazi uniform and all these punks went crackers. He goes, "Yeah and that's what you're gonna get if you don't smarten up!" It didn't go down well, it was supposed to be a tongue in cheek joke but it missed, it was like a scene out of The Blues Brothers, they were throwing bottles at us. Wild! We were the house band for Rabid Records, we were called Gyro, you didn't need drugs it was just hilarious, it was so Dada, nothing made any sense, I loved it, everything was totally unhinged. Roger was good for all that, because he was right there for it, he loved it, he thought it was brilliant. Tony Wilson and loads of others took their colours right out of Roger's paint-box.

Will Sergeant: Our first gig was on a Wednesday night and Julian (Cope) said to us, "Do you wanna support us?" It was just me and Mac then and we said "Yeah." We used to go to Eric's every night it was open. We were there one Sunday night and someone said something about a bass player and we didn't really understand what a bass was and Les goes, "Ah, I play the bass." We found out that a lad who used to go in Eric's called Robbie had a bass and an amp for sale, so we went over to somewhere in Bootle and picked it up, it was this tiny little crappy practice amp and a bass with 3 strings on it. I asked Clive Langer what sort of amp would I need, he said, "You'll need at least 30 watts." Our first gig when we supported Julian was a party, Julian used to go to this teacher training college in Prescott and it was an end of term party. I had a Mini Pops junior drum machine and a guitar with a couple of strings on.

Bob Harding: I did the sound for the first ever Echo & the Bunnymen gig. There was a band that Roger was managing called Pink Military, I was doing the sound for them. In fact Tony Bowers, who was the bass player in both the Albertos and The Mothmen, and myself produced the first Pink Military album. So they were

190

playing that night and it was Echo and the Bunnymen's first gig. Roger introduced me to them and I said "Which one's Bunny?" which didn't impress them too much. This was when it was just the three of them with the drum machine, it was the era when some bands would have a reel to reel tape recorder in the background, just for effect really. The drum machine was called Echo. I had it down as Bunny & The Echomen.

Bob Bellis: One time when The Clash played at Eric's and they came to the flat and Roger lent them a tenner because they were starving, they hadn't eaten since the afternoon before. Roger lent them a tenner to get some food and he and Bernie Rhodes had this big argument because Bernie reckoned he shouldn't have given them any money. His thing was to keep them hungry and under control, that was quite amusing.

Jayne Casey: Roger and I had a fallout which is quite funny in retrospect, we diverged a little bit. Eric's played reggae all the time and Roger had the most humungous record collection but there were no black kids going to Eric's. When Big In Japan played their second or third gig it was at a festival on Hope Street. We were the last thing on after The Yachts, they'd over run and the neighbours by this time had got tired of the noise. When we hit the stage we were the final nail in the coffin for the neighbours, who called the police. So then the police turned up.

At this gig were loads of black kids from Liverpool 8 at the front of the stage, and we just refused to get off the stage, it was like this was our new big thing, we loved being on stage and we absolutely refused to get off stage. So the police got on the stage and they're trying to turn the PA off and I was screaming down the mic, so they kind of ended up dragging me off stage but they didn't take the mic off me. So I'm over this policeman's shoulder, this little bald girl and I've still got the microphone plugged in. The black kids couldn't believe it, they'd never seen anything like it in their lives.

So the following week this group of black kids walked into the club. At the time we had our own table which was at the bottom doors as you entered the club, there was a little platform and that was our table and no one else was allowed to sit there. They just walked up to the table and said "We saw you play last week and we found out you were from this club and we know it plays reggae so we just had to come." So we all became big mates and suddenly there's this punky-reggae thing going on and Roger just thought it was the best thing ever and you know I've done my job, I'd brought him a whole new audience from Liverpool 8 and they absolutely loved the club.

One night Roger said "Come back to mine",
And I said "Well I've got a few people with me",
He said "Who is it?"
I said "It's the black kids",
He said "Oh, are they alright?"
I said "Yeah yeah, they're fine",

And they were absolutely fine, and you know I'm still friends with them. But obviously when they saw his record collection they couldn't believe it. Then they went out and they must have talked you know? "You wanna see the dude's record collection" and he got broken into and all his records robbed, this was when he was living on Canning Street in a little flat. We had a massive row about it, I was such a dysfunctional little thing anyway and he half blamed me, and there were certain triggers in it for me, you know 'She's a bad girl', and I just flew, I was calling him a hypocrite blah blah. I mean he'd lost all his records, at that point we diverged a little. But he would still come round to the house and stuff. So the period after Eric's I wasn't involved in watching what he was doing.

Pete Fulwell: Very early on a kind of tension grew between Ken and Roger because Ken fancied himself booking bands as well. In the very early stages he was the one that went down to

London and set up the relationships with the agencies, which you needed to do. So there was a little bit of frisson there which came to a head nine months in. Ken used to work all hours God sent and he overdid it in many ways, so his brain was fried doing the bar. We were also getting robbed blind from people working behind the bar, we weren't aware of security measures, we probably wouldn't have minded overly much at the time. Ken forgot to re-apply for the license, and we nearly missed it. This incensed Roger because if we'd lost the bar license it would have just imploded. It would have been back to the drawing board and start all over again, renegotiate with the guy we were buying the club off because we'd paid the deposit and we were paying the rest out of cash flow and takings.

Whenever we had to discuss stuff we'd go down to the docks, there was none of this redevelopment then, it was pretty much as it had been since the war, it was a wonderful place actually. So we'd go for a wander down there and Roger basically gave me an ultimatum, "I can't take this anymore, it's me or him" and to me it was a no-brainer, because without Ken, ok you can get a bar manager but without Roger you haven't got anyone to book the bands. In my mind there was no contest, it was Roger's lifeblood, it was his reason for living, it's no exaggeration to say that he lived to put gigs on.

Jerry and Brenda Kenny set up Naffi HQ on the outskirts of a deserted airfield between Manchester and Liverpool. Initially a space to record their own music, a session recording Half Man Half Biscuit for Probe records in the early 80's enabled the purchase of better equipment. NAFFI Universal Studios became the recording facility used by Probe for a good many of their releases in the 1980s. Recording and gigging under many guises including the jazz influenced 70's band Inside Out, Naffi Sandwich, Jerry's The Minister of Noise and Sir Freddy Viadukt. Brenda contributing with Brenda & the Beachballs and more recently Brenda Ray.

Both Brenda and Jerry have appeared as session players on many artists' recordings, from both Manchester and Liverpool.

Brenda Kenny: We started going into Liverpool and playing gigs with the jazz band Inside Out and I remember Roger turning up at one we did at The Pen and Wig on Harrington Street, this must have been about 1979, getting towards the end of Eric's. We never really went to see a lot of bands at Eric's, we were more the Manchester side. We did eventually play Eric's but I remember The Pen and Wig and Roger being there at the gig and within the next week he'd phoned up and said "Will you come and do a gig at Eric's?" That's when we started going to Eric's, about '79.

Jerry Kenny: The music we were doing was based around the bass and drums with different soloists. At the same time we also had this offshoot called Naffi Sandwich which was experimenting with tape recorders.

Brenda Kenny: So that's how the friendship with Roger started. He'd come over and visit here and we'd go and visit him when he lived on Huskisson Street in Liverpool, he lived in a top floor flat. When we actually played at Eric's I can still remember him going up the stairs with his vinyl and he went "Look what I've got", and it was Ornette Coleman 'Dancing in Your Head', I said "Oh we've had that for ages."

Jerry Kenny: Eric's was incredible, it's nothing like this shit now, where everybody looks the same and is the same. If you'd have gone with your granny she wouldn't have been out of place. We'd go on stage there playing jazz after a punk band and people would stand there and cheer, it was an incredible place.

Bob Harding: I can remember one time the Albertos were doing a gig for Roger at Eric's and I think it was my birthday or something and he came and gave me a couple of records, both by Big Youth, 'Green Bay Incident' and 'Pope Paul Feel It', so I said

"Oh I'll have a listen" because there was a deck there in the club. So I put the record on, I put the A side on first and Roger goes "Hmm checking the vocal first, how odd." Roger would always check the dub first.

Penny Henry: I went out with CP Lee for a while and I also used to live with Tony Bowers. I remember one time we all went over to see something at Eric's. Roger saw us when we got there and he shut the door and said "Don't let them in, don't let those horrible Mancunians in my club!"

With Eric's only a stone's throw from the Probe shop on Button Street, the idea of both businesses benefiting from one another would seem an obvious conclusion to make – Geoff didn't seem to think so.

Geoff Davis: Not particularly.

Norman Killon: I think it was a two-way thing. The Probe shop in Button Street opened up at pretty much the same time as Eric's, which was fortuitous.

Geoff Davis: Well yes it definitely connected, if that club hadn't been there the shop would still have been successful.

Norman Killon: Yes but with a different clientele, they would have been young but not necessarily punks.

Geoff Davis: Well the punk thing was happening anyway when Eric's opened but Liverpool was never a punk city, there were very few punk bands in Liverpool.

DOCKLAND PROJECT

Doreen Allen: I must have gone everywhere with Roger to look at bloody premises, he wanted to open a rehearsal studio down in the Albert Dock. We were in Eric's one night and he says "Come on we're going down to the Albert Dock." The Albert Dock was derelict in those days. I think Martin Dempsey was with us that night, I think there was some really good band on in Eric's and Roger drags us down there to look at this derelict building. I was always in on his plans and schemes.

Martin Dempsey: Around that time there was also this fascination with a place on the docks. Everyone went down there and did bits and pieces of work to try and get it up and running, Roger was going to have an office there that was the idea. It was an old dock-keepers cottage type of thing, a really interesting place. There's quite a few photos of Wah! Heat and Wylie hanging around that building. He was involved with this docks idea when he was living on Belvedere Road.

Brenda Kenny: I remember we ended up down Liverpool Docks at about four in the morning one time, this was when Roger lived in Huskisson Street. He took us to this place and it was just a stone building, it was fantastic, a ship had just docked. He was saying he could see himself living there and perhaps have music going on. There was this one building and he was saying, you know, I want this place.

Roger Eagle: Originally I was working on a project to set up a four-track recording studio in an old customs house down in Liverpool's dockland. However, just about the same time Eric's was closing the building burnt down.

Martin Dempsey: He got a lot of his records nicked at one point, we were all at the club and somebody had got in. It was all the reggae stuff they were after, it was probably somebody local who knew who he was and where he was. He moved out of there and moved to the end of Devonshire Road and he shared that with our drummer Bob Bellis. They lived in this flat and they had to climb in through the back window at one point, this was probably about '79 and just before he moved into The Warehouse, he shared the place with Bob and this tall gangly guy called Stretch

Barton.

At one point the front door was jammed closed with a Landrover back axle and Jayne and Holly used to live in the basement next door. You'd climb in through the window at the back and there was this big flooded area. I remember going there in the winter and there was obviously a leak upstairs, and there was ice forming on the walls, half of the floorboards in the place had been ripped up and burnt. I remember Tony Wilson going round there and being completely wasted and not being able to get out. This place was on the corner of Devonshire Road and Belvedere Road, not long after that the whole building was pulled down, it was a big terrace, very run down.

Jayne Casey: I remember Roger living on the corner of Belvedere Road. Eric's was still going then, I lived next door to them, I lived in the derelict basement in the house next door. That was quite a bad time, he was living with Bob Bellis. Eric's was going then, but there was never any money.

Geoff Davis: Then he lived in that place with Bob Bellis and they were burning all the floors and the staircase on Belvedere Road. They lived on Berkeley Terrace or somewhere down there, they've knocked the building down now. They were with that tall, quiet fella as well, at one point they were the last people in the building, they were all broke and they had an open fire, and they were taking wood from the rest of the building and using it as fuel, the stair handrails were going, the floorboards.

Henry Priestman: I suppose Yachts were one of the earlier bands on the scene, also Roger shared a flat with our drummer Bob Bellis. They were a motley crew; Roger in the front room, Stretch Barton and Bob Bellis. I remember his room, there were loads of records, and for me suddenly seeing stuff like the first 'Love' album, all these amazing records. It was a crazy house, they had a real fire and they would rip shelves off and just keep feeding them into the fire. It was this mad house and it seemed so exciting living there. It would drive you mad probably, I don't know how Roger stuck it. They knew the building was being knocked down so it was a real shithole by the end.

Doreen Allen: You walked in the door of Eric's from Mathew Street and into a little hallway bit on the right you had the pay desk and a little office behind it. One day I heard Roger banging about with some bits of wood, I thought what the bloody hell is he doing? He'd locked the door between the pay desk and the office, I couldn't get into the office. He was dismantling chairs to take home for fire wood. He had a red bag which was a Steve Hardstaff design and he always had bits of wood poking out of it, it was for his fire.

Bob Bellis: The only way to get in and out of this flat was to go round the back and climb in through the kitchen window, which was kind of fun. We used to go round to the local building sites and get scaffolding planks and just feed them into the fire, the punks that would come round and visit used to love all that, because it's definitely rock 'n' roll. The place was a shambles, the front door was held shut with a Landrover back axle and Roger moved out when a couple of people thought it would be a good idea to petrol bomb the door. It was a bit of a range war between myself and a couple of other people and we were blaming everyone but the people that did it, the black lads got it, Holly got the blame, Pete Burns got the blame, everyone got the blame for it. We were convinced at one point that it was that lot next door, so Stretch and I went round there armed with lump hammers, and I had a moment when I was bashing holes in the wall around Holly's head trying to get him to admit it was him that had set fire to the door, and then realised it wasn't because he was shitting himself.

I found out a couple of years later who it was, I was coming off stage at a Yachts gig and this bloke says could he talk to me? I said "Yeah alright", it was Tim Whittaker the Deaf School drummer, it turns out it was him and another bloke called Steve, they thought it was going to be a bit of fun, tripped off their nut I imagine, and two years later they finally admitted to it.

Val Randall: He used to live in Toxteth as well when he worked at Eric's, I went to visit him because he'd not been well, he had all that heart trouble after Eric's was closed down. He had heart problems and I was really worried about him. I don't know if he was hospitalised but I was so worried about him because his voice sounded thin, you know without it's usual resonance. So I trucked over to Liverpool to see him and he said "Don't be put off, the bottom part of the house is boarded up, but I'm living upstairs." It was just typical of him. I went to see him and there's just this upstairs flat on the first floor of this terraced house, everything in the row was boarded up. What I loved about him was he didn't give a shit about possessions. He never owned a bed, wherever he lived all he was bothered about was his vinyl and his sound system.

Bernie Connor: There was a book came out many years ago called 'Liverpool Explodes' about The Bunnymen and The Teardrop Explodes and in it there's a great picture of Roger Eagle. He used to smoke Renos, American menthol cigarettes, and in the picture he has on this white dinner jacket that he wore for years, it was a kind of lightweight jacket. On the lapel of this jacket he had a badge that just said 'Netherlee', which everyone at the time thought was awesome because Netherlee was such a shit hole, you know, concrete jungle. It's a fantastic photograph; it's Roger sitting with a fag in his hand, the caption underneath it said 'Roger Eagle – All these people work for me.'

The photograph Bernie mentions graces the cover of this book, it was taken in the Grapes pub, quite near to Eric's by the acclaimed Mancunian photographer Kevin Cummins.

Mike Badger: I was going to St. Helens Art college in 1979, and around the Christmas of that year I mustered up the courage to go and speak to this giant. I said "I'd like to hire Eric's for St. Helens Art College Christmas Party, I've got some great bands to play and all that." One of them was a punk band I'd started hanging around from Huyton called Neuklon. It was on the 18th December 1979. So I put this gig on, a band called the Go-thongs played doing songs about surfing the Mersey and dodging the oil and glass, they had a surfboard, a beat machine, a bass and a guitar.

Then Neuklon came on and they were like horrible punks, they had Sevvo on drums in his tartan bondage kecks and a bike lock round his neck which he'd lost the key of, Lloyd on lead vocals and synthesizer and a lad called Robbie on keyboards. They were a riot. They were like Iggy Pop meets Kraftwerk, a really hardcore band from a hardcore place in Huyton called the Bluebell estate. Roger saw them at this Christmas party and thought they were magnificent. He thought they'd crystallised what it was all about, and he actually did say "They are the future of rock 'n' roll" this was before Lee Mavers joined them though. Consequently because Roger liked them so much I took on a sort of managerial role, I didn't know what the hell I was doing, I was blagging it.

So I approached Roger and said "Would there be any chance of getting a support?". He said "I'll see what's coming up." The next thing he's got back to me with "Would they like to support OMD?" this was a real coup because OMD were just breaking with 'Electricity'. So the night of the gig came round and I turned up at Eric's to get in and the doormen wouldn't let me in because I didn't have a ticket. I said "But I manage the band", they said "Two other people have just gone in saying they were their managers." It turned out that the band had agreed a deal where these people said "We'll do better things for you" and they'd not told me about it. By this time Lee Mavers was playing with them.

Mick Hucknall: We did this mad show at Eric's as Frantic

Elevators and that's where I met Pete Wylie and Ian McCulloch – they were all hanging out in Eric's. Some of them used to work in the record shop, Probe, across the road. We did a show at Eric's – Roger got us back and we got an extra tenner! It was a great time because of the ambience, all these other bands starting out – Teardrop Explodes, The Bunnymen, Wah! Heat, and I remember spending time with those guys in the club and how enthusiastic they were about the madness of the place.

Bill Drummond: Roger managed Mick Hucknall early on, Mick was living with him in Liverpool. Mick Hucknall then, seventeen, completely and utterly stunning. I have this very clear memory of this boy with short cropped ginger hair singing The Beatles tune 'Don't Let Me Down'. I know Roger must have been thinking "This guy's got it completely" because none of us did, Jayne Casey couldn't sing, she just screamed, she was a presence, a force. But Mick Hucknall could genuinely sing because it was a soul voice, Roger would have loved it.

Doreen Allen: If a band didn't turn up at Eric's, Roger used to say to me "Get the Frantic Elevators!" this was with about two hours' notice. I'd have to ring the callbox outside one of their houses because none of them had phones. God bless 'em, they used to get a van at ten minutes notice and get over from Manchester.

Penny Henry: The first time I knew of Mick was when Roger said, "I've seen this fantastic singer who's in this band called The Frantic Elevators, you've really got to come to their gig". So me and Tony went and we took Elliot (Rashman) with us. Elliot managed The Mothmen and various other bands, he tried all these things out but nothing worked.

Bill Drummond: Roger's personality could be overbearing, it wasn't like we could be buddies, he was 36 when I was 24. He always liked to let everybody know that he knew what was good and what was bad. Norman Killon will tell you what a bully he was. In some ways I worship the man but at the same time I know what he was like.

Norman Killon: I think you'll find everybody will say the same thing about Roger, he could be a bully, it helped for him to be the size he was, particularly for someone my height. Quite often he'd come in and be dead enthusiastic about certain things and he wanted you to know about that. Henry Priestman and practically everyone will tell you, on his good days he was great. If he was in a bolshie mood you were in for it.

Bernie Connor: Tim O'Shea said a great thing, Tim O was even younger than me, and he was DJing in Eric's when he was 14, Tim O used to do the Matinees on Saturday. He was a great DJ and he should have stuck with it. We were in the doorway once and someone had said something about Roger and he said – "Fuck La, don't say that, you say anything about Roger, a big trap door opens in the ceiling and ten tons of heavy dub falls on your head, seriously heavy dub!!"

From an interview with the author conducted in 1994 Roger Eagle speaks about the latter days of Eric's.

Roger Eagle: You have to exercise a very strong quality control over who you book. It's like survival in anything else, if you're not ruthless you don't get the best and the punters know it straight away, they know when you're faking it. If you haven't got anything good on you know. In the latter days of Eric's I was forced to book rubbish like Slaughter & The Dogs just to keep a few punters coming through the door, so we could pay the bills, I hated it. We had them once that was fine, they did their act and went away again, it was alright, you know? But it rapidly became a joke and fizzled out and we started to book them because there was nobody that was doing anything interesting. The ones that were going to make it at that time had already made it, they were already big money bands, so that cycle was over quite quickly.

Bernie Connor: One of the things about Roger was that he hated punk, he didn't rate the music. He put punk bands on because it made him enough money to put the stuff on that would maybe lose a little money, things like Sonny Terry & Brownie McGhee, Muddy Waters or bring over Dillinger.

Jayne Casey: There isn't any money in a 300 capacity club, so it was a rough ride financially. They'd sussed what was wrong and that was the capacity and the fact that they were getting all these amazing bands on the way up but they'd sussed that once the bands had made it big they couldn't make any money on them, so they started promoting at other places, when The Police played at Liverpool Empire they did that gig. There was a plan, they knew it was gonna crash but based on their goodwill towards those bands that had played Eric's on their way up, if they promoted their bigger gigs then they stood a chance. So there was a plan, it wasn't just, "Let's burn" it was let's hold on and wait 'til we get to the next stage but they didn't get there. That was the world that Roger inhabited, it's hard, you've got to make quick decisions.

From an interview conducted after the closure of Eric's, Roger talks about the club and also his motivation regarding club promotion.

"Generally people think to run such a club as Eric's would be great. To own a club in Liverpool is great in theory but not in practice. As I've said, people would only see the big groups, the 'safe' groups. Due to a lack of money, people weren't prepared to take a chance on a group they'd probably never heard before. Some people would but the vast majority wouldn't."

Jerry Kenny: I'm a barber by trade and when Eric's was going Roger and Pete would come to me to get their hair cut, I had this shop called Nova Mop, I had pictures in the window of women with no hair, shaven heads. This was in Newton-le-Willows and

Roger would call whether it was 2 in the afternoon or 2 in the morning, he'd drop in with whoever was driving him around. We seemed to have a mutual spirit.

Bernie Connor: I love it that people can affect your life so dramatically. A lot of my mates thought he was curmudgeonly, they thought he was a bit of a cunt really. I liked him a lot. A lot of the time he couldn't even be arsed to remember your name.

THE END OF ERIC'S

Pete Fulwell: The popular external perception was that the police closed it down. What happened was, I mean I don't know if the police intended to close it down, when something like that happens then self-justification starts to roll. The police put out statements at the time to the effect of "Why not? There was this happening, there was that going on." But I really don't think they intended to close it down, they didn't realise how fragile it was. Because what happened was they didn't actually close it down.

A couple of weeks before it shut there was a big raid and a couple weeks before that a couple of police officers came down on what was a regular, annual visit. They went round all the clubs and I was there on my own when they came down. I was asking them if there were any problems they thought I should be addressing. They replied, "No, no, no, everything's fine, you're keeping a good house." One of them said while we were talking "I really fancy a drink."

I said, "Oh right, let's go down the bar then."

So we're down the bar and I said "What do you fancy?"

He said "Well, no alcohol on duty, but I do fancy a drink",

So I said, "Do you fancy a coke?"

He said "Yeah ok I'll have a coke",

I think this was my naivety, I think what they meant by a drink was a bribe. I'm offering them a drink, but they didn't want a drink.

Anyway two weeks later they turn up mob-handed, about fifty of them and it was almost like a pantomime, the police were wearing school ties. They just came steaming in and treated people atrociously, they were dragging people up the steps by their hair. They weren't uniformed, whether they were Drug Squad or not I don't know. What had happened was one or two of them had come down earlier in the evening and sold drugs to people, so when the team burst in they picked out the people they'd sold drugs to and dragged them up the stairs. There was mayhem; Pete Wylie was the support band, I think the Psychedelic Furs were playing, someone like that. Pete Wylie was support and they started playing 'I Fought The Law', turning it into a show, as he would.

Word got out after that very quickly, the next day the creditors who we'd been keeping quiet on drip-feed cash-flow panicked because they thought the police were trying to close it. So they all piled in for their money and down we went, within days it just collapsed.

From an article published in *The Guardian* four months after Eric's closed down, Roger commented on the events that occurred on the evening of March 14th 1980.

"It was shameful, they were using tactics against us they would use against the IRA. All of a sudden you had the representatives of law and order literally running in and hurting people. I'm not anti-police, I respect the values they're there to protect. They'd raided us before for routine licensing reasons and they'd always been very courteous and correct. But the police knew it wasn't a club where they had to pitch in. In three and a half years they hadn't been called down once."

Stan Hoffman: I was led to believe when Eric's shut that there was a lot of trouble on the last night, well there was this giant punk who worked for Roger and he brought him to our house in Manchester and said "Can you hide him in your cellar? He's public enemy number one!"

I said "Come on Roger!" He said "Oh please, please." A giant punk, like the kid out of 'The Young Ones', but five times as big.

I said "Roger, I can't put him in the cellar." Apparently he'd done something this guy and Roger had got him out, I don't know how, he was a giant, and Roger brought him to Manchester. I think he was from Liverpool, he didn't say much, he just grunted, we kept giving him gruel and things (laughs). He stayed with us for about a week, in the end I just got sick of him, I phoned Roger and said "Come and get this guy he's driving me mad" and he took him away again. I can't even remember his name.

Doreen Allen: Talking about the last night at Eric's I got a Customs and Excise VAT notice put in my hand that day. I ran over to Pete Fulwell, he was in the Armadillo, and said "Two official looking people have just handed me this at the door." He said, "Oh I was expecting that."

In the evening at the gig I was taking notes of what the police were doing, I must have looked official I don't know why. We took the Psychedelic Furs out to Paddy's Market the next day, and they actually said to me "We didn't realise you worked at Eric's, we thought you were the DS."

Pete Fulwell: At that point there were two feelings really, firstly we had to set up a meeting with our creditors to reach an agreement with them, it was either that or go completely bankrupt and that was unpleasant, it was like presiding over your own funeral in a way, horrible. We managed to reach an agreement with them and we're driving back through town and we're both conscious that we're the only ones that know it's gone, there's people waving at us and we felt like shit. So to cheer ourselves up we went round to visit Jerry Kenny to heal a bit. We'd go and visit Jerry and Brenda quite a bit, he's a barber, we'd go round, he'd cut your hair and he'd play amazing music while he did it. They were out on the edge, but to Roger and I they were very central. That was the first place we thought of to go.

So then there was one more gig left and some people were intending to have a sit-in at the gig but we knew it was pointless, it would have just given the police an opportunity to batter them and it wouldn't have saved it anyway. It wasn't the fact that they wouldn't give us a license, it was the fact that we were up to here in debt. So we did the last Eric's gig in Manchester, I'm not sure where, it was Siouxsie.

Bernie Connor: After Eric's shut rather abruptly they still had bands booked and artists booked, one of those was Siouxsie & The Banshees, who they ended up putting on at the Osborne Club in Manchester. I worked in Probe at the time and I remember us selling tickets for them.

Pete Fulwell: At the end of the club we didn't fight tooth and nail to keep it if the truth were told. Because we'd come into it with the perception of it, Ken as well, perhaps a bit less so, of it being on the margins. That's where we wanted to be, we wanted to be on the margins and it had become mainstream, it had become the club in town.

Because the club on Mathew Street had closed, the last Eric's gig was held at the New Osborne club on Oldham Road, Manchester on 19th March 1980 with Siouxsie & The Banshees, Robert Smith from The Cure played guitar for the Banshees at this gig.

Pete Fulwell: There was a march through town, I was grieving as we both were, but I was angry as well, because if all those people who were out there protesting now would have come to the club more often, we'd still be there. They were all remembering it from the nights they went, and they only went when the big acts were on. They weren't really treating it like a club, they were treating it more like a concert hall. So when they went and it was heaving, they thought it was always heaving but it wasn't, we put some classic things on and there might be thirty people turn up. I remember saying to Roger "I don't want to talk to the press, I'll end up saying something I'll regret later." So Roger did the obituary really.

Brian Jackson: I think the closing of Eric's and what happened subsequently hurt Roger quite a bit. It was probably the best club there's ever been. I mean where else could a local band find itself with an international type audience, and vice versa, an international band with a local audience, the support band was local and you had headliners from Europe and around the world, so your local band got a big audience and it was great for launching people. Where would Mick Hucknall be without Roger?

Because Eric's captured the essence of Britain's live music scene of the mid-to-late 70's many writers have tried to put into context the influence of Eric's as a social and cultural phenomenon. The club can easily be compared to such esteemed venues as London's Marquee club in the mid-60's, New York's CBGB's in the mid-70's or Manchester's Hacienda club in late 80's. Here Pete Fulwell, Roger Eagle's business partner for the majority of the club's tenure, gives his view on the club's historical importance and whether the idea of Eric's has been misrepresented.

Pete Fulwell: It's that old cliché of trying to find out what an elephant looks like in the dark, it depends where you were looking at it from. It wasn't wrong, it just wasn't the whole story, and they extrapolate from the bit they saw into that being what it was, and it wasn't. It's been misrepresented in that its personalised and seen as being more to do with the people that ran it, rather than the people that went there.

The people who went to the club made the place. It wasn't just a case of community, horrible word but it was one. With all the hatreds and loves that went on, like a family, with sibling rivalries, all that stuff bubbling away. It wasn't just that, what we

R & B SCENE 1/6

VOL. 1. No. 6. APRIL 1965

BRITAIN'S LEADING
Rhythm & Blues
MAGAZINE

CHUCK BERRY
JAMES BROWN
LAZY LESTER
HOMESICK JAMES
WILLIE MABON
SCREAMIN' JAY HAWKINS

— PLUS —

Record Reviews
Rhythm & Blues Quiz
Readers Letters
The Horror Scene
Say Man

REAMIN' JAY HAWKINS meets Brian
ith. The reason why we put a photo
our photographer on the cover may
ver be fully explained, but we do
ew the reason for the tremendous
cess of Jay's tour. SEE INSIDE

R'NB SCENE 1/-

AUGUST, VOL. 1. No. 2.

HOWLIN' WOLF

Also in this ▶ Issue

JOHN LEE HOOKER
SCREAMIN' JAY HAWKINS
CARL PERKINS   SPENCER DAVIES

PLUS Rhythm and Blues Record Reviews

R'NB SCENE 1/-

NE. VOL. 1. No. 1.

FATS DOMINO

lso this ▶ sue

SONNY BOY WILLIAMSON
GEORGIE FAME   BOBBY BLAND
JAMES BROWN

Plus: R'N B Quiz · The Northern Club Scene · John Zacherle

FREE

R'NB SCENE 1/-

VOL. 1. No. 3.

MUDDY WATERS

In this ▶ Issue

THE MUDDY WATERS STORY . BOOKER T.
EDDIE BOYD . CYRIL DAVIES . SUGAR PIE
DESANTO . MEL TURNER . TOMMY TUCKER
Rhythm and Blues on Record

t covers from the R&B Scene magazine, put together by Roger, Brian Smith, Neil Carter and Roger Fairhurst in conjunction with the Twisted Wheel. c 1964.

The Magic Villa
front door on Cromf[
Court, Manches[
The building u[
knocked down in [
early 1970's to ma[
way for the Arnd[
shopping cen[
c 19[

The coffee bar at the
Magic Village, with
Roger Eagle centre.
c 1968
Both photos Maggie
Backhouse

Roger Eagle, Manchester c 1971. - Photo Stephen Hopkins

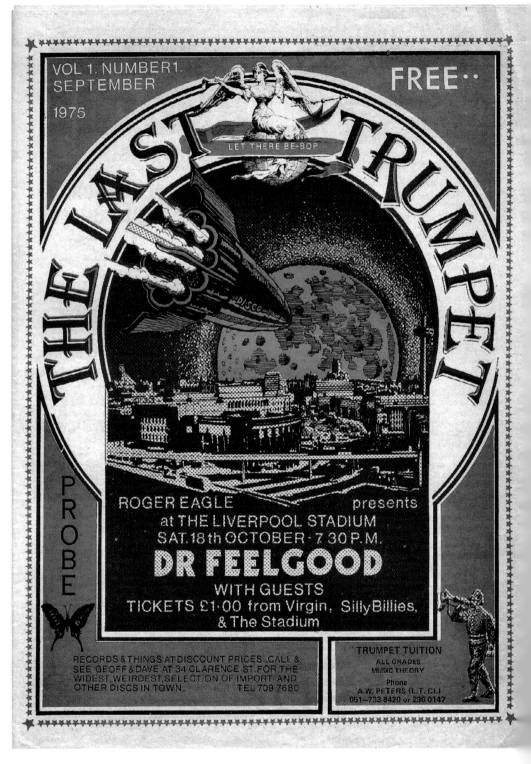

The Last Trumpet Issue No 1. A free magazine put together by Roger and Steve Hardstaff, distribu... free around Liverpool in 1975. - Artwork by Steve Hardstaff.

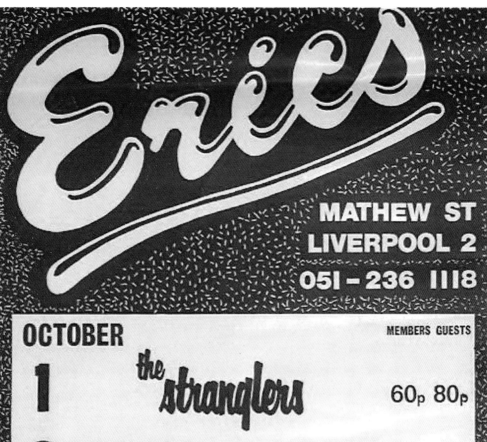

Eric's flyer from the first sessions, October 1976.

Roger Eagle behind the ticket desk at Eric's c. 1977 - Photo Bob Letsche.

Tel: 051-236 7881

Big In Japan promotional print. Roger booked gigs for Big In Japan and also managed the band bri

The Frantic Elevators featuring Mick Hucknall around the time Roger looked after them. Taken at their rehearsal space, Brittania Mill, Buxworth Derbyshire.

Photos: Dave Eaton.

Eric's club night. Artwork by Steve Hardstaff.

put on was shaped by that, they told us what to put on. So they owned it as much as we did, there was a core of maybe 50 people that this applied to, lots of others dropped in and out, but there was this core. The creative people carried the club forward and obviously since some people are more articulate than others, they're more likely to publicize their ownership, their contribution and their views. So it's seen through those lenses but the truth is, Roger included, if he was here now, none of us could have said what it was like, we all had our point of view. None of it was true, it was all partly true.

Eagle's nurturing of local talent set the stage for a whole new Liverpool music scene, ten yards and a million miles from the Cavern club and the Merseybeat sound. Eric's became the setting for debut gigs by such characters as gorgeous scene stealer Jayne Casey who, with future Frankie Goes to Hollywood singer Holly Johnson, fronted reverse supergroup Big In Japan. Bill Drummond, who nailed the club together, played bass and guitar with Big In Japan and Lori & The Chameleons, and went on to much bigger things with the KLF. Lightning Seed Ian Broudie's guitar playing also graced the Big In Japan line-up. The same band also featured future Slits and Siouxsie & The Banshees drummer Budgie. Another future Frankie Goes to Hollywood member Paul Rutherford fronted Liverpool punk band The Spitfire Boys.

Pete Burns, with his biting wit and challenging androgyny, played Eric's with The Mystery Girls and Nightmares in Wax. Psychedelic dream poet Ian McCulloch, whose career with Echo and The Bunnymen has lasted more than thirty years, played his first gig at the club. Julian Cope played his first gigs at Eric's with the nascent Teardrop Explodes. Pete Wylie with his rock 'n' roll heroics, dangerous mouth and ear for a melody, played his first gigs at the club with the Spitfire Boys, the Mystery Girls and Wah! Heat. British synthesizer pioneers Orchestral Manouevres in the Dark debuted at Eric's and went on to great success in the 1980's.

The La's lead singer Lee Mavers played his first gig at Eric's with Neuklon. Not forgetting square peg in a round hole Mick Hucknall who played some of his first live gigs at Eric's - inspired by the initial urgency and vibrancy of punk, eventually finding his blues/ soul voice with Simply Red when his musical direction was encouraged and nurtured by the great Roger Eagle.

These are just a few of the many names that Eagle influenced and supported during his time in Liverpool and although he encouraged competition between local bands he also encouraged a sense of community and familial ideas. Roger, with his vast knowledge of different musical genres, his enthusiasm for putting on interesting acts - both international and local - coupled with his support and education of local artists, helped to drag Liverpool from beneath the shade of the enormous cultural shadow cast by The Beatles and set in motion a new idealism and optimism for future generations of musicians and music fans. He helped create the best late 70's live music venue in the UK bar none. His effect on the city's musical landscape up to the present day is as important as the river that runs through it.

Martin Dempsey: When I came to Liverpool the only band of any note that wasn't prog rock was Deaf School, who were a theatrical show band type of thing with interesting and clever songs with a bit of attitude. Everything else was sub-Beatles stuff, Beatles influenced or prog rock.

Mike Badger: One thing I will say about Eric's is there was absolutely no affiliation with The Cavern club and it was literally five steps across the road from where Eric's was. It was like 'Yeah it was great all that, but we're doing this', you're talking about the biggest musical phenomenon in the world. No one was doing Beatles songs, or talking about The Beatles.

Jayne Casey: An illustration of Roger's influence - he told us all never to listen to The Beatles... He stressed it upon us all in such a big way... "You'll all be fucked if you listen to The Beatles."

Recently me, Wylie and Ian Mc were sitting in a bar talking and Ian looked across the table and said to me, "Have you listened to them yet?" "No, not conciously, have you?" he said, "No"

We both looked at Wylie, he said "No".

Not one of us asked "Listened to who?"

8 - Crackin' Up, The Lord Buckley and Colne

From an interview after the closure of Eric's, Roger Eagle took some time to explain what went wrong at Eric's and the reasons for the club's closure.

"It was really a financial thing. Basically people didn't really come to see new groups. It's hardly surprising really as it probably cost about £10 between say two people after bus fares, admission, drinks and everything else. When people came to see the more famous bands after maybe a success in the charts, or an appearance on the television, the place would be packed. They took this to mean Eric's must always be packed and it must be making a lot of money. This was just not the case. For example The Specials played four times before the club made any money and we broke even. It didn't seem to matter though as I wanted to be able to give new groups a chance and maybe 'discover' them."

Pete Fulwell: After Eric's closed we decided to do a few things like tours, keep that side going. We did a few gigs, northern legs of tours and things as Eric's promotions. There was the club, the label and the promotions. The other thing was, there was still a problem with debts with the bank and the arrangement with the creditors.

Doreen Allen: He buggered off, he ran away didn't he? You see I carried on, I was working for Eric's Records and Pete Fulwell and Roger's name was obviously dirt. He left Pete with all the debt didn't he? Roger and I lost touch then. When I was working for Pete, Roger's name wasn't to be mentioned because he did leave Pete in a lot of shit.

Geoff Davis: He was trying to get something going after Eric's finished.

Norman Killon: He did Rafters.

RAFTERS

A week after he had put on his favourite Motown act Junior Walker, Roger was interviewed by Erlend Clouston for *The Guardian* about the new venture he'd begun at Rafters on Oxford Street in Manchester. It was tied in to Eric's promotions and called the 'Zodiac' club. After the demise of Eric's and the large amount of debt that had accumulated, Roger was obviously trying to get a profitable project off the ground. Here he makes a telling point about the state of the music business. A point that is still pertinent more than thirty years later.

"So few people have any real affection for the music, look at the bookers, the bookers are like door-to-door salesmen. I used to get the most terrible pressure, the most appalling amounts of grief off people to book a band that would be heavily subsidised by the American parent company, phone calls every half hour, "Don't worry about the money..." Well you can smell an enormous rat straight away. I really seriously doubt whether the straight music business can tell one band from another."

Dougie James: I used to have this place in Manchester called Rafters, I started it off with Paul Young from Sad Cafe. Then I met Roger through him doing Eric's. He used to come over to Manchester to see me, and I'd go over and see him in Liverpool.

Mick Hucknall: After Eric's Roger managed us (The Frantic Elevators). He really liked us, him and Pete Fulwell but Pete was more involved with Wah! at the time. Roger would try to get us gigs but he wasn't really a manager. Roger; he had a passion for music, such passion. I was already into soul music but he had a lot more than I did and it was a lot more R&B based and from the fifties, compared to the more modern soul I was listening to. He turned me on to dub reggae, Charlie Mingus and Charlie Parker – he had a big musical influence on me did Roger.

Penny Henry: I've got a letterhead of Crackin' Up productions and Roger's card from when he was doing the nights at Rafters. Roger used to come round a lot to see me and Tony (Bowers) and he said he was going to start this R&B club, I thought well if Tony's off doing stuff in music I'm going to start working, so I said to him "Roger can I work on the door for you?" and that's how I began working for him. He used to come over and stay on the Saturday night and me and Tony would always feed him, Mick Hucknall used to turn up quite often as well. Roger used to sit on this little chair I bought for my son next to this tape machine and he'd go "Have you heard this?" and shove things on. When Roger was round it always seemed like the room was sweating. He was travelling over from Liverpool to do the R&B night, this was around 1981. There were a few very dedicated people who would go to that but it was never really successful, by the time I'd got back from working at the club I was quite exhausted really. Roger used to worry incessantly about it you know? About not making any money. I don't think I ever got paid, it wasn't because he didn't want to pay me, it was because he didn't make any money.

While I was working for Roger I met Alan Wise and I also did nights for him at Rafters, it was at Rafters that I met Ginger (Howard Jones) who became the manager of the Hacienda, I also started working at the Hacienda in 1982.

This was about a year before the Hacienda. It was when Ginger was working for the Spastics Society and he'd put gigs on at Rafters for them. Ginger combined his love of music with his work, making money for charity, that's how I met him. He saw what I would do, he got fed up of Alan Wise letting people in for nothing, I actually used to ask the bands how much they needed to be paid.

Howard 'Ginger' Jones is known for being the general manager and one of the founders of Manchester's Hacienda club. He later left to manage the Stone Roses. It's well known that Tony Wilson was unhappy with Jones moving on from the Hacienda and this could be the main reason he took a disliking to the Stone Roses.

Howard 'Ginger' Jones: Roger's night at Rafters was one of the nights I used to go to. I knew Alan Wise more than I knew Roger and I didn't make the connection that it was the same bloke that was booking the bands at Eric's. I think Alan and Roger are cut from the same cloth, Roger knew the music and understood the music and was more of an artist, or on the side of the artist. Alan is definitely of the same entrepreneurial school. How can I put it? If they'd been of another generation it would have been vaudeville, it would have been snake charmers, jugglers all of that. I think there are some people in life whose vocation is to provide entertainment for other people.

Les Hare: I worked at a record shop in Chorlton called King Bee and Roger used to come in and sell stuff, he was replacing some of his vinyl with CD's and having a general clearout. I knew him from after he'd finished at Eric's, he came back to Manchester and did a place called Rafters, an R&B club night, this would be 1980/81, I think I've got a flyer somewhere. He was doing this R&B night on a Saturday night in a basement on Oxford Street, I think it only lasted 12 months, something like that.

From the previously referred to 1980 *Guardian* newspaper interview with Erlend Clouston, Roger again commented on the workings of the music business.

"There's not a lot of new music around just now that affects me. The scramble for money now is so intense. The straight business of the music world can't understand someone like me. They keep ringing up trying to seduce me. They see your name in the papers and think 'We'll buy him'. They do this to a lot of people, not just me. They don't realise that if they

bought you and you got inside the organisation, you'd only be a fifth column. The big companies are despised now. If your local band signs up with a big company they immediately take a credibility dive and in most cases are never heard of again. The Buzzcocks are an extreme example. Their first record 'Spiral Scratch' is still selling by the truckload and the UA stuff has just flopped completely, not that United Artists are a bad company."

Nicky Crewe: I also worked at Rafters with Penny, and Roger used to stay with me as well. I lived in Longsight with my boyfriend who was called Jan. Roger would come over to do this R&B night and he'd stay with one of us. It was heaven for Jan as Roger would leave his records, Jan would record everything during the week. When he stayed he and Jan would smoke a lot of dope, we'd get back from Rafters and it would be intense – listening to music and smoking really. There were quite a lot of people who were quite intense to start with and smoking would heighten that intensity. It made it more acceptable as well. The thing about Rafters was it was an R&B night and it was Roger playing all his old favourites and this was at the end of the punk era, it was very low key, it was just Roger and his records. To be in fashion now you can be as retro as you like, it was a strange time to be listening to that music.

I went to Morocco in September 1980 and it was happening before I went. He would travel over from Liverpool as far as I can remember and he'd sleep in our back bedroom, and he'd leave the records there. If you had asked me I would have said he stayed with us every time, but obviously he didn't, it felt like a lot.

Howard 'Ginger' Jones: Penny ran the door for me when I did Rafters, she ran all my charity shows to be honest. It wasn't a long running thing, because Factory came in and asked me to do the Hacienda. I was the general manager and one of the founders of the Hacienda, and I took Penny with me, it was part of the deal.

Again from *The Guardian* interview with Erlend Clouston, Roger reiterates his mission and admiration for the achievements and qualities of the musical pioneers he admired.

"Forever, and I mean forever, the universe will be in debt to these people, they're dying out and nothing can take their place. It's only permutations and twists now. You go back to the founders and you respect them, you salute them, and that is why I do it."

ADAM'S

Bernie Connor: Then he opened a place called Adam's on Seel Street in Liverpool. Adam's was where he put Bo Diddley on.

Steve Hardstaff: Of course Roger put on Sonny Terry and Brownie McGhee, Junior Walker and Bo Diddley at Adam's, in fact he put Bo on, on several occasions. A big love of ours, a common love was Bo Diddley, I've always loved Bo Diddley. Adams was Roy Adams son's club (Roy Adams owned the premises where Eric's was situated). I don't like meeting my heroes much but Roger engineered a meeting which involved me going out for a curry with Bo before the gig, he was a really nice bloke.

Mick Hucknall: When we were coming to the end of The Frantic Elevators, around 1981, we used to rehearse over in Liverpool and we'd get on a National bus every Saturday morning, and stop over that night, in his flat in New Brighton. We'd stay up listening to records.

Henry Priestman: Roger had some great vinyl round there, he had some punk stuff, psychedelic stuff, all his dub and all his soul. Going round there was amazing, I was at that age when all that I wanted to do was listen to tunes, for me a whole new world of music was opening up. He would make tapes up for you, I asked him to put a particular track on, and when the tape was finished it was a bit of a slap on the wrist, "I don't normally do requests

Henry", I'd asked for 'Soul Finger' by the Bar Kays. This was around the time of Adam's.

Adam's wasn't going for long, maybe a year, I was in a band called It's Immaterial and we played there. The band who played there on a regular basis were The Lawnmower and that featured Mick Hucknall doing blues covers with Al Peters, they were the house band, they played every week. I also remember seeing Bo Diddley there.

Mick Hucknall: Alan Peters had a great deal of enthusiasm, and he used to organise things as well. He liked the madness of a rockabilly, soul-abilly band which was The Lawnmower. I'd never worked with anyone else and it was fun. That would have been around '82. I was DJing down at Adam's. I'd go down there on the bus on a Saturday, I'd do the DJing and then Roger would put me up in his flat. We'd go and have a Greek or Indian meal or something afterwards because Roger had a big appetite and loved to eat and so did I. When I was DJing I'd play a lot of his record collection, and they'd have acts on. As The Lawnmower we opened for Bo Diddley, Junior Walker and the Allstars, Sonny Terry and Brownie McGhee.

Doreen Allen: He also did Adam's, that was maybe going for 3 months at the most. The Lawnmower used to play and Mick Hucknall used to get up and sing with them, Mick also did the DJing. He used to stay at mine sometimes when he couldn't get back to Manchester, he'd get a return on the coach but he never had the money to get into town the next day so I'd have to pay his 10p for the bus.

Jerry Kenny: Soon after the Junior Walker and Bo Diddley gigs he had to leave Liverpool quick for some reason, I don't know why it was, but we had half his record collection, and that was a house full of records. After that these cassettes kept coming through the post, Roger compilations. Having listened to dub for all those years from these cassettes it's only in relatively recent years I've found out who these people were. After he got settled he took his records back, but we had them for ages.

The gigs Eagle put on at Adam's in Liverpool seem to have been set up with a little more foresight – he would have been trying to build up a club with a view to promoting gigs on a regular basis, with the possibility of a regular income from club goers and friends who knew him from Eric's.

CRACKIN' UP

From a fanzine interview conducted after the closure of Eric's, Roger Eagle explains his plans for opening a recording studio in the heart of Liverpool and talks about his hopes for the Crackin' Up project.

"With a lot of help from designer Steve Hardstaff and Jill, I've set up Crackin' Up productions based in Temple Street in the city centre. The building's got several floors and when it opens in September it will have a rehearsal studio, a four-track recording studio, a dance studio and facilities for art and design, where people can help design album covers along with tee-shirts and badges. There was not a lot of money left over after Eric's. In fact this venture is being run on a shoestring budget.

"I think the Liverpool scene if it can be called that, is still very healthy, but over the years there has been something lacking; a focal point for groups in the area, a centre for groups to go to. It will be a place where groups can come for advice/recording/referrals/contact with radio, television and newspapers. The only thing the group will need is enthusiasm for what they are doing. I don't think it will be everybody's cup of tea as the studio will have its own distinct atmosphere. On the one hand the recording studio itself will have its own atmosphere which not all groups will like. But the building on the whole will be a place for social contact which I believe is invaluable. Record companies will be able to come up and listen and also chat to the groups, so it will be a place where groups with no

connections can come into contact with media men, giving groups the chance to communicate quicker.

"I want it to grow naturally, but I've got no plans to push it towards growth. If it becomes bigger, all well and good. You see there is a difference between running a business and doing something you really want to do."

Steve Hardstaff: After the demise of Eric's he lived in a flat off Catherine Street in Liverpool and people were bailing him out in terms of paying his gas and electricity. I think it got so embarrassing for him to be living on handouts, because he'd never sign on. He was making bits and pieces of money, but not enough. He was living in penury really.

I think he moved to the warehouse after that, he moved around quite a lot and he did move in with Tim Whittaker. Things happened concurrently; the warehouse thing was interesting, it was bitterly cold and Roger built a shack almost and lived there, but not for that long, it got so gross in the warehouse there was no glass in the windows, it was freezing. As winter came on my missus and myself said "Come over here." Which he did, then I can't remember what happened after that. I can't remember why he left here, we certainly didn't kick him out. I think again Roger was very sensitive, he was far too big a personality and physically to fit in, in some respects. Also we didn't have the room, we had five kids at the time. His lifestyle was such that I think he felt awkward.

Geoff Davis: I went to visit the Crackin' Up place, Roger was making cassettes and selling them. I actually took a band in there and did some recording; a punk band called Public Disgrace, it was one of my first singles. We had to abandon the recordings because the sound was so crap. We redid it in SOS. We started off in 1980 doing it in that warehouse where Roger was living.

Brenda Kenny: At one point after Eric's he lived for a while in an old warehouse, fantastic that, we visited him there twice. He had no money but of course it was pure music all the time, it was fantastic. In other ways it was quite a sad time because he deserved so much more, if you're going to put history right, but he wasn't there that long really.

Henry Priestman: He was at the Crackin' Up place with Tim Whittaker, that's where he gave me the tape. I think they had almost pre-warehouse parties there. It was this big warehouse place and again another mad place, typical of Roger to live there.

Martin Dempsey: After living at the place on Belvedere Road he moved to the warehouse, he moved in there with Tim Whittaker, who was the drummer in Deaf School, he also played with Pink Military. The warehouse became a rehearsal studio downstairs called SOS, Roger was living upstairs basically, this place was freezing, he should never have been living there, totally unsafe of course. At the front door there was a guy who was living under this archway, he sniffed butane gas this kid, he lived rough in this hole under the warehouse, really tragic. At the warehouse Roger did do some promoting.

Bruce Mitchell: After Eric's closed Roger was skint to an astonishing degree, he had nothing. He moved in with The Yacht's drummer Tim Whittaker into the roofspace of a warehouse quite near to Mathew Street. It was in the winter and they built two plaster-board sheds within the roofspace, and it was gigantic. They had one, one hundred watt bulb between them for the whole area, and they used to move it, that's how skint they were. Into this space Roger moved his sound system, his records and a mattress.

I went to pick him up from there once and it was one of the most moving incidents of my life. I'd gone to pick him up to take him out for something to eat and we were doing a gig later on. So he's getting ready and because there was just this one lightbulb for this one hundred yards of roofspace, with moonlight coming through the skylight and he's playing very heavy duty King Tubby, and he was very chirpy, he's dancing about, y'know, "Hey! we're going out!" – it was so eerie.

I knew he was skint, he actually had nothing, the one hundred watt bulb underlined it all, but there's a guy who's really enjoying himself, the right speakers, the right tunes. I didn't know whether to laugh or cry.

Bernie Connor: After Eric's closed, that's when Tim Whittaker entered the scene. Roger and Steve Hardstaff had this little arts centre going in this big old warehouse. Pink Military used to rehearse there, Roger and Steve set up this place, they'd got little membership cards and you could go and hang out there, you could get tea and coffee. Bands would come and play in there y'know? Mike Badger used to do poetry evenings there. It was Mike that formed The La's, before Lee it was Mike's band. This place was called Crackin' Up', it was named after the Bo Diddley tune of the same name. It was a great idea but there was one incredible flaw in it though, it was in the winter and it was fucking freezing. I think at that point when he was doing Crackin' Up it was a difficult period in his life. He had no money at all and he was heavily in debt as well, as you can imagine.

Mike Badger: When he was living at the warehouse, that's when I got to know him better, by this time I was 19/20 and I was knocking about town looking for places to hang out. So I'd go round there, see if the big metal door was open, and if it was you'd just go in, go all the way up these stone steps to the top of the warehouse and just see who was there. If Roger was there I'd chat with him about Beefheart and stuff.

At the warehouse they had a noticeboard and I'd put up a notice that I was playing Bongos and I was telling Roger what I wanted to do and that I was into Beefheart, he said "I know the guys who'll really suit you, they're called The Mothmen." Eventually I formed my own band called Kindergarden Paintset, we were kind of like art/percussive, almost like Rip, Rig and Panic, Roger was into us and he put us on at Adam's with The Frantic Elevators.

He was putting everyone on at Adam's, I saw Martha Reeves & the Vandellas there, they all had suits and tuxedos on. I remember Roger being sat in the ticket office on the way in and seeing a poster with Bo Diddley on it, I was going "Bo Diddley's not playing here is he?" and Roger went "yeah, he's on whatever date", and I'm like "Really? Bo Diddley?", Roger says "Yeah I've got him on." I couldn't believe it. Then we played with The Frantic Elevators in about '82, and they were doing more rhythm & blues, American influenced rhythm & blues, they were pretty good I thought.

Steve Hardstaff: At the same time we were also doing Crackin' Up Records, which consisted of just three of us; me, Roger and a guy called Dave Owens, who I think put some redundancy money into it. We released 'Jukebox At Eric's' with The Frantic Elevators third single because Mick Hucknall was a big chum of Roger's, that was called 'Searching For The Only One' backed with 'I Feel Like The Hunchback Of Notre Dam'. Then we did the Freeze Frame single, Freeze Frame being a Birkenhead band that would have been down to Dave Owens as Dave comes from Birkenhead. Then, after Roger had lost interest, Dave put out a Davy Graham LP.

Taken from an interview with Paul Whelan in the book 'Liverpool Eric's' by Paul Whelan and Jaki Florek, Dave Owens explains the reasoning and ideas behind Crackin' Up.

"I was introduced to Roger in 1980 at Steve Hardstaff's house and Roger was looking for partners to form an enterprise called Crackin' Up that would involve multimedia activities in the arts and music industry, I was bought in as an assistant to Roger and the music was up to him. Roger required a building as his headquarters for operations, and finally we decided on a disused warehouse, Colonial Chambers, numbers 3 to 11 in Temple Street next door to The Pyramid club. The Pyramid used to be The

Iron Door club in the days of Merseybeat and rivalled The Cavern club with it's own history. Roger had access to the Pyramid club because he knew Roy Adams who was the owner and Roger would be able to present gigs there by arrangement. A twenty year lease was taken out on Colonial Chambers and that became the headquarters for Crackin' Up productions.

"In the first instance we had an arrangement with Prudential Insurance who owned the building that during refurbishments we would have a rent-free period of a year and they would contribute 50% of all developments that we needed to have done. There were four storeys - ground floor to third floor, basement, sub-basement and a sub sub-basement. We were required to have toilets and washrooms installed upstairs and sinks and a coffee bar - not for the public, this was for the people in the building to have as a recreational room and inevitably a jukebox in the corner, and Roger's record player and record collection.

"Tim Whittaker, the drummer from Deaf School, he rented a room, he was painting pictures for an exhibition he had coming up and Dave Balfe would drop in and Bill Drummond and they'd hatch plans with Roger to present Club Zoo. On the second floor was a dance rehearsal studio and an art gallery, we had a private collection and that was on display there. On the second floor Steve Grace, who was in Stevie and The Stopouts, had a woodworking sort of design studio that he rented, and the third floor we rented out occasionally for group rehearsals but it would be mainly the basements that we'd hire out and groups would rehearse there, so there was some income from that.

"Anyway, due to financial pressure and by arrangement with the owner Roy Adams, Roger took on another (smaller) club which was Adam's in Seel Street, where he had Mick Hucknall performing with The Lawnmower and rehearsing soul numbers, working towards what became Simply Red - certainly the interest in soul music generated from Roger's collection of music. During the time that Roger was there, the Christmas of '81, he had a four track or eight track recording machine there and they did the session with The Frantic Elevators and they actually recorded an *early version of 'Holding Back the Years'.*

"We were negotiating with Liverpool Development Agency for a grant to cover the other half of the costs. We'd built toilets that cost thirty grand and finally to do the full lot it would have cost a hundred and fifty grand. They then decided that because we'd built the toilets we had pre-empted the grant because work had already started. I think it also coincided with a number of other projects they had going on like the Tate Gallery and the developments on the docks. Perhaps I didn't present it that well... We were printing T-shirts for Dead or Alive and they were going "Who are they?" - we were only just starting so we couldn't produce sales figures... the whole process dragged on for a year and finally we got no assistance at all. Roger bailed out and I had to drag pals in to work for nothing and we did what we could.

"It's understandable in terms of the ginormous figure involved, to go for that kind of investment you would have to spark a lot of confidence in the investor. Was it a white elephant? Did we need such a giant building for our project? In some respects you might think we were wishful thinkers trying to conjure up a lot of cash, because we certainly needed it. There was a lot of administration and details like that but Roger was primarily involved and driven by the music and everyone was inspired by Roger - so if it was cleaning up pigeon mess or tidying up downstairs, it all had to be done."

The Crackin' Up project was Roger's attempt to regain the money that was owed to debtors from Eric's club - it was a venture that should have had a large degree of planning and forethought attached to it but sadly not enough. A construction industry refurbishment of a damp and derelict building is a huge undertaking for a team with no experience of putting a project like this together.

Any ambitious plan for prosperity in Liverpool at this point would have come up against a severe economic downturn. Unemployment rates in Liverpool in the early 1980's were among the highest in the UK. The city answered the government's political and monetary policies with social unrest, riots in Toxteth and thousands leaving for employment elsewhere.

Saying that, an entertainments complex on the scale Roger Eagle was contemplating would have been a wonderful addition to Liverpool's cultural legacy. If it had worked it would have brought revenue as well as a potential environment for artistic development in the city.

Crackin' Up was also a track released by Bo Diddley on the Checker label in May 1959.

Steve Hardstaff: Roger and I discussed putting out the 'Jukebox At Eric's' LP on CD, but it was a bootleg of course and the copyright still existed with the original recordings, he said "No I'm not interested Steve." Originally it was going to be number one in a series of ten. It would have covered modern jazz, reggae and soul. The rock 'n' roll one was number one, we soon realised we were going to have terrible copyright problems. People are always badgering me to put it out again but Roger did say he didn't want it out.

The reel to reel master tapes from the 'Jukebox At Eric's' LP were placed on Roger's coffin by Steve when he was buried at Bangor cemetery in 1999.

CLUB ZOO

Bill Drummond: I managed The Teardrop Explodes in the early 80's, they'd had this pop success and I just thought "this is useless, they're falling apart, they need to get some guts back into what they were doing." So I came up with the idea of Club Zoo, where they had to play every night at the same place in Liverpool. It completely demystified them, you could go and see this reasonably big band, gold album, top ten record. They were playing 7 nights a week. I was thinking somewhere along the lines of "You haven't had your Hamburg bit."

I was paying Roger to front the club, Club Zoo, so Roger was on the door, he was on his uppers at this point, he was living in the warehouse. Mick Hucknall was there a lot of the time, he was living half in Liverpool and half in Manchester. Roger was getting like cash in hand, which seems horrible and like a reversal of things, but he was up for it.

Doreen Allen: Roger also did Club Zoo, I worked on the door when The Teardrops did Club Zoo, I did all the secretarial for that actually.

Bernie Connor: Then The Teardrops did Club Zoo at The Pyramid. The Pyramid was a nightclub which was situated in the same place as the 1960's Liverpool club 'The Iron Door'. Roger had something to do with that, he was always there and of course he was living in a warehouse across the street dying of hypothermia. Club Zoo was winter 80/81, so he was still in Liverpool then.

Henry Priestman: All the old faces turned up there, that was nice. I saw The Ravishing Beauties there, The Teardrops played for a week there and I DJ'd on one of the nights.

When Roger worked the door at the Club Zoo gigs in Liverpool for Bill Drummond and The Teardrop Explodes, he accepted the jobs to keep the wolf from the door. He didn't claim social security benefits until quite late in life and these gigs would have helped out a little.

Steve Hardstaff: Then Liverpool got a bit hot for him in as much as the gas, electric and phone companies were after him, he stayed here because we had a spare room. All of the Eric's shit came over here and went into my attic, there are probably still a few things up there. He came back afterwards and took anything that was valuable to him. There were, at one point, lots of Eric's posters and band contracts, stacks of singles that hadn't sold, the

Big In Japan first single. I don't know what happened to them he must have taken them.

Pete Fulwell: There was about £30,000 to find which in those days was a lot of money. I said to Roger "Of the two of us, I'll pay the first half of it, I'm gonna get on my feet quicker than you are." So I did that. In the meantime the bank had agreed, "Yeah, we'll do it that way". When my bit was done Roger did a runner. I don't really know where he went, there were rumours that he was in the West Country or somewhere down in the South-West, anyway no-one could find him. I didn't know where he'd gone, so I had to pay the rest of it off

It would have been completely understandable for Pete Fulwell to have reacted with animosity towards Roger's poor financial standing. But it seems that with having worked closely alongside him, he knew the man better than most. Asked whether he had bad feelings toward his ex-business partner this was his reply.

Pete Fulwell: No, no, I knew him, no I honestly didn't, and that's no blag. No ill feeling at all. It was like I'll do the first bit, when I said that in the back of my mind, no matter what he said. You know, maybe he will, but the reality was, I can't talk about his relationship with other people but in our relationship I never felt there was ever any malice or any of that. So I just thought if he's going to fuck up, it's because he's fucked up, because in that area he's weak and it won't be anything more than that. That's how I saw it, I never saw it as anything else.

THE LORD BUCKLEY

Mark Thomas: The next time I met Roger I was living in a house in Upper Bangor, in a kind of bedsit. I knew the guy that owned the house, Robert and he wanted some work doing. So I was

digging a trench at the front of the house and one day Roger
Eagle walked out of the front door wearing a neckerchief and a
faded Captain Beefheart T-shirt carrying a pick axe and got into
the trench with me. I said "You're Roger Eagle!", he said "Yeah
that's right", I said "I live here", he goes "Well I live here too, I've
just moved in." As it happened Roger had a girlfriend, a lady in
Beaumaris. It was quite interesting because people would come
and visit him, Mick Hucknall came over, and other people from
Liverpool and Manchester. I didn't really have much to do with
him, I just lived in the next room to him. There was always this
thunderous dub coming from his room and a strong smell of
hashish, he also had loads of pulp fiction, yards of it.

I think the biggest impact he had when he was in Bangor was;
because he was quite a scenester, he'd find out if there were any
local place for hire. He went to this place where a lot of local gigs
were put on in the 70's and 80's called the 'Jazz Room' which was
in the basement of the student's union at Bangor University. So
Roger took his record collection or part of it and started putting
dance nights on and he was playing reggae, which had never been
done in the area before. There was rock and a bit of a northern
soul scene, that was about it really. Anyway he put these reggae
nights on and within two weeks the place was heaving. It was only
a small room but it was jumping, this was completely reggae.

A couple of local guys, Ron Taylor and Dylan, had their sound
system kick started by Roger, that gave them the impetus, they
would help out. When he moved out to Bristol they assumed the
mantle, and they're still going now.

Ron Taylor and Dylan Fernley started the 'Tribulation
Rockers' sound system after hearing Roger play reggae at a night
in Bangor, Roger thought a lot of Ron and the sound system and
would later move back to the area to recuperate after his operation.
Here Ron explains how he came across Roger.

Ron Taylor: The first time I met him he was putting a sort of reggae dance on in the local students union, and it was a poxy room and a poxy PA at Bangor University. It was when he'd sort of done a runner from his debtors and Eric's had been busted out of sight, you know? He was staying in some poxy upstairs room, a tiny room where the roof leaked and all this kind of thing. He was just DJing at the Uni and I think he was getting £30 a night. They supplied the PA, but the speaker boxes were tiny. All the reggae I'd heard was the standard fare, Marley and so on, I'd never heard proper Jamaican stuff and it rocked my boat. I've never been a great dancer but I found my rhythm with reggae, because you don't have to do anything you just have to move, it came naturally and I couldn't get enough. I used to be the first there y'know? He did a few of these gigs, it didn't last long, I think it was fortnightly. He was having to deal with stage crew and entertainments secretaries and basically they were idiots. So he just stopped because he'd had enough of it.

In the meantime I'd met him in town and invited him back to my house, he'd come round with a carrier bag full of tunes and say "Here play these!" and just plonk himself down in the corner and smoke a load of black hash. I used to play the tunes exactly as he'd put them in the bag in order and record them, he'd go "And the version of that one." I probably made about 25 tapes and that's how our friendship developed. It was during this time that he met this woman from Beaumaris, and consequently did his runner, I lost contact with him after that.

Because of his influence, not long after he left, I took my whole record collection, weighed them in and bought reggae with the money. Shortly after I was introduced to a mutual partner who does the sound system with me now. Roger had started me off on a track in the sort of roots of Reggae but this fella is more into modern stuff like Mad Professor and stuff like that. He changed my life Roger Eagle through the sound system, it was him that inspired me.

Lord Buckley was a prime exponent of what was known as 'Hipsemantic', another word for jazz speak, hip speak, jazzoetry or jive talk. He would deliver monologues in an English accent that were totally influenced by black street talk. The material he chose was remodelled versions of well known stories, Shakespearean material, biblical tales or even contemporary topics such as civil rights issues or the Hydrogen bomb. His friends included many jazz musicians and he worked at one time for the legendary mobster Al Capone. He can certainly be described as one of America's most original comedians. Lord Buckley was one of Roger Eagle's great heroes, if you were privy to his company for any length of time you would learn of Lord Buckley.

Bruce Mitchell: Well the next thing that happened is he goes, probably with creditors in his wake, to stay with friends in Bangor. He goes to Beaumaris on Anglesey, and there's a restaurant there run by a Swedish woman, a very popular restaurant, and she falls for him. She was a very elegant blonde lady who knew how to run a restaurant, a very successful restaurant with her husband. She meets Roger, gets infected with his enthusiasm, like all of us, then they do a runner, she just ups sticks and they move to Bristol. This was where they opened the Lord Buckley Cafe, it had a big front window, and a picture of Lord Buckley in a pith helmet.

Elliot Rashman: There was this woman who offered to bankroll him in Bristol, so he said "I'm going to Bristol to set up 'The Lord Buckley', I want you to look after The Frantic Elevators", so I inherited them, that's how I got them. He knew I'd heard Mick. I'd already put them on, a member of the Albertos had been to see The Frantics in Liverpool, and he said to me "You've got to put them on they're dead funny."

I remember phoning up Brian (Turner) and saying "Will you do a support for £50?" and he somehow wangled £60 out of me, and I was really impressed because I had this rule never to pay more than £50 and somehow through his cheek he got £60.

They were booked to play in the bar at UMIST where I was Entertainments Manager and I remember walking through the bar while they were sound-checking and Mick was singing on his own, 'I asked for water and she gave me Gasoline' by Howlin' Wolf and I kind of saw my life flash in front of me, the opposite of backwards, forwards. But they weren't a bunch of musos, they were all drinkers, big drinkers. Brian's trick was to see how many pints he could get in him before he got on stage, the trick was whether he could stand up. I loved what I'd seen just from that one thing.

So that's when I started to manage Mick and The Frantics, and The Frantics very quickly fell apart, partly because Mick had become obsessed with black music, he wanted that excellence, and James Brown became his obsession in life, still is possibly. I'd be happy if I never heard a James Brown record again because I heard so much of it over and over again.

So Roger went down to Bristol and I went down to visit him once. They'd set up this fantastic restaurant that was empty. It had this great neon profile of Lord Buckley with a pith helmet and he had his jukebox there, he still had the jukebox which was world famous, because it was the only jukebox to have Charlie Parker singles on it. It was the Eric's jukebox, and to me it was the most eclectic jukebox I've ever heard and if somebody could put that jukebox back together it would be fantastic because it was pretty fixed, it's Charlie Parker... you play Charlie Parker to punks. Roger was only attracted to punk music because of its dynamic.

But she had money, and what basically happened was they ran away to Bristol, it was like eloping, almost a midnight flit. I think it was because she had money, and he thought 'I can fulfill my dream'.

John Eagle: I went to the Lord Buckley, it was in Clifton - a Ferrari on every street corner. Roger told me to keep my eyes on the ground because the money was just lying in the road.

Bill Drummond: I did go and visit him in Bristol, I had an idea for a film which I was evolving and developing, and I wanted Roger to be in the film. It was to be a film set in Liverpool and it involved some lads who decide to put on a show down in the docks. It was based on some kids I knew from Liverpool. They put on a band, do a runner with the money and set fire to the place at the end. For some reason I was wanting to involve Roger in this. So we went and visited him, we went for a meal at the restaurant. I was surprised at the girlfriend, she was blonde, I'd never seen him with a woman before other than Doreen. It was quite a domestic situation down there. I was going to call the film 'The Big Killings', I never made the film, got the script somewhere. I think he was interested in the idea of being part of the film.

As manager and agent for the 70's progressive rock band Stackridge, Mike Tobin was in contact with Roger when he promoted at Liverpool Stadium. Throughout the 1970's Mike was also involved with various record companies, working as a PR and promotions man. In 1980 Mike moved back to his home town of Bristol having been away for twelve years and, while having a drink with friends, met Roger by chance in the Lord Buckley restaurant. At this time Mike also kept a personal diary, the following is taken from Mike's diary from 1983.

Mike Tobin: I remember there was a jukebox downstairs stuffed with really good music, and what he wanted was to encourage the Bristol music fraternity, musicians if you like, to use it as a place they could feel free to go without actually having to buy a meal. They could always have a drink in the downstairs bar and listen to the jukebox. I don't remember anything about the food and of course this was a time unlike today when Bristol wasn't packed with restaurants of every conceivable variety and quality. So it was probably pretty new that there was something unusual and inspirational going on in a restaurant at all.

Sunday 22nd May 1983: Popped over to Clifton at lunch time and had a drink at the Lord Buckley, met some old friends. Also met the bloke who runs the Lord Buckley, Roger Eagle, who I knew as a voice on the phone when he was promoting in Liverpool.

Saturday 11th June: *Took Susan out for a birthday dinner at the Lord Buckley, had a very good meal and stayed on until 1am chatting to Roger Eagle and Maria the Swedish cook.*

Tuesday 14th June: *I met Roger today and we went for beers and a meal at the Lord Buckley.*

Tuesday 21st June: *Met with an old friend Phil Baker, who was working for Arista Records. Went to 'The Studio' to see The Lotus Eaters, then went for a meal at the Lord Buckley.*

Monday 11th July: *Worked at BBC Bristol until 3pm, then went to see Roger Eagle at the Lord Buckley. He is making progress in South Wales re: promoting gigs and wants my help.*

Wednesday 27th July: *Had coffee with Roger Eagle in Clifton, he wants to get promoting gigs off the ground and to pursue signing some bands.*

Monday 8th August: *Met Roger Eagle for coffee in Clifton.*

This is the last and final diary reference and I seem to remember that prior to the day in question or on the night before I got this weird phone call from Roger, and I've got this vague memory that he sounded really, really stressed. He begged me to help him because I was the only person he knew that had a car and he had to get out of Bristol. He was saying it in such a way that he sounded terrified. So I very reluctantly agreed to do it because it meant driving to Oxford, and I should also say I only had a little VW Polo, and I'm quite a small person but as you'll remember Roger was quite a big bloke, the back seat and the boot were absolutely stuffed to the roof with his belongings. I also have this vague memory of Roger getting us lost a couple of times as we drove around Oxford trying to find where his mother's place was.

Wednesday 10th August: *It was very, very hot, had to volunteer to drive Roger Eagle to his mother's in Oxford. He split up with Maria last* *night and had to leave the Lord Buckley and the flat. When we got to Oxford we sat and talked in his mother's garden and later at a very nice pub, 'The Trout', by the river. He really wants to start promoting with me, but I'm not sure if it's what I want because he's talking about places other than Bristol. Got home at 9pm.*

From that point onwards in the diary there is no other reference to him, so I obviously never saw him again. My only other memory is that the Lord Buckley was closed within days, if not on that very night.

The Lord Buckley was Roger coming to a serious career and life crossroads. The incidents surrounding the demise of Eric's and the failure to get the Crackin' Up project off the ground must have been a very frustrating time for him. He'd worked with the public ever since leaving school and now he found himself in a relationship, with all the possibilities of starting a family and a new life with someone whose skills complimented his own. On the one hand he was attempting to start afresh by bringing a long held dream of combining good food and good music to life. On the other hand his disappearance to Bristol could be looked upon as a neglection of his responsibilities to Pete Fulwell and the debts they'd accrued at Eric's.

Bruce Mitchell: I think we were all enthusiastic about it at the time. He was doing front of house and she ran the kitchen because she knew how to do it. In the end they split and Roger's words were "It's this jealousy thing Mitchell". His story was, he was doing his usual thing going into the kitchen getting the plates and taking them out to the punters, which must have been terrifying if you were a punter, anyway he's down in the kitchen and there's a waitress who apparently fancied Roger, and she lifted her top up to Roger, and just as she did this the Swede walked in. But you wouldn't tolerate that, you'd just go. I think he went to his mum's.

Elliot Rashman: The problem with Roger again was he was ten years ahead of himself. If he was to open a place like that that now it would be a bar and it would be called the Lord Buckley and it would be rammed and it would be on some regenerated dock somewhere. He was a pioneer and pioneers always get a rough ride.

Bob Harding: God knows how big his record collection was, there was a period at the beginning of the eighties when I moved to Oxford, and as you know Roger originally came from Oxford, I think just prior to that he'd been living in Bristol. Anyway he ended up in Oxford living at his mum's. I went up to his mother's house a few times and he took me up to the loft, and it was just full, absolutely rammed with records. He said to me something like, that's just part of the collection. I don't know where the rest of it was, probably all over the place.

He quickly started a Reggae night at the local gay club, and he and I were DJing, in fact he'd leave me to DJ while he took care of business, you know checking the door and stuff, of course I was hopeless at DJing but with Roger's collection to DJ from you can't go too far wrong. This night in Oxford didn't last very long because we didn't get many people in the club really, but, y'know, that was Roger. If he stayed someplace he'd want to get a night going. I can remember it because it was around that time that Prince Far I got shot.

On September 15th 1983 gunmen burst into the home of reggae singer/DJ Prince Far I in Portmore, St. Catherine Jamaica and shot him and his wife. Prince Far I died in hospital, his wife suffered serious injuries. Known as 'The Voice of Thunder' due to his distinctive vocal technique, Prince Far I was 39 years old.

Brian Jackson: Roger stayed with me for a while, he went on the run. It was after Eric's had shut. I'd said to him, ill-advisedly of course, "If it ever gets hairy Roger, I've got a spare room and I'm in the middle of nowhere, so you'll be alright." Of course it came to pass. About 1 am there was a loud knock on the back door, I opened it and there's Roger looking like a bear in this black fur coat, as he often did anyway, with a couple of oppos carrying bags and boxes all full of records. He said "Hello Planet, I'm here for decades." I said, "Well you'd better come in then."

I said I'd like to hear some of your records and he did a test on me, a test of whether I was any use or not, it was very simple. He'd only been here about 10 minutes, I made a cup of coffee and we were sat down. He takes a white label 12 inch disc out of the box, no information on it at all, puts it on the turntable and says "Right Planet, concentrate, who produced this?" Well the drums kicked in and I say "Oh it's a Lee Perry" he took it off immediately and said "That'll do" and that was the end of the matter as far as he was concerned.

He stayed for two or three months, he was very difficult to live with, difficult because, to be honest and fair to the man, we were very similar people. We were both obsessive about music, it was a constant fight. I would say "Roger, listen to this cassette" and he'd say "No, no no, listen to this, you've not heard this." This was happening regularly, also he was completely unhandy about the house.

Steve Barker has DJ'd and been involved with the BBC Radio Lancashire radio show 'On The Wire' for more than 25 years, a show which has continuously given airspace and time to experimental and marginal forms of music, as well as classic rock 'n' roll, rockabilly, reggae, roots, dub, R&B and soul. In fact anything that is of great quality and ignored by daytime radio and the commercial stations is given airtime on Steve's show.

Brian Jackson: I introduced Roger to Steve Barker when he was staying here with me. I said to Steve 'I have a Mr Roger Eagle staying with me at the moment, not only has he got a phenomenal record collection but he would be a wonderful studio guest, he could play some tunes and talk about the tunes.' So he went on the show under his soubriquet 'Juke Box Johnson'. I remember taking him to Steve's show and Steve being fascinated by this man and, you know, Roger being Roger he almost took over, Steve didn't mind though because he knew he was a pro.

The reggae and dub maverick and legend Lee 'Scratch' Perry appeared on Steve Barker's show on three occasions, 1984, 1986 and 1991. From the sleeve notes of a CD recording of the shows released in the UK on the Pressure Sounds label, 30th January 2001 (PSCD 32), Steve Barker outlines what happened when Roger Eagle met one of his all time heroes.

"The plan was for me, a mere reggae fan and Roger Eagle, a total Perry fanatic and dub disciple, was to chat to Lee and play a few tunes. Before the show Roger handed Lee a stack of Ja 7" pre-releases - all bearing the imprimatur of Scratch, whether credited by script or sound. Scratch balanced a pair of NHS specs on his nose 'Jack Duckworth style' and began to tick with a ballpoint pen the labels of those tunes he recognised, stopping to ponder those which he actually could not remember. So to Roger each 7" in turn became a quasi religious artefact - touched by the hand of the master."

From another Pressure Sounds Lee Perry release called 'Voodooism' (PS09), on which Roger chose the tunes and annotated the sleeve notes, this is Roger's version of the 'On the Wire' story.

"In 1984 I co-hosted an edition of Steve Barker's "On the Wire" show for BBC Radio Lancashire, Lee Perry was the one and only guest for three hours. Hoping to obtain more information on matters relating to tunes, I produced a stack of rare gems and proceeded to pass each one in front of Lee. He raised his ancient spectacles high on his forehead staring at each one in turn with a frown of concentration. Pausing as he read the details of every label, he brought out a biro from his bag of many things and solemnly ticked them one by one - good play Scratch!"

Steve Barker: I have stacks of Roger tapes. He shacked up in Blackburn between Liverpool and Manchester and we did those shows together with Scratch and demo'd the releases that came out on Pressure Sounds! He always used to come down the Beeb and I'd let him use the phones to make a zillion business calls.

Jerry Kenny: Steve Barker had Lee Perry on his 'On The Wire' show on Radio Lancashire and Roger was like a kid at Christmas and he just fucked everything up, you know what I mean? He was so excited. Steve Barker phoned me up and said "Can you do us a jingle for the programme using Lee's voice?" I said "yeah" but I wasn't going to try and do a reggae thing, I did this kickin' R&B type thing with his voice on. At the end of the show there's a masterpiece where Lee talks over his own dub track, it moved me to tears. Lee was made up with what they knew about him, they were telling him about records he'd forgotten he ever made.

Allan Frost: Then I think he started doing some gigs up in Colne in Lancashire at a pub called The Union. Mick Hucknall, Roger and I used to go up every Thursday night and do a blues disco in the Union pub. Roger would be mostly just hanging about, Mick would do most of the DJing.

Mick was living in one of the flats in Hulme, the big council run bull ring flats. He had a small place there. I remember the first time I met Mick, he'd just had to push his push-bike home because he'd got a puncture and he was pissed off about that. So we went back to his flat I think, I seem to remember he had quite a lot of books and records and we got on well. I met him a couple of weeks later, I think on Stretford Road in Manchester, which has been all pulled down and built up again now. We went in a pub and had a drink and later went down to the gig at Colne where he was DJing.

At that time he wasn't well known, he'd finished with The Frantic Elevators and Simply Red hadn't started, we were at one of those nights in Colne, and he was packing away his records, and while he was doing this he was singing a Buddy Holly song, and he had such a sweet voice and this crowd of about half a dozen girls who were the last to leave, stopped as they walked out of the door and came back in just to listen to him singing. He had such a gorgeous voice, when he finished they went. I'm not sure what song it was, it might have been 'Wishing'.

Brian Jackson: I was hoping that while Roger was here that the main reason he was here was to hide out while he found somewhere. There were some fairly cheap properties round here, so I introduced him to folk round here and put the word about. When he said he'd found a place in Blackburn I thought, cool, it's a better town to be in than Colne, better transport network, a bigger town. You could actually do something there, because he did try a couple of things here. He did a few gigs up here at the Union Hotel, Mick Hucknall and I put the tunes on. It would have been '84/85, I remember that was the last time we had a proper winter, a snowy winter, it was cold. I remember at one of the gigs at The Union Mick was singing along to one of the songs to himself and one of the neighbours said "Hasn't he got a lovely voice?"

I once asked Roger what he was looking for in life, and one of them was to find a nice little R&B band, I think he found that with The Frantic Elevators which led to Simply Red. The other thing he wanted was to find a club to do it in. He found one in Rochdale called 'The Lamplighter' which was in the centre of Rochdale. It was run by this guy who was a dead ringer for Arthur Daly, y'know with the hat and the coat. It was a little club with an upstairs room and a small staircase. The size of the sound system was dictated by how many bins you could get up there. This was the same time that he was here with me, he called it something like 'Dub Til You Drop' or 'Wall To Wall Dub'. It was one those that didn't quite make it. It was ok, or it could have been ok, it's just that there weren't enough people there. I think it was on a Thursday night, it could have done with being on a Friday or a Saturday it would have been better.

Allan Frost: Roger always did it at a price people could afford, that's why he was never a millionaire, he wanted as many people as possible to hear the music that he loved.

Nicky Crewe: I would say for certain Roger never had any money, you almost felt he was of no fixed abode most of the time. That always seemed a shame.

Brian Jackson: He stayed with Barbara for a couple of weeks, then he stayed with my girlfriend for a while, Janet, Janet Cook, he'd blot his copybook though and people would get tired of him. Eventually he kind of sensed things were going wrong so he says, "I'm thinking of going to see some people in Blackburn." So he gathers up his things and we throw them in the car and I run him to Blackburn. When we got there I said "Are you staying here?" and he said "I think so", I said "Should I come in or wait outside?" He said "Wait outside, I won't be long". After about two hours I knocked on the door of this house and said "I've gotta get back actually because I'm working" he said "I can't possibly go now", I said "Well look I've got to get back Rog!" He said "Well go then!" So I went home.

For years afterwards he said, "You dumped me in Blackburn!" and really he asked me to run him there. So I found Roger's recollections of things were at a variance with reality. I found this to be true with other people I spoke to as well.

9 - The International and R.T.R.

The International club was situated on the corner of Anson Road and Dickenson Road in Manchester. In the 1960's it was known as 'Ocean's 11', in the seventies the club was known as 'Genevieve's', a generic discotheque club and regular Travolta paradise. The club's name changed to the International in mid 1985.

Bruce Mitchell: When he did a runner from the restaurant, it wasn't long after that he got headhunted to do The International. Everything was entrepreneurial with Roger, he would make an impression on people. A lot of the time he would promote gigs out of his own enthusiasm for an act, I don't suppose he made any money.

Dougie James: I'd performed with my band (Dougie James Soul Train) there, we were one of the last bands to play there when it was Genevieve's. The guy that owned it, a friend of mine Barry, said he was going bump. So I said "Oh I might have a go at this," I had the idea of turning it into a live music venue and putting groups on like I'd done at Rafters.

Alan Wise brought Roger to see me, he was living in Blackburn or somewhere. He was skint and Alan brought him to see me at the hotel I had in Didsbury, The Andalucia.

Alan Wise: He was living with some people I didn't know in Blackburn. At the time I was working with New Order, I had a show and I gave it to him, which he put on at King George's Hall, upstairs and downstairs. We set it up for him and we gave him the show.

New Order played St. Georges Hall, Blackburn on January 26th 1985.

Steve Hopkins: I'm not exactly sure of the year, but he also lived outside Blackburn. We'd heard a rumour that he'd become very down and reclusive, so Penny Henry and I went to visit him and that did seem to be the case. We said to him, "What are you doing here Roger? this is the end of the earth." I remember him muttering "I can get something going in a pub up the road", you know, this and that.

I've never really thought about it before but perhaps he did have a depressive illness, he had kind of manic episodes. We said to him, "What do you need?" and he said, "I need a venue where I can promote." As it happened I knew Dougie James and he'd just got involved with the International Club in Manchester. I said to Roger "we'll ask Dougie if he wants to give you a night for a start". So I asked Dougie and he was delighted, yeah he remembered Roger, "get him down, when can he start?"

It all happened, and Penny and I were amazed really that anything happened at all. But a week later Roger was back in Manchester, Dougie probably put him up, I think he had some dodgy hotel on Palatine Road.

Alan Wise: Then The International came about and I was in London, I told Dougie to get Roger. In fact I went and got Roger, I drove him over, I went with Steve Hopkins, we found him and brought him back. It was me that thought of him, everyone else had lost contact with him. When he started at The International he lived at Dougie's hotel, The Andalucia which was in Didsbury.

Dougie James: Alan brought Roger round to see me. I said, "Right you can stay at the hotel", because he had nowhere to live. So he lived at the hotel rent free, with food and board, and when it opened I paid him a wage.

Stan Hoffman: When Dougie and I got a bit of money we bought the hotel on Palatine Road, The Andalucia. When Roger came back on the scene he started living in the hotel, he was going to be booking the acts at The International and also DJing.

Penny Henry: Another thing was when Roger was living at the hotel he put all his records under my bed, he said he couldn't take them to the hotel because he thought somebody was going to pinch them. They were under my bed for about a year and I felt a real responsibility to look after them. I knew they were so precious to him, I was terrified somebody would take them. He must have trusted me a lot.

Dougie James: Roger said, "What are we gonna call it?" We sat down and wrote loads of names down and Roger came up with The International and I picked that name.

FIRST NIGHT

Doreen Allen: I think the next time I was in contact with Roger was after he rang me up and said he'd got involved with The International. I'd started this club night in Liverpool called Planet X and The International were interested in me doing a Planet X night there. Roger phoned me up and I went over to Manchester and we had a meal at some hotel. I remember they had a stuffed Donkey. We went to the opening night of The International, I remember Mick Hucknall being there and he said to me "Can we play Planet X?"

In an interview with Ray King for the *Manchester Evening News* dated Friday May 24th 1985, Roger explains his plans for the International club which had only just opened.

"The International is going to be the Mecca for record company talent scouts. I want an adult rock club, not a sweaty hole where the bands come on at midnight and everybody reels off into the night at two. I've done all

244

of that and I'm getting too old for it. Rock has been with us now for 30 years. People have grown up with it, it's a mistake to think it's the preserve of the 16 year olds."

Joe Strong: It was a style of club that was a throwback to the 60's or 70's, it was sticky carpets and chrome lamps on the tables. A sprung dancefloor, the music system was shot to pieces, when Gareth and Mathew took it over they didn't spend a penny on the place. Originally it was a place for Dougie James' Soul Train to play and it was a hangout that transferred to the hotels around Withington and Didsbury, where you could go for late drinks and stuff like that, maybe pick up a prostitute and score some drugs and stuff like that. That was before it became The International. When Roger started booking the acts it had an enormous amount of success, unbelievable, it was packed 5 nights a week.

Dougie James: Unfortunately I was involved with two crooks, one was called Mathew Cummins and one was called Gareth Evans. They were also my partners in the hotel, all the money that the hotel made was used to finance the club. When it came to dishing out the money after the first few weeks they said, "What have you done?" So I said "I'll tell you what I'll do, I'll take you two to court, and I'll have you like you've had me." So I was in court with them for five years in Manchester. Until my court case was over I couldn't go in the club.

Brian Jackson: The other thing I did was help to turn Roger on to African music. He'd not really heard much of it and I played him some stuff. I particularly played a lot of Thomas Mapfumo and His Blacks Unlimited from Zimbabwe; a fabulous band and just to show that Roger did occasionally listen, the next I knew within a month he'd booked Thomas Mapfumo to play at The International in Manchester. I went to the gig and they were wonderful, in fact most of Roger's gigs were wonderful.

CP Lee: At the time of The International I'd removed myself from music, so then I was merely a fan, so it was interesting to go to The International. Roger had this amazing ability to grab the zeitgeist and had started putting on a lot of world music. I hate to be elitist about it but people with sophisticated tastes, we knew all about blues, we knew all about R&B, Irish music, whatever and there comes a point where you're looking and you go, "Have you heard these guys from Zambia or have you heard these guys from Algeria, or Mongolian throat singing or this, that and the other?" Roger was exactly the same, he was always looking for good music, it didn't matter to him where it came from. For him The International, the very name signifies to me that he perceived world music, before there was the phrase 'world music'.

So what I also loved was Roger's idea of what you could do with a demographic, he knew what his demographic was. His people were, for better or worse, about thirty; they could be school teachers, social workers whatever, they were the ones who had disposable income, they were the ones who nobody catered for.

In an Interview with Peter Bossley printed in the *South Manchester Reporter* in late June 1985, Roger explains some of his ideas and booking policy for the the newly opened International club.

"Excellence in live entertainment is what I'm trying to achieve with an interesting mix of African, American, British and European. Our booking policy is simple; we aim to have the best possible. African bands are new in this country and they are exciting. They always put on a great show and the audiences love them. When we had Somo Somo on, the whole club was jumping and dancing."

Dougie James: Roger also used to bring Mick Hucknall round to the hotel, he'd tell Mick what songs to do.

Howard 'Ginger' Jones: The International was a hellhole, it was in one of the worst parts of Manchester, impossible to get to, but by sheer willpower and booking nous Roger turned it into the only comparable club to the Hacienda.

Anthony H Wilson: I didn't see the Hacienda and The International as connected at all really, it seemed to be a bit kind of grotty. I mean we'd built a New York style discotheque, which is what we wanted. With New Order we'd been to New York and seen these wonderful clubs and gone why haven't we got one of these in Manchester? The fact that somebody had opened a typically Mancunian grotty music venue was of no interest to us whatsoever. It only really came to my attention when Bernard started hanging out there with Gareth. Bernard Sumner and Gareth Evans, the nutter.

Jerry Kenny: I couldn't believe The Hacienda, what a crap sound it had, they had the best gear you could buy. If you're going to open a place that has music you make sure you've got a good sound, that's the first thing you do.

Here's Roger again from the interview in the *South Manchester Reporter* in June 1985.

"I don't believe in insulting the audience and the artist with a shabby place to work and enjoy themselves. We are aiming for the best, the club has a good sound and it is easy to get a drink. Basically there is not a club in the North of England with a booking policy as aggressive as ours; I use the phone 15 hours a day. A band must have something a bit more than what the record company want to see and they must entertain. You can hit people over the head with the product, the product, the product, but I like to credit audiences with a bit more intelligence than that. The whole alternative movement in 1977 was about getting away from all that and it is something I still identify strongly with."

Joe Strong was one of the original DJ's at The International, he worked at Manchester Polytechnic alongside Elliot Rashman and also DJ'd the Friday night disco there. Here he explains how he got to know Roger, and through him went on to run the London music venue Dingwalls, and eventually Ministry of Sound.

Joe Strong: My first contact with Roger was through working with Elliot Rashman and through Elliot I fell in with Mick Hucknall, through those people I came across Roger. I didn't know him that well but when he was booking at The International, I somehow became resident DJ there. I think he saw me as some kind of whippersnapper who was into the new music scene, which perhaps was not his area. So he would occasionally ask me "What do you think of this new band Prefab Sprout? Do you think they could sell out?" I'd go "Yeah put 'em on, put 'em on", and invariably it would work out.

Judy Williams met Roger at The International club and would later forge a friendship that would last until Roger passed away in 1999. Aware of the hierarchies and red tape within the NHS, Judy would later be invaluable to Roger regarding his recuperation and care following his hospitalisation in 1996.

Judy Williams: I got to know Roger at The International, a friend of mine, Rick, was helping out moving equipment onto the stage, and Roger came over to speak to me.

Dougie James: I remember walking into The International one time and Gareth Evans was jumping on Roger's back. Roger had to throw him off.

Judy Williams: I'm not good at remembering song titles or actor's names or singer's names but I do know what I like, I'd talked to him about a piece of music and that it was before I was born, but I could never describe it to him. I can remember him saying to me "Well that's rubbish, you can still appreciate a Rembrandt." So he gave me the information about the music I enjoyed, so that was very helpful to me. His tapes are very valuable to me, if you listen to them carefully and listen to the inserts of humour such as The Goons. He liked to observe life and society and the irony of life. He was a very educated person.

Joe Strong: The Monday nights were a night that I started, it was my night. I said to Gareth Evans "Why don't you let me do the Monday night?" It was dead quiet anyway, put 3 or 4 local bands on, get them to bring their crew down, you'll do a bit over the bar. Also it'll give these bands a chance to do stuff. We had bands on like The Railway Children, it was also around that time that bands such as Inspiral Carpets started giving me demo tapes.

Tuesday night was student night, we'd get a thousand people down there every Tuesday, I'd play everything from LL Cool J to the first house sounds. Through the rest of the week we'd have all sorts of stuff, right across the full spectrum; folk artists like Roy Harper. Roger didn't have barriers as far as his booking policy was concerned, he was very knowledgeable about everything.

He never told me what to play, that's why he wanted me, because I knew what I was doing, and he knew it was different to what he was doing. He could quite easily have employed a young Roger Eagle but what would be the point of that? Roger could do it himself. He wanted a DJ who could give him an insight into the new and up and coming bands.

Brenda Kenny: When he was at The International Roger phoned us and said I've got Courtney Pine on, and we'd not played with the jazz band for years, absolutely packed out it was.

Jerry Kenny: We had a fella called Jaffa from Manchester on piano, and Tim Franks on drums from Manchester, they were all part of the band 'Inside Out' at one point. We got back together after 10 years, we went on at The International supporting Courtney Pine and we blew the place apart. It was packed. But Roger knew it would be like that. Courtney Pine came on with 'I'm a serious jazz musician' and everybody just fucked off, we really played him off. It's a pity there was no-one reviewing that gig.

Brenda Kenny: At the time he'd just signed with Island records and they'd set him up with gigs all over the country, he was terrible. Roger wanted us to get a review for this because he knew we could blow him off. Everyone was dancing, it was great. We were thinking we must get a review for this because every other week he'd played and got these fantastic reviews you know. Do you know something? That week there were no reviews.

Jerry Kenny: I remember the next time we went in the barstaff were going "Oh your gig was fantastic." I remember we got on stage and Tim Franks said "What we doing?" I just said "Listen man we're in G – Tim go!", and he started and we played like a dream, it was one of those gigs you couldn't do again.

Jerry and Brenda's band The Flying Viadukts were listed as supporting Courtney Pine at The International on Friday 21st November 1986.

Brian Smith: I'd not seen Roger for a long, long time until he started doing the booking at The International, he was the first to put Robert Cray on.

Les Hare: I think he played there a few times, the first time I saw Cray there he was out of this world.

From an interview with John Crumpton, here Roger gives an insight into how he would DJ, and what sort of tunes he thought were important to fill a dance floor.

Roger Eagle: If you're a DJ the trick is to play that one track that defines an artist's whole career and puts the artist right there in the frame. That's what I try to do. When I DJ in public in a large club or something, what I hear is "Why haven't I heard this before?" and they're looking at the record spinning round. You've picked out that one track that is going to get to them, that is the secret of being a DJ. I'm not talking about the specialist DJ's who play for a particular dance crowd; it's all fragmented into highly specialised areas today, I'm talking about playing for the wider public.

For example I DJ'd a couple of Robert Cray gigs, Robert Cray is a nice guy as it happens, he was looking through my records when I was DJing. I booked the guy to play and I did very good business with him twice. I DJ'd the shows as well and Robert Cray fans tend to be middle of the road blues fans who don't know an awful lot. I distinctly remember playing 'Smokestack Lightning' by Howlin' Wolf and to me it's very, very well known, a standard, staple blues tune. And at least six people came up and said "What is this?" they'd never heard 'Smokestack Lightning' played through a big rig in a club before. Which is a different experience to playing it at home.

When you're playing to a thousand people in a club and you play something like 'Smokestack Lightning' – the power of that record confirms your own faith in it. You see people dancing to it and it's a frisson, it's a shock for people, they haven't heard this stuff before. Then you might play another obvious record, you might play 'Bo Diddley' by Bo Diddley, and funnily enough a lot of people haven't heard that record before, they've heard other people do it, they've heard the rhythm a million times. But they haven't actually heard that record played as a dance record in a club context, which is different. Then you might hit them with a heavy dub track, and it's got them rocking, and they're going 'What is this?'. You can play them all kinds of stuff that locks into that groove, it's a fascinating science.

Brian Smith: Joe Louis Walker, he had him on at The International a couple of times, Albert King, I think that was the only place Albert King played outside London.

Les Hare: He put Jimmy Smith on there and they put in seats, like cinema seats on the dancefloor.

Brian Smith: We all went down there to watch Lee Allen, who's the legendary sax player who plays on all the New Orleans stuff, all the Little Richard stuff, everything. The most distinctive sax player I know. He was on with a band called The Blasters, they backed him on two numbers, I don't think they even gave him a solo, he just riffed. One of the best sax players on the planet, and he could still play; so we all piled into this rat hole of a dressing room and there's about 20 of us all piled at one end with him, nobody took the slightest bit of notice of the star group.

In 1986 Roger guested on Radio Lancashire's 'On The Wire' for a second time with reggae legend Lee 'Scratch' Perry. From the sleeve notes of the Pressure Sounds release 'Divine Madness... Definitely' (PSCD32) the show's host Steve Barker recalls the occasion.

"Two years later Scratch reappeared 'On The Wire', this time in the company of Adrian Sherwood, with whom recently he had cut his best post-Black Ark album 'Time Boom X The Devil Dead'. Adrian spent most of the show watching football on TV. Scratch bought in a video camera. The show was already being caught on camera by Brian Jackson a.k.a. Planet Jackson a.k.a. Prince Boppa a.k.a. Rasta Foureyes. At one stage Scratch was found to be sticking a feather in an electrical socket and pouring water over it. When I got home I found a ten pence piece nailed to my wall and an evergreen tree covered in silver kitchen foil."

Jerry Kenny: We went to Steve Barker's and Lee was staying there over the weekend. He said he never saw Lee, he was playing with the kids all the time. He said the next day he got up and they'd got a tree outside the kitchen window and it was covered in silver foil. He said the silver foil got a bit outrageous, he kept putting it in the mixing desk you know?

Judy Williams: I went to Radio Lancashire with Roger on one of the occasions that he appeared on there with Lee 'Scratch' Perry. Adrian Sherwood was with him because there had been a show at The International as well over that weekend. I remember Lee Perry poured water over all the electrical sockets and everything before starting and I think that's how the studio burnt down. Then lighting his joint under the wiring; the opening to the show was Lee 'Scratch' Perry saying "Good morning Buckingham Palace!" it was just so funny.

Bill Sykes: The first time I met Roger Eagle was at The International venue in Manchester in 1986. He booked the bands there, and my mate Steve Longden and I had heard his name mentioned and thought we'd take a tape in with a view to getting a gig with our then band Ministers Of The Groove. We were a seven piece band trying to do our version of Northern Soul and we'd heard his name in various publications associated in some way with the scene.

As most people remember him at this time he was stood by the small bar on the left hand side just as you walked into the club, he had on a loud Hawaiian shirt and his size struck you straight away. We eventually managed to pluck up courage to hand him the tape which he pocketed and said he'd listen to. Obviously he wasn't going to phone an unheard of band and offer them a gig so we made our way down there to catch another gig, probably Zoot & The Roots or something similar, a couple of weeks later and sought him out. He didn't really say what he thought of the music, but he liked the energy.

I think we got offered a Saturday night gig when another band had dropped out. I remember going to The International quite a lot at this time, it was really the only venue in Manchester where you could see a large cross section of bands and styles from local first timers to Internationally famous artists. The legendary Hacienda, on the other side of town was cold, the sound was shit and no-one went there, until 1987/88.

I'd always chat with Roger, and try and tap him up for musical tips, when he knew you were into music he'd give you tapes, carefully put together in a genre crunching manner, with a photocopied front cover and typed sleeve; tough rockabilly making way for the heaviest dub, then a slice of doo-wop segueing into some 60's proto-punk garage. These tapes made way for a later Roger concept of 'The 20th century jukebox', a good 20 years before Bob Dylan mumbled "Dreams, Themes & Schemes" on his Themetime Radio show, even longer before Mark Lamarr came up with the 'God's Jukebox' concept.

This music was my education, you couldn't and still can't hear this stuff on the radio, it's way too dangerous; the innovators, the terror men and women of the 20th century. If you speak to people now about Roger's tapes, they will explain how very precious they are to them. Roger must have put together hundreds of tape compilations for friends, some duplicated, some simply one-offs. Imagine titles like 'Bathtime With Beverley', 'Giant Tunes Pts 1, 2 & 3'. 'Heavy Gravity', 'That Was The Wheel That Was', 'Barefoot Rock', 'Blackstar Liner', 'Rhythm Of The Rebels', 'Iron Leg', 'Ballistic Dub' and 'The House of Dread'. The list is long and Roger's rules were simple; rare vinyl and later when digital technology arrived, tunes that hadn't yet been put onto CD.

Roger also invited me to his flat above the Manchester Arndale Centre a few times, he'd put the kettle on, pass a well loaded spliff and go 'Right! Sit down and listen to this!' I had no choice but to listen, I was partially incapacitated anyway; strange environment, hep music professor, big speakers and heavyweight dub. I remember hearing Funkedelic's first album in his front room for the first time and it totally knocked me sideways. To this day it's the best album I've ever heard. If you haven't heard this by the way do yourself a favour. You can almost hear the synapses being frazzled in the studio. It's Hendrix, with female gospel backing singers, deep bass, a massive snare sound and space, loads of space... Oh and the must have prerequisite for all great rock music, a touch of insanity... and as Roger explained - Black men on acid playing rock music.

Roger would come to manage our band later on, getting

reasonably paid gigs for us around the North-West and introducing us to music business people he believed could help us. He also helped to get us a small national tour with an internationally famous group who'd just had their first number one, the singer is another of Roger Eagle's students.

Ron Taylor: When I saw him again he was living in the middle of Manchester above the Arndale Centre. What staggered me most about him was the spread of his musical interests, I mean I love reggae but his command of other genres was astonishing. He'd DJ reggae for a night, rockabilly, rock 'n' roll, he could DJ R&B and soul.

Joe Strong: I went to visit Roger once a week when he lived above the Arndale, he gave me records and tapes. He would also do a lot of compilation tapes and send them out to people like Bruce Mitchell, Mick Hucknall, Elliot Rashman and Bill Drummond, people like that I think. A lot of the music he played was pure out and out rockabilly, he played loads of records to me when I went round there. Whenever Roger had a minute to sit down and listen to music it would always be rockabilly, pure and simple, which surprised me. I think he'd passed through his R&B phase and his dub phase and onto the rockabilly phase. He'd also tap me up about bands that were touring at the time and ask me if I thought they'd pull a crowd or not.

I think he enjoyed my company, because I was younger. Even though he'd have difficulty communicating, he wanted to have people around him and that's what he'd do with the club. He used to facilitate people getting together and listening to music and stuff like that. He didn't really participate that much, you'd never see him on the dancefloor or anything like that. He did it for everybody else really. In that sense he was very altruistic. The amount of people who were introduced to types of music they would never normally have heard must be phenomenal. The debt people owe him in that respect, and then for him to end up in a kind of destitute state.

Brian Rae: Some time in the late 80's, I'd not seen him for a number of years and Atlantic had released an album boxed set of soul stuff, it's called the 'Rhythm and Blues years' or something like that. I walked into the HMV in Manchester, next to the Arndale Centre at 9 o'clock that morning and Roger was in there. So I went sidling up to him, and he was actually looking through the boxed set, what the listing was and what was on it. I said something like, "I think there's only seven tracks I haven't got" or something like that, he turns round and says "Bloody hell!" lifted me up and all the rest of it, and he said "Well there's only three I haven't got", then he says "Come upstairs and have a coffee." This was when he lived on top of the Arndale. As he made the coffee I sat down in his chair and there's a big pile of Stax stuff, the early stuff and slightly later stuff. I ended up with fifteen Booker T singles that I didn't know out of this pile and I thought I knew Booker T pretty well.

Judy Williams: I certainly didn't give him anything that linked him to the music world, I had no music knowledge or anything like that. Roger liked to help people develop their careers and their talents, more often than not the people he helped to get promoted did really well. Somehow he seemed to be kind of left behind, I don't mean in every respect.

Joe Strong: Roger used to say to me that he could tell by the tone of voice of the agents that would phone him up, whether or not the band they were trying to flog him was worth having on or not. He certainly had a bit of magic as far as booking bands was concerned. The International was a goldmine, not that he saw any of the money. Anybody that works with Gareth Evans is ripped off. If he reads that he'd be proud of the fact, he's a hard-nosed businessman. The way he became The Stone Roses manager was nothing to do with music, he didn't have much of a clue. He'd come to me and say "Joe, tell me the truth, you know this band The Stone Roses, are they any good?", I used to say "Yeah, they're alright, yeah."

At The International Roger got totally used, he would have been on a fixed salary, maybe £300 a week. Honestly I'd go into that little office every single night, it was like a narrow corridor, you could hardly fit the money in there. As you went into the venue it was on the right hand side, there was just enough room for two chairs. I used to go in every night to get my money, I'd say "I've just DJ'd and I want my £25". They'd be counting the money, it was ridiculous, they were just sticking it into bin liners, thousands and thousands of pounds, and Roger's there on a fixed salary.

He tried to change the terms of his employment but obviously they weren't having any of it. They said "If you don't like it Roger, fuck off, we've got the name of the venue, we can put our own bands on." Obviously Roger wouldn't walk away because it was his lifeblood you know? He was never in it for the money. It's just a shame that when things started to go wrong for him that he had nothing to fall back on, you know?

Judy Williams: Mathew and Gareth were always very polite to me because I was with Roger, but I also knew they were very difficult characters. They wanted to get what they could from him but they didn't treat him well. His knowledge got the place going.

Brenda Kenny: It ties up with the time I was at The International when he pushed me in this small room with his brother John and said "Look after the money", and he went off, he was sweating, there must have been something going on, "Look after the money!", I remember Martin Hannett being there that night.

Tommy Smith was to become a part of Roger's circle of friends and helpers, he was already a DJ when he first met Roger and because of his enthusiasm and knowledge of music became one of the regular DJ's at The International. He would also later help Roger out by guesting on his radio show on Piccadilly Radio, and chauffeuring some of the major stars whose gigs Roger would promote. As well as continuing to DJ, Tommy also spent time working in the specialist collectors music shop Beat'n'Rhythm on Tib Street in Manchester.

Tommy Smith: I guess Roger's name was part of urban folklore when I was growing up, kind of youth clubs and stuff, older brothers or the people who went to the second Twisted Wheel, stories carried on the grapevine if you like. It's amazing how it came about really, there was no internet, nothing was written down. He must have had such a strong personality and influence at the Brazennose Street Wheel, he was, I suppose, a bit of a local legend. I'd also seen an interview in *The Face* magazine with Mick Hucknall and he name checked Roger and credited him with his musical grounding.

I'd also heard of this place called The International, and I heard Art Blakey was playing, I missed that, but then I heard Bo Diddley was playing, and I thought "what is this place?" So as a punter I went to see Zoot & the Roots, a top class soul revue band, with of course Snake Davis. At that gig Joe Strong was DJing, so I just went over and had a chat, probably to compliment him on what he was playing, which was a very eclectic mix, very similar to the kind of stuff I'd play when I DJ'd. I happened to mention that I DJ'd myself and would love the opportunity to do what he was doing. He said "Well I'm busy next Saturday night, can you cover the Jimmy Smith gig for me?" I thought this is unbelievable, this was one of my favourite artists and I jumped at the chance. He said, "Right I'll introduce you to Roger to make sure it's ok."

Henry Priestman: The next time I saw him was when The Christians played at The International, he was at the corner of the bar, he was dead friendly, and he was made up that we'd had a couple of hits. He said "Well done Henry!" he was very pleased. It was like yet another was coming along, that was in '87, everybody else had broken through. I think 'Space', who used to go to Eric's matinees, were the last of the lot. I suppose Ian Broudie and the Lightning Seeds also came quite late.

Tommy Smith: The first time I saw Roger he was sat on his usual perch at the end of the bar near the door in a Hawaiian shirt. My first impression was like "Is he gay? Is he an old queen or something like that?" Turns out he wasn't. I was aware of his presence and stature and the way he carried himself; a sort of aloof, lofty figure of a different breed than the likes of us, a sort of military wing commander type of bearing, slightly eccentric, but not on the fringes of lunacy. From the word go he had a way of bullying you. From that day on I put my enthusiasm across and we kind of bounced off each other. The conversations you'd have with him were always blunt and abrupt and if he had some gossip he'd embroider it to make a Bayeaux Tapestry of it before he'd deliver it. His passion for real music that he wanted to get across to people will always stay with me, I'm also eternally grateful for it. His passion for music often got the better of his judgement financially.

Les Hare: Roger put Bobby Womack on who was a bit of a disaster; he was a real clot, putting shit up his nose. But he came back a couple of years later and played a blinder. He put Gil Scott-Heron on as well.

Tommy Smith: A great example of Roger booking stuff by the skin of his teeth was the Bobby Womack gig, it couldn't be done now. I had to drive Roger from Cromford Court above the Arndale to The International, and he's saying "Bobby Womack's not confirmed or signed the contract, he should be there, I'm 99% sure he'll be there." I remember the car I was driving ran out of petrol about 100 yards from The International, you can imagine how stressful that was. We had to push the car into a petrol station, fill up and continue the journey, we were all silent in the car, all a bit tense. The whole thing was, Bobby Womack may or may not turn up and there was a big delay in him coming on and that was hyped by whispers and rumours. There was no contract like you would have today and Bobby Womack certainly wouldn't be playing somewhere like The International now. The place had sold out, we opened the doors at 8 o'clock and I started DJing, it got to 9 o'clock, no sign of Bobby, the place was absolutely heaving and I'm keeping people dancing, you know? I think there may have been a 12 o'oclock curfew, anyway it got to 11 o'clock, still no sign of him. People were asking me "Where is he?", the mood was very tense and basically at a quarter past 11 this car turns and the gig went ahead.

Mick Hucknall was also there and he went across to meet him as he arrived, they went in the office with Gareth, Mathew and Roger. Roger suggested that Mick join him onstage for a couple of songs and Bobby Womack said "Let's hear how you sound, get an idea of your voice", so Mick sang 'I was born by the river' and Bobby Womack said "Yeah, sure you were son" that was Roger's story anyway. Then I had to go into the dressing room behind the stage to bring him on, I'll never forget it, to catch his attention I had to hold his arm gently and say "Bobby it's time to go on", I remember the feeling of his arm was like touching a prosthetic limb, it was cold and plasticcy, a very odd feeling. He went on and I introduced him. I went back to the DJ booth and Mick's stood in there with me while he did his first few songs. Mick was saying "I don't know whether to go on with him or not" I said "Go on!" I was trying to push him, I said "Do it, people are expecting it now." He went on and came back off after two songs, really pissed off, saying "He sang over the top of my lines, he had no respect for me", he was quite annoyed about it.

That was a typical Roger Eagle show, by the skin of his teeth, nearly didn't happen but eventually it did. It wasn't unusual that kind of thing.

Judy Williams: I think he wanted people to experience something vibrant, and I think he came from such a very formal background. He wanted to get away from that Oxfordshire middle England life. I think that part was always there, I think it showed up in his interest in literature and the arts, he had a very full knowledge of the arts, all aspects, and politics.

On the 6th December 1987 Simply Red put on a one-off gig at The Ritz in Manchester as a tribute to Roger Eagle. The majority of the songs played that night were blues and rhythm and blues standards, Roger also DJ'd the gig under his alias Jukebox Johnson.

Bruce Mitchell: Simply Red did a special gig at The Ritz, it was Roger's gig but they didn't want to burden Roger with any work, so they brought in their own promoter, Stuart Galbraithe to run the gig and he had to do it for nothing. I like the idea that they decided to do it for Roger. Andy Dodd and Elliot (Rashman) felt Roger was on hard times, he was always skint anyway.

Although still employed at The International, by this time Roger had met American ex-athlete Zane Branson who was in Britain representing New Orleans in a city twinning project with Liverpool. Along with Zane, Roger set up the company RTR (Rock The Ritz), putting gigs and club nights on at the Ritz on Whitworth Street in Manchester, probably hoping for a bit of student overspill revenue from the Hacienda which was two minutes walk away and very successful at the time. They also went on to do two shows with the American blues legend John Lee Hooker and two all day festivals at Bodellwydan Castle in North Wales.

Joe Strong: Zane became his right hand man, he spent an

awful lot of time with him. Zane and Roger put all kinds of things on at The Ritz, it was his kind of place after The International. The gigs weren't as regular as The International, there it was practically every day of the week.

Zane Branson: I was working on the official city twinning of Liverpool and New Orleans with Connie Atkinson, we did several events with the two cities. A guy who was in a band called The Lawnmower, Al Peters, told me about Roger. He was doing a radio show on Piccadilly in Manchester, I went to see him and he invited me onto his show where he asked me about the twinning and all kinds of things. He actually invited me to watch the band Ministers of the Groove play – that was the first time I went to The International. So Roger and I talked and we decided to put on a couple of shows together. That's when we started RTR Promotions. Roger knew that The International was coming to an end, he wanted to do something else. I told him that he obviously had a lot of talent and knowledge, and he'd done such influential things at the Liverpool clubs and in Manchester in the early 60's. It's remarkable, if you're a music fan you can't not appreciate what Roger did.

In 1986 the success of The International venue encouraged Mathew Cummins and Gareth Evans to branch out. They chose a venue at 210 Plymouth Grove, an old Irish ballroom known in the 1960's as the Astoria and in the 1980's as the Carousel, then briefly Slosky's. They named it International 2, so now Roger was booking the acts for two major venues in Manchester.

INTERNATIONAL 2

Brian Smith: Didn't he book the bands at International 2 as well? Didn't he put on Otis Clay and Ann Peebles?

Les Hare: Yeah, the 'Hi' label one.

Brian Smith: That was fabulous. It was Willie Mitchell, the whole crew, the full 'Hi' package or road show, Otis Clay, Billy Always, David Hudson.

Tommy Smith: Joe (Strong) did a night called 'A Night In Tunisia' which was on a Tuesday, and also the most popular student night in town at the time, so I went down and listened to what Joe was playing. International 1 had a thousand capacity and that's how many people they would get in, and I thought I'd love to do this, play this sort of music to an appreciative audience. It was actually quite a challenge to take over a night that was already successful. I kept the same mix of music that Joe had been playing but put my own spin on it and it kept going for the next couple of years.

Zane Branson: When I first met Roger he introduced me to Bruce Mitchell, we went up to Roger's flat above the Arndale. Roger's was always laughing that Bruce should have died many years ago because he had this medical problem. When we did shows at The Ritz we always rented the lights from Bruce, he sometimes come in on this fold-up bicycle, wearing a white boiler suit, down Whitworth Street, right up the ramp and in through the front door, drop off a cable and ride back out again.

Bill Sykes: Roger first introduced me to Zane Branson around 1989, in the Railway public house in Whaley Bridge. Roger and Zane had with them the blueprints for a Mississippi steamboat. The boat, a registered National Landmark, was situated in Louisiana, Roger and Zane were looking at shipping the boat over to the UK and placing it in a dry dock in Liverpool. It even went past the first stages of approval. Zane suggests the project never came to fruition because funding from the Merseyside Development Corporation ceased.

Zane Branson: Roger and I had done a consultancy for Bingley's. They were a company that dealt mostly with restaurants and some of the finest such as Browns in London, places like that. Somehow they'd acquired this pub/venue and they didn't really know what to do with it.

A friend of mine, Jim, had a club called Tipitinas in New Orleans and Ronnie, who was Bingley's representative, happened to be in New Orleans and spoke to Jim and said he thought that Tipitinas was the kind of thing that was needed at Dingwalls. So they flew Jim over, he called me and I got Roger involved. Roger and I went to London for two or three days to watch everything and they put us up in a nice hotel.

They took us for a meal at Browns in a private area upstairs; there was Ronnie, Jim and his wife, Roger, Joe Strong and myself plus the manager of Dingwalls and his wife. It all started off very amicably, everyone was joking and everything, we'd given Ronnie our report while we were talking, everything was great. Then this guy Ronnie brutally tore this manager apart, and while the dinner was going on he had security people taking things out of his office. Then they had the guy arrested right in front of us. This was right up Roger's street, this was like a dream come true for Roger.

The guy was ripping the place off, Roger knew all the tricks, he knew all about running that kind of business and that knowledge got Joe Strong down there as the manager of Dingwalls, Joe was hired on the spot.

Joe Strong: By February 1988 I'd left Manchester, I was in London. I ended up in London when the company that ran Dingwalls in Camden had got in touch with Roger and asked him to go down to London from Manchester and look at their club and tell them what was wrong with it, as it was losing about £1 million a year. A lot of money was going down the swanee. So Roger went down over a weekend to have a look at it. I got a telephone call to go down to London immediately, halfway through a football match as it happened. So I finished the football match and jumped straight on a train down to London and booked in a Holiday Inn. I thought "Jesus what's this?" Then I went out and met this businessman with Roger, and Roger said "This is the man you need to take over your club." All I'd done really was resident DJ at the International, Ok I'd run the Poly, but Elliot Rashman had always run the business side of things.

Zane Branson: Taking over Dingwalls was a good boost for Joe, he didn't have much money at the time, he actually had to borrow money to get down to London when we contacted him, he went on to run Ministry of Sound after that.

Joe Strong: The next thing I'm moving to London, I lived in an hotel for two weeks while I found somewhere to live. I took over Dingwalls, sacked a load of people, did all the dirty work and managed to turn it around. Unfortunately within six months of moving down the whole company, which had nineteen restaurants and one solitary nightclub, went into receivership – which sounds shit for me but it turned out to be brilliant. The receivers that came in knew all about restaurants but nothing about nightclubs and because they had to keep the club open as a going concern, they had to keep me because I was the only one who knew anything about nightclubs. That more or less gave me free reign; there was no check on the money, profit, loss or anything. So I put different things on every night of the week, we had film shows there, all kinds of things. Can you imagine running a club where money is not a concern? Put what you want on, have what DJ's you want on, pay the bands what you want to pay them.

Zane Branson: Roger was talking about that whole story for months after that. If you knew Roger you'd know those were the kind of things that would make him tick.

★

The International also put on many gigs that contributed to the so called 'Madchester' scene, including early sets from local bands, many of whom went on to much bigger things such as The Stone Roses, World of Twist, Inspiral Carpets, The Charlatans and The Happy Mondays. Roger's influence on the whole late 80's Manchester music scene was to give a space for these bands to hone their material in front of their own crowd.

Tommy Smith: I must also mention Gareth Evans' more than eccentric state of mind in handling any given situation. Regarding The Stone Roses he came up to me and said "Here's the new single 'Elephant Stone', after you've played the last record you put this on, full tilt." Well I didn't put it on full belt, maybe because the doormen were trying to clear the club and it wasn't helping them. Towards the end I let it fade out, then Gareth came over and said "Right that's the last record you'll ever play here, I told you to play it full blast, that's it." I thought "what?" It was a very odd thing to say. Anyway the next morning I rang Roger and said "I know you've got me in for some gigs there but Gareth's just got rid of me", he said "Leave it with me." Anyway he got back to me later and said "I've had a meeting with Gareth and Mathew, and I've made it quite clear that I won't be working for them anymore if they do that to you." I don't care whether this conversation took place or not, but for Roger to suggest that was just fantastic.

Zane Branson: The first show Roger and I did together was James at The Ritz, we sold that out. That was when students still had grants and all that. I think the 3rd show we did was Was Not Was, we put The Fall on a couple of times. There's a big list of bands we put on at The Ritz. Roger got to a point where he was tired of doing the promotion and I was happy to learn from him, to be there at the clubs all the time and do the stuff.

John Lee Hooker's career had pretty much petered out by the 1970's after his collaboration with Canned Heat. On the back of the great bluesman's 40 years of work and reputation alone, Eagle was prepared to promote two big shows at the Manchester Free

Trade Hall. These gigs didn't revive Hooker's career but in the U.K. they certainly helped put him back into the popular frame. As a young man Hooker recorded many tunes that he did not receive royalty payments for, this would have not gone unnoticed by Roger Eagle. To be a successful promoter one has to be willing to take a gamble – and certainly the first of these two gigs that would have been the case. After struggling for most of his life The Healer album with guest appearances from Carlos Santana, Bonnie Raitt, Robert Cray and Los Lobos gave John Lee Hooker his long awaited payday from the music business.

Zane Branson: The John Lee Hooker gigs were Roger's idea. He was still living above the Arndale at that time, certainly at the time of the first John Lee Hooker gig. That was the first time Hooker had played Manchester since the sixties or early seventies, the first gig was a bit before The Healer album. At the time I noticed he only did two gigs, one at London's Town and Country club and the Free Trade Hall in Manchester with us, that's all he did in England.

The first gig must have been 1988, that was on Roger's birthday, July 15th. Hooker's tour manager was signing autographs in his name because he couldn't write, but he did sign Roger's, somebody had done a drawing of Hooker off an album cover for Roger's birthday and they got Hooker to sign it. The second gig was on the day of the Football World Cup final (8th July 1990), England almost got to the final but they ended up going out in the semi-final. We still sold out the show, that was around the time of The Healer album.

Tommy Smith: I think one of the highlights of Roger's career must be the first John Lee Hooker gig that he promoted. You've got to remember that two years later his album The Healer came out. That made him globally famous and put the money in his pocket that he'd waited all his life for. This gig was two years before, when he wasn't hot property.

I had to go to The Rampant Lion, I had a Mk 4 Cortina which I used for a private hire taxi work during the day. Roger said, "Go and pick him up from The Rampant Lion on Anson Road near The International". It wasn't a particularly glamourous hotel, it was ok. I had to go and pick him up and bring him to The Free Trade Hall. I thought, "wow this is great! I get to meet one of my heroes". So I get to the hotel and I'm knocking on his door and there's no answer, and it was really quiet. I thought "God, he's due on stage in half an hour," so I knocked again still no answer. So I thought I'll try the door. The room was in complete darkness, and I could see he was in bed asleep. I thought "Shit, I'm responsible for getting him to the gig which is in front of many hundreds of people at The Free Trade Hall". So I just gently tried to push him and said "Mr Hooker, it's time to get up now", and he's saying "Leave me alone, leave me alone, my stomach's really poorly." I thought if any of his fans could see him now, lying there, it was like waking your granddad up out of a peaceful sleep, you know? You'd leave him to rest. So I had to tell him, "You're due on stage shortly, it's time to get up." Ok, so he said "Pass me that jacket", but the jacket was completely covered in mud from the shoulder to the waist, he must have fallen over, I said "You can't wear this", and I found him another coat, got him dressed, got his hat and walked out of the door.

In the foyer of the hotel there was a music journalist who asked me if it was ok if he had a lift to the gig, he showed me his ID and I said ok, fair enough. Driving to the gig I handed over a piece of paper and a pen and said Mr Hooker could you sign this and dedicate it to Tom? I could tell there was something wrong and he felt uncomfortable about it. The journalist, who probably knew a damn sight more about him than me, was shaking his head a bit, then it dawned on me, he couldn't write. He came from a time and place where there was no real education for black people. I've still got the autograph now, he wrote 'To Tom from the Hook'.

I had no idea.

He was still quite drowsy when we got to the gig, it wasn't long after he'd had an operation on his stomach, but he went on and played as if he were a young man in my opinion. As soon as he got on stage he was very lively and he entertained everybody. After the gig they had to surround him in a kind of guard of honour to get him out through the back door. He asked for a couple of blondes to escort him back from the gig and I took him back to the hotel.

Brian Rae: One of the worst experiences I had with Roger and we had a few, was sometime in the late 80's when he put John Lee Hooker on at The Free Trade Hall, this was the first show out of the two he put on. At the time I was working for Charley Records and I did the displays in the foyer, we had quite a bit of John Lee Hooker material. I'd been to see Roger the week before and I think he'd put his house on the line. John Lee Hooker was one of these characters who wouldn't go on stage until he'd been paid, he wouldn't even bother because he'd been ripped off so much over the years. Roger said, "The advance tickets aren't selling, it's going shit." I think he'd done about 400 or something, he needed to do 1200 to clear, I think The Free Trade Hall would do something like 1700 flat out. So I said, "You're still going ahead with it aren't you?" he said "Oh yeah." So I said "I'll come down at dinnertime on Friday, meet you at The Free Trade Hall and I can put the display up." So I met him on Friday and he was worried to death by then, I think it had only picked up by a hundred or so. So I took him out for something to eat around tea-time, he was really worried by this time. But when we got back to The Free Trade Hall there was a queue half way round the building, people had got coaches from as far away as Newcastle and Carlisle without tickets, the place was absolutely packed.

John Eagle: One of the most memorable times for me regarding Roger was going up to Manchester for the evening from Oxford in the car in 1990 to see John Lee Hooker at The Free Trade Hall. It was my job to drive John Lee Hooker from the hotel to the gig and then back to the hotel again afterwards. At the gig he was just about to do the song The Healer and I was told to go out to the car and wait for him as he was going to leave soon afterwards.

I think my mother was proud of Roger but I think she was a bit upset that he borrowed so much money from people.

Roger Eagle: When you DJ and you meet the public, the committed fans are a pain in the arse, believe me I know. They're always whingeing on at you about this and that and have you got this version? Can you play that track? They'll come up to you when you're trying to get a club cooking and you want people to enjoy themselves and dance and all the rest of it, and they want to hear something that is totally unrealistic. I know a DJ like that up in Blackburn, he'll DJ a show and he'll play stupid slow blues tunes and obscure things, and you can tell that there's a handful of people enjoying them but the bulk of the people are shuffling their feet and looking at their watches and buying another drink.

What I want to do is rip into that crowd and really turn them on. I'll play one or two reference tunes like maybe 'Green Onions' by Booker T and the MG's - I know that record inside out, backwards, upside-down etcetera right? But still if I'm out DJing for a wider public I play that because it gives a reference point. They think 'It's not as weird and mad as I thought it was going to be'. 'Green Onions' is a blues tune and it was originally released as a B-side not an A-side. When you play a strong record like that it blows the rest out of the sea straight away.

Tommy Smith: I also did a radio show with Roger and Jillian Cowie. Jillian I think was freelance but she had her own regular Saturday show on Piccadilly in Manchester. Roger must have persuaded her to do this 'Jukebox Johnson' guest appearance spot on her show, so he could go along and play in his words 'Rare and rocking tunes' and these were the major principles he wanted to bully across to people right from the start. You really must know the importance of Little Richard, Bo Diddley, Chuck Berry, James Brown, Lee Perry and King Tubby, without those your education was incomplete. It was very exciting, I think it went on for a few months, I only went in about 3 times. I remember one time I was at my flat in Audenshaw early on a Saturday evening and my phone went and it was Roger, "Why aren't you here? You're supposed to be here with me now, I'm on the Radio!" So I had to jump in my car and drive down to Piccadilly and do it. I didn't think I was on that night but Jenks hadn't turned up, so he needed somebody with him to bounce off.

Joe Strong: The International didn't last long when Roger did eventually leave, and I do believe strongly the reason he left was because he was still on the £300 retainer. I think he also told me they didn't pay any of his National Insurance or Tax.

Zane Branson: Then we started this thing called The Temptation club, which was on a Wednesday night. The only nights available to us at The Ritz were Sunday, Tuesday and Wednesday. We decided early on to do a club night. So I got some DJ's from Liverpool and some students who hadn't really DJ'd but had some ideas. So we did it and we had 1700 in on the first night. This club went on for 10 years, it went on until The Ritz was actually re-vamped, we were told one week they were going to close for six weeks from the next week. When it opened again we did it for another year and a half but it was never the same.

Tommy Smith: When Zane and Roger set up RTR, Roger said to me "When I leave The International it'll close, so you're better off jumping ship now." I told Gareth and Mathew and they said it's probably best if you don't work here if you're working for Roger. So a student night started at The Ritz and they ended up getting a team from Liverpool to do it, so I was put out of a job there. These things happen.

Commenting here on the, at the time contemporary dance music scene of the early '90's, Roger's opinion could be seen as behind the times in some ways but also with a huge element of truth.

"That's why I feel so sorry for kids today, because they've got such a load of fucking rubbish to look back on in their middle age. Are they gonna be playing all this rave stuff? I don't think they are quite frankly, I suppose they might now and again, but there's very little to get hold of that's really memorable."

Although Roger Eagle wasn't involved with the phenomenon that became acid house and rave culture, as could be said of Tony Wilson, his influence on youth sub-culture had already made its mark. Dancing until the early hours of the morning to repetitive beats aided by amphetamine based drugs was something Roger was only too well acquainted with. His contribution to the 1960's sub-culture of modernism and rhythm and blues, which gave rise to perhaps the biggest underground music sub-genre ever known is undeniable. Of course to suggest that the the 90's rave scene originated at the Twisted Wheel is rather tenuous but Eagle's influence and musical knowledge can certainly be tracked back through a similar, dance music based, cultural lineage.

10 - Whaley Bridge

Before Roger stopped working at The International, he moved to the small town of Whaley Bridge in Derbyshire. He wanted away from the city; the air, the hassle at The International from the greed heads and baby gangsters, and the stress which at one point he thrived on, but could ultimately have contributed to his later illness. It's also possible that this move signified a downturn in his general well-being, he may have considered a move to the hills of the Peak District as potentially beneficial to his health. By moving to this small town Roger had seen a gap in the clouds, he was optimistic about getting a small scene going, one where his creative abilities and musical knowledge could be realised, at the same time as getting the rent paid.

Doreen Allen: I remember when he moved to Whaley Bridge he said, "Oh you've got to come out here for the day." I was like, bloody hell where's Whaley Bridge? I couldn't understand why he moved out there.

Dougie James: When it came to the court case (with Gareth Evans and Mathew Cummins) I needed Roger to be a witness. He came to my lawyers' office and he was a great witness, fantastic. But because he was still working for Gareth and Mathew he said he wouldn't go to court and testify. So I said "Roger, don't worry about it", he was living in Whaley Bridge at this time. He got on the train to go home and as soon as he got off at Whaley Bridge I had somebody there with a subpoena and £10, so he had to do it. My man knocked on his door and gave him the paper. In court he was brilliant, one of my best witnesses.

Pete Fulwell: When I finally saw him again he was living out at Whaley Bridge some years later and we went down to The International. He was saying he'd lost the appetite, it wasn't the same as it was at Eric's and he wasn't there all the time. I think he got bored, he didn't hang out at the club. When I worked with him he'd be there from the soundcheck until cashing up at the end of the night and the staff leaving and buzzing off it all. When I saw him he wasn't, he would go down and sit at the bar for a bit, he said "Some nights I don't even go down." So you knew he'd lost the appetite a bit. The Roger I knew just lived for it, he studied the music papers like a betting man studies race form, totally immersed in the whole thing. In love with the idea of putting a show on.

Val Randall: I went to see him at the cottage in Whaley Bridge. He said he'd moved out of Manchester because of his health, nothing of the nature of what happened later was suspected.

Roger Eagle: I couldn't really see myself doing anything else. I mean I'm not a career person, I'm not a worker, you know? I'm not a wage slave, although I would love some wages, now and again. You just do it, you know what I mean? It's like putting your money where your mouth is. I stumbled into promoting the same way I stumbled into DJing, I had no plan, I didn't know what I was doing. But that's how things start you see, that's how things do start.

Judy Williams: I can remember Roger being really enthusiastic about helping Mick Hucknall, the sadness about Mick Hucknall was that Roger made the pathway and introduced him to music which was apart from what he was writing at the time. After all of that, once he'd made it there was an arrogance about him.

I'm concerned because when Roger was really struggling in Whaley Bridge and was short of money, the help that he asked for was not given graciously. I think they did help him get his house, but it wasn't seen as a gift really, he owed them for that.

Pete Dunn: He said to me one of the reasons that he moved to the Peak District was because of the fresh air.

Mick Baker: He smoked 40 fags a day.

Pete Dunn: He had worries and anxieties all the time, he was worried about the air being polluted in Whaley Bridge.

Judy Williams: What he used to talk about when he moved to Whaley Bridge was the fact that he was out in the country. I think he started from a position where it was all going to be very healthy. He'd become preoccupied with those issues and gradually he got to know the area, and he'd go around, then he'd show me all the pollution. He'd point out all the industry going on around, the water's polluted, the air's polluted. I think the tragedy of all that is that he ended up with an appalling cancer, cancer is in his family, his Mother had it I think.

It seems that after years of working for Gareth and Mathew at The International, Roger had finally had enough – his wages were never going to alter and he wasn't his own boss. Plus the court case with Dougie James and Gareth Evans must have helped force his hand and by 1992 he'd left The International behind. Roger's big hope had been his partnership with Zane Branson, somebody who was enthusiastic and with huge potential to create a business more in keeping with Roger's ideas, but for various reasons this wasn't all plain sailing. Over the next couple of years Roger would have many projects on the go, a club night here, a couple of gigs there, nurturing young bands, compiling tapes, putting together records for the Pressure Sounds label and generally trying to keep the wolf from the door in any way he knew how.

Zane Branson: I used to go up to Whaley Bridge on a Wednesday, have a cup of tea with Roger, then go for a walk for a couple of hours up on the hills and around the area. This was always a good time to chat about shows we were putting on and general stuff. At the end the business was becoming difficult because we were losing shows, and Roger was trying to get more shows in but no matter what, the more we tried, the more the shows lost. That was the same for every promoter at the time just about, and we didn't have the financial backing to keep it going.

A contributing factor to Roger and Zane's continuing failure with RTR to secure successful gigs was the popularity of the contemporary dance music scene of the early 90's.

Roger Eagle: The trouble is that half the market is gone that used to be there for bands, at least half of it has gone to dance.

Bill Sykes: As I lived relatively close by, I'd see Roger occasionally. Usually on a Sunday morning sat on his doorstep, reading *The Times*, coffee at hand, some very heavy dub on the turntable, mingling with the American menthol Kools cigarettes being smoked as medication. He'd sometimes call me over "Morning Sykes! Come and have a listen to these tunes I've got from London." He'd say tunes in the way it was said on the TV advert (For the cough sweet Tunes) after the effect of the sweets had enabled the sucker to speak in perfect Queen's English. Something like 'Teyoons'. Of course you didn't turn the Eagle down, he'd take you in the house, make a coffee, "Would you like a cup of hot water?" hand you the spliff, then he'd drop the needle on the deck, leave it for thirty seconds or so at a tremendous volume and say "Who's this Sykes?" Woe betide you if you got it wrong, "Er, is it Tubby, Rog?" He'd say "Go-od", then the next tune would commence "Come on, who's this?" , well it sounds very similar, he wouldn't put Tubby on twice, "Is it Sir Niney?" "No, no! You fool! Its Prince Jammy!" – and onwards my education proceeded.

YESTERDAYS

Brian Smith: He was always trying to get live gigs going, he did Yesterdays at Alderley Edge which was on a Thursday night, starting at 10–10:30. I think the rarities, if you can get them, are the gig lists, probably for the first few weeks he'd have on the Big Town Playboys, The Lawnmower, Kevin Brown – the blues singer from Bath. I don't know if shows 6–12 ever happened, I don't know if it lasted. I went there to see The Big Town Playboys who would always fill a place. But a gig that far out on a Thursday night, and at half past ten, no public transport, even for when it started, never mind when it finished.

Roger Eagle: When I DJ nowadays I always try to play the originals wherever possible, people will come up and say: "Haven't you got such and such a version? Why are you playing this?" and I say "Well this is the original." Somebody said to me recently that 'Little Red Rooster' by Rolling Stones was this great classic record, etcetera etcetera, and I said: "Have you heard the original?", and no, no they hadn't, and it's rather painful because you end up going round the same old circuit.

Tommy Smith: Thursdays was the night Roger put on at Alderley Edge. The very first night I went out with my partner Emma. Our first date was picking up Roger from Whaley Bridge and driving over to Alderley Edge to have a meeting, he thought it was a night I could possibly DJ at. We went over and met up with Dougie James, I think we did something there once, it never really took off.

In an article in *Cut* magazine in 1989, Craig Ferguson described Roger as Entertainments Consultant (along with Zane Branson), irrepressible music enthusiast and quiet man. The writer also mentions Roger's involvement with The Ritz in Manchester, Dingwalls in London and a new roots night in Alderley Edge.

Roger's comments regarding the night in Alderley Edge were:

"For me the music business is a personal business, for a lot of people it obviously isn't - it's just money. The secret is getting the balance right. Sadly, it's a rare thing to find a club run by people who care about, and understand, the music they're putting on stage. That's why the north is different, the great strength of the north of England is the people here - you can't mistreat them.

"There's a genuine interest in the twentieth century as a whole and the music it has produced, people want to trace back the sources, the roots of rock 'n' roll if you like. To me, how music forms is the exciting thing, when one influence meets another and sparks off a third thing. Good music, whatever it is, comes through in the end."

Brian Smith: I ran into him again at the time of The International, didn't he put a Mississippi blues night on with Zane Branson at the Ritz, with Little Milton and ...

Les Hare: Oh yeah with Latimore and Denise Lasalle, yeah I went to that.

Brian Smith: Millie Jackson as well. I think Zane put on Kris Kristofferson at one point.

Roger Eagle: It's all there waiting for you in the music stores, but the problem is there are no radio programs where you can actually hear it, because it's never presented in the correct way. You'll hear a show playing deep blues and you'll end up not listening to it because they're not playing the right stuff.

If you put a blues track up against a dub track and you follow it with a funk track, a soul track, a rock 'n' roll track and a good rockabilly track, and you go back and play something else, a Beefheart track, some good underground stuff. As long as you lock it into a frame that the punter can enjoy you can get it across to people. There's no point in being too specialist or too elitist about it, when I DJ on the radio I always play driving tunes, they're all uptempo, they all have a good groove to them, a good rhythm to them.

Bill Sykes: At one point in the early nineties Roger had his own radio show. It was in Stockport, near Mersey Square, and at the time the station was called KFM Radio. His show was hosted by his alter ego 'Jukebox Johnson' when he did the show he was living in Whaley Bridge and I used to go down with him and carry his records and help him out with the show, finding records and noting catalogue numbers down for the PRS; this was very important to Roger as he knew only too well that some of the performers from the tunes probably needed every small PRS cheque that came their way. His spot was from 5pm to 7pm on a Saturday, his remit, as always, was to play rare and rocking tunes from the 20th Century Jukebox, I think I did it for about a month with him. The shows theme tune was Slim Jenkins' Place by Booker T & the MG's. It used to severely pain him to play the advertising jingles.

I have this memory from one of the shows, Roger had turned me on to early Funkadelic, I really loved that stuff, still do, I wanted the band I was in to sound like them. Anyway it's 5 o'clock on a Saturday afternoon, you can picture the shoppers on their way home from the Merseyway shopping precinct in their cars, or football fans on their way home from Manchester or indeed Edgeley Park, which was just around the corner from the studio, and the first track he puts on to start the show is Funkadelic's 'Free Your Mind and Your Ass Will Follow' in it's entirety, and it's like ten minutes of psychedelic acid mayhem. I just thought what a great move to put that song on at that time of day, to that audience. You couldn't get more subversive than that. That simple act was in the true spirit of the subject matter of the song.

As far as the listeners were concerned it would either drag in the curious, who would maybe want to know who would dare to play this stuff, or people would immediately change stations or turn the radio off. Maybe the people who were financing the radio station and the advertisers would have viewed it slightly differently. When it had finished – and he didn't fade it out, he turned round to me and said live on air "What about that Sykes?", I think I was a bit dumbstruck, I didn't know what to say, then I think he probably said something like "Good evening I'm Jukebox Johnson, and while Bill recovers from that I'll tell you what's in store for the rest of the evening's show." With hindsight I think when he asked me to help him out with the show he wanted somebody to spar with, at the time I didn't really have the confidence.

Speaking about the one person who could be considered a contemporary, here Roger pays tribute to the popular music icon John Peel, while also reflecting on his own motivations when DJing on the radio.

Roger Eagle: He's a great man John Peel, he's a kind and generous man, the only criticism I have of Peel is he plays a lot of demo tapes from all over the place which aren't necessarily that enjoyable. So if I listen to the Peel show I have to wade through loads of stuff to get to something I like. But like I said he's a generous man, he will play that stuff, he's got great taste and he's on the side of the underdog. He enjoys what he does and he worked hard to get himself into that position. I'm the opposite of Peel, I'm a very, very minor figure compared to the mighty Peel. But when I do a radio show I'm trying to hit the ordinary punter who is not specialist and doesn't know anything about what you're doing, but will react to it.

Mick Baker and Pete Dunn were neighbours of Roger when he lived in Whaley Bridge. They got to know him through their mutual love of music. Pete is an aircraft technician and Mick is a trained engineer and mechanic, they both play in bands from the Whaley Bridge area.

Pete Dunn: Roger was already living on Reservoir Road

when I moved there, that was in 1990.

Mick Baker: I moved to Reservoir Road in 1992.

Pete Dunn: Roger always went in The Railway and gambled on the fruit machine.

Mick Baker: He'd spend a pound on half a beer and put £10 in the fruit machine, every now and then he'd venture across the road to The White Hart to try a different fruit machine.

Pete Dunn: We couldn't avoid bumping into each other, I got to know him slowly, I'd occasionally bump into him in the pub. He wasn't an easy bloke to get to know, when he went in The Railway he didn't mix with everybody, he'd very rarely sit down and chat.

Mick Baker: You'd hear the music coming out of his door, he used to leave his door open.

Pete Dunn: I didn't have a clue about his history or who he was.

Mick Baker: No me neither.

Pete Dunn: I didn't realise he was as well known as he was. It wasn't until after he died that I found out he was a pretty famous guy. He was just my grumpy neighbour. When I got to know him properly it was through sitting on my front step on Sunday mornings, hungover, reading the paper. He'd be sat on his step three doors away and he'd say "Alright Dunn?" I'd say "Alright Roger?" then he'd make some wry comment and go back to his paper.

Martin Eagle: My grandmother died from cancer of the colon in January 1940, my mother died from cancer of the colon almost 50 years to the day later on January 14th 1990. My Mother said that if she was in Ireland she wanted to be buried in Ireland. With less than a day to live I said to Mum "we're going to Ireland"

and her eyes lit up. I don't think Roger had ever flown before, in fact I'm sure he hadn't. He flew from Manchester to Dublin, and then from Dublin to Killarney, to this small aerodrome there. It was a day of tremendous storms and a fishing boat had been washed up onto a small island nearby. I drove over to Killarney to meet Roger and it was sort of dusk. He was flying in a small aeroplane known as a Short Sky Van and, as it was approaching, this thing was hardly making any headway flying against the wind, but finally it landed and Roger got out looking rather shaken. In fact the same aeroplane had flipped over on its back at Bristol around the same time. I don't think I told Roger, he was a rather nervous character, for all his size and bravado he could be remarkably timid. My Mother died very early on the Sunday morning.

As Roger neared fifty his awareness of potential money making schemes had improved considerably. Because he'd spent a large part of his life either trying to make a living out of musical projects or helping to kick start somebody else's career, he was aware of what was and what wasn't possible monetarily. He knew what would sell, he knew the mindset of advertising executives, he knew how ruthless record companies were and he was completely aware of how popular music was becoming commodified. The vast history of rock 'n' roll could now be re-activated at any time by a beer or denim jeans TV advertising campaign, which could open up the possibilities of a completely new market for some of the great music of the 20th century.

Roger Eagle: When some advertising executive who has an enormous account, Budweiser for God's sake, with huge amounts of money to spend. It's awesome the power these people have, and they go and pick 'Smokestack Lightning' by Howlin' Wolf, and it took 30 years but there it is on TV.

When you're in the kitchen because the ads are on TV, and

you suddenly hear Howlin' Wolf come bursting out of your TV set – that is what gets through to people, and will tell them about Howlin' Wolf. More than any number of reissues, fan club magazines or clever articles in *The Guardian*. It's when it's on TV and there it is. Because that record is a magic genius record that will stand up forever. It's immortal. That's what I'm saying about immortality. Immortality isn't the rambling highways and byways and opinionated people like myself, immortality is; "Can that record cut it for the public?" And if an American beer company can choose it and put it out there, then it has achieved immortality, and it has. 'Stand By Me' – Ben E King. Suddenly you've got John Lee Hooker becoming the major artist that he always was in the first place because they put him in a frame that's acceptable to the public.

Towards the end of the RTR period, Roger and Zane sometimes differed over the acts that they should put on, this resulted in the setting up of another company which would do similar music based promotions, Blues North West.

Zane Branson: At the end, sometimes Roger wouldn't want to do a show so I would do it myself. I bought over Albert King, a friend of mine from New York helped me put that one on.

Tommy Smith: At the end of it Roger and Zane were working separately, Roger's love for the music overrode the commercial side as always. Roger thought the world and his wife would want to go and see these acts because they were wonderful and full of energy but they didn't you know? Whether it was the fact that their time had come and gone, or the location of the venues was wrong, they couldn't create a buzz.

Zane Branson: We also did the Bodelwyddan Castle gigs; the first one had Snooks Eaglin, Earl King and Bobby Radcliffe. The second one we had Bo Diddley and African Headcharge, that was Roger's idea but it was fantastic, we also had an old New Orleans piano player named Jake something. Also Zachary Richard the zydeco guy, Walter 'Wolfman' Washington and Davy Graham. We put Davy Graham on around dinner time, we had like jambalaya and all this great food there too. We had about 6000 people there that year, it was quite a big thing. We would've continued, there was no trouble with it or anything, it was really well done. Basically the venue was sold, they made it into a holiday camp for retired people and of course they didn't want the kind of thing we were doing. The head of the local area council was a Blues fan and he was trying to help out but in the end they sold to a private company who leased it and made it into a hotel. But the last show was great, the weather was good and we had an interesting line-up. The association and story of Roger and I kind of came to an end here.

Mick Baker: Roger got me to get a coach together to go over to this R&B festival he was putting on in Wales. That was in '92 or '93, eight or nine different artists played. At the festival he came and found me in the crowd and said, "There's somebody I want you to meet" that's when he took me backstage. He marched me into this tent and said "Baker this is Bo – Bo, Baker", he didn't introduce me as Mick, and he didn't call Bo Diddley either. That was in this huge marquee that had nothing in it apart from a few chairs, there was no hospitality or anything just a pink and white tent. Bo Diddley was supposed to be headlining but African Headcharge were so late turning up that they had to go on last. Roger seemed slightly stressed, marching in and out of different areas. It ran until 11 o'clock in the castle grounds, and there were four more acts on in a local nightclub as part of the festival.

Judy Williams: We did crazy things together, we drove all the way to Sellafield for the irony of going to have a look at an environment that was incredibly dangerous. I also remember driving to Lyme Park and watching families playing, and he'd see the hilarity of families ending up in arguments having hoped to go out for a nice day.

THE JODRELL ARMS

Roger Eagle: If I was to run a wonderful venue tomorrow – my dream gig out in the hills, where everybody would have a welcome and a really good time. I'd be putting on all sorts of esoteric, difficult stuff, but at the same time – because the whole thing would be good, the food would be good, people would discover the joys of the music of the twentieth century.

One of Roger's long term plans was to find a country pub with the potential for a scene. His proposal was very simple, after finding a place with potential, eg. a stage and a kitchen, maybe slightly out of the way and past it's prime. The four things that would ensure success were/are:

1. Good down home food, local dishes, stews, soups etc .

2. A good Jukebox, with a well chosen and eclectic selection ...

3. Good beer...

4. Live music...

People will travel miles if these simple requirements are met. The first two are essential and so simple it eludes the majority of prospective entrepreneurs...

For 6 months maybe more Roger found his pub; great transport links, a good chef, and a separate function room with a PA. The jukebox was there, but ownership by the brewery made it difficult to convert it into the 20th century jukebox that would no doubt have proved popular and influential to another generation of seekers and all two minutes walk from his front door. The Jodrell Arms in Whaley Bridge was the last venue in the North-West to benefit from the Eagle treatment, he DJ'd most of the nights he put on there, with local and touring bands such as the Bhundu Boys, even Frank Sidebottom made an appearance. But all to no avail in the end, the woman running the place decided it would be a good idea to do a runner with the week's bar takings, so for Roger it was back to square one… again.

Mick Baker: I remember the opening day, they had a free barbecue on the car park. The pub had been shut for quite a while because they had to take asbestos out it, that cost something in the region of £200,000, the place was riddled with it. It was general knowledge that it was costing a fortune to get rid of the asbestos, the building regulations would have insisted on this. I think Roger helped them to get a late license until 1 o'clock as well, because they had a function room and were serving food.

Pete Dunn: I remember Roger putting gigs on at The Jodrell, I don't remember the name of the woman who was running the place but they converted the function room into a venue, he booked the bands there as well. I remember going down to The Jodrell to see The Bhundu Boys, I was with Mel, I thought they were brilliant, they were doing like African chanting. I think Roger assumed the people in the area were going to be broad-minded.

Penny Henry: I went with Jon Savage to a gig in Whaley Bridge it was The Bhundu Boys. I brought Jon with me because Jon had never, ever met him (Roger), I thought Jon ought to meet him, there was hardly anybody there.

*

Bill Sykes: As Roger settled into the slower life of the Peak District he would often talk about the literature, art and obviously music that inspired him. One of his favourite writers was Hector Hugh Munro, better known as Saki – a British writer who satirised Edwardian society with witty and often macabre short stories. He was intrigued by Charles Bukowski and had a predilection for

1950's science fiction writers such as Isaac Asimov, Ray Bradbury and Alfred Bester. His favourite artist was the overlooked English painter Edward Burra. I remember him being excited about the fact that the Chuck Berry song 'Johnny B. Goode' had been sent out into space with the Voyager I space probe in 1977, along with many different musical styles from around the world to represent the human race. Wherever Roger lived he always had a large photograph on his wall of a very animated Orson Welles, also a photograph of himself with Captain Beefheart, as well as one of himself aged about 22 alongside Bo Diddley, posing with one of Bo's guitars slung over his neck.

Prompted by the onset of commercially available digital technology in the late 1980's, the start of 'house' music – the last original musical genre of the 20th century – signalled the beginning of the end for pop music as an original and ever changing art form. Recycling seems to be standard in the present day.

By 1994, when these interviews took place, Roger had known 30 odd years of the music business in the UK. Studying the politics, the media and the music itself – watching the drama of each era unfurl and able to utilise a critical and all-seeing perspective.

Roger Eagle: None of the contemporary bands I've heard are coming up with anything permanent, they're not cutting a very deep notch. They're doing ok on a surface level, probably selling quite a few tickets and albums. But they're not cutting down deep into the body of it, where you get constantly reissued. Out of what I've heard in recent times I think only Nirvana will be around for a long time in the reissue racks, maybe one or two others.

The thing about about the original R&B and soul and other music, a lot of other music was that it took time to grow. The problem now is that the time span is so short. If a movement starts in London this week, it's in the NME next week being touted as the next big; the week after it's dead because it didn't get a chance to grow.

That's why I feel so sorry for kids today, because they've got such a load of fucking rubbish to look back on in their middle age. Are they gonna be playing all this rave stuff? I don't think they are quite frankly, I suppose they might now and again, but there's very little to get hold of that's really memorable.

Mick Baker: I remember when he was learning to drive, he couldn't get to grips with a manual gearbox so he had to learn in an automatic, a manual gearbox was a bit too challenging for him. It was a red 1600 Montego automatic with oil leaking out of it from every orifice, he regularly drove to Liverpool in that.

Pete Dunn: I asked him to manage our band at one point, it was when we first started Mr Pharmacist. I said, "You know a bit about the music industry, will you manage us?", he said "You'll have to change your direction, you've got to have a gimmick." He wanted us to change the band name to 'Thor of Gog'. He said "If you change your name to 'Thor of Gog' from the Peak District it'll give it a bit of a hook."

Mick Baker: He said to me one time, "Baker, I've got this song I think you should cover" and it was some old R&B song and with what we were doing it just wouldn't have worked.

Pete Dunn: He was keen for us to cover quite a lot of stuff, just going round to his house he'd give you tapes, the majority of stuff he gave me was in the R&B direction, R&B and soul.

Mick Baker: There was one time I had to fix a tap washer for him in his bathroom, it was running constantly and he was hopeless with anything like that. Whatever he thought of me I don't know, but when I'd finished he gave me a huge tumbler of Whiskey as a thank you at 11 o'clock in the morning.

Pete Dunn: I don't think he ever called me Peter once.

Mick Baker: I was definitely always Baker.

Pete Dunn: I don't think he knew my first name.

*

On October 23rd 1992 LaVern Baker played a set at Liverpool's 051 club, it was the first time she had played in Britain. Roger always name checked LaVern as his favourite female singer and it must have been a dream come true to finally be able to promote a show for one of the greatest female rock 'n' roll singers to come out of the 1950's American R&B explosion. Undoubtedly Roger lost money on this gig but to Roger this was not about money – it was about paying respect to the great in music. Tommy Smith helped Roger out again at this gig, these are a few of his recollections.

Tommy Smith: I'll always be thankful that Roger introduced me personally to so many great people, such as Albert King and Bo Diddley, actually one of the most memorable was LaVern Baker. Roger was instrumental in bringing her over from America, and I was asked to go down to London to pick her up from the airport and drive her up to Liverpool, I spent a lot of time with her. There was one occasion that comes to mind in particular, I was carrying LaVern's bags into the Adelphi Hotel in Liverpool. I pushed through the revolving door and stood at the reception desk was Gil Scott-Heron, eating a Mcdonald's. I just felt that I should be introducing these people, these two great figureheads. I could tell she wasn't quite familiar with him but he was in awe of her. They had a short chat, you know, discussing what each other was doing. It was a wonderful moment for me, I couldn't let them walk past one another.

I'm not aware of her coming over to the UK at any other time, I think that was the only time. It should really have been better documented, I think Granada may have filmed her so that may surface one day.

What a great experience it was, I also took her down to Great

Yarmouth where she was playing at a rock 'n' roll weekend, and we had dinner together, I was sat opposite her at the table. I had a small tape recorder with me and asked her if she minded me asking a few questions about Jackie Wilson, she more or less cut it short there, she said "That's all private business."

Brian Rae: One of the last times I worked with him was at a gig with LaVern Baker in Liverpool. She was over here to do a weekender in Hemsby I think. But she was also going to do this one gig in Liverpool that she was going to treat as a rehearsal for the gig down at Hemsby. Me and Roger were the disc jockeys. Roger played things like Elmore James, he always tried to catch people out, he liked a lot of Travis Wammack stuff as well. The gig was supposed to finish at two o'clock and LaVern Baker is still on stage, at three she's still on stage, at twenty to four the management came and pulled the electric on her, she was well upset - she felt she hadn't finished her set, which was quite funny. We thought she was tremendous to be quite honest.

Brian Smith: She was bloody fabulous, and she wasn't really very well but she put a great band together for it. Roger was virtually robbing the slot machines to pay for it, no-one tried to blag a freebie that night.

Bill Sykes: Roger had been looking forward to this gig for years, he always insisted LaVern was his favourite female singer, but he must have been concerned about not breaking even on it. I remember he asked me to go with him to Liverpool to the 051 club to carry his records. He'd recently learned to drive so we jumped in his car and went over to Liverpool. The show was seriously under attended but LaVern put on a great show, she looked great, her voice was strong and her band was tight. After the show LaVern was sat in a roped off VIP area, Roger said to me "Go and talk to her!", but not knowing her back catalogue that well I just said "No, I wouldn't know what to say" but he kept on at me "Go on, go and talk to her!", I really didn't want to make myself look silly but Roger kept on at me "Go and tell her you enjoyed the show!", maybe he saw me as a younger version of himself, so for him more than anything, I went over. After negotiating her minders I asked her permission to sit down and chat, not having thought about it I said "I really enjoyed the show Ms Baker" I think she said "Thank you very much" then I said "Did you start singing in the church ?" to which she replied "We all did honey", I think I made some more small talk, made my excuses and departed.

In 1991 LaVern Baker was inducted into the rock 'n' roll hall of fame, second only to Aretha Franklin, who was inducted in 1987. LaVern died from coronary complications on March 10th 1997.

In an article published on November 12 1992 in *The Independent* entitled 'Introductions necessary', Roger was interviewed by Martin Kelner about his then current projects and thoughts on the music industry past and present.

"It never occurred to me to go into management. I don't have that business look on things, although that's not to say I haven't made money out of some of my projects. People like me are necessary in the music business, otherwise nothing new would ever emerge. The big corporate structures are not built to recognise new talent. Look at Elvis, The Beatles, punk rock - all rejected initially by the majors."

Martin Eagle: I went to see Roger in 1993 from here when he was living in Whaley Bridge, he picked me up. I stayed with Roger for three or four days and after the third day we were beginning to get on one another's nerves. We'd planned to visit the Derwent Valley and Roger wouldn't get up. We finally managed to get out at 11 o'clock in the morning, it was a beautiful November morning and by the time we got there, there was nowhere to park, I think we ended up not speaking to each other and having a pub lunch somewhere near Mam Tor. We were not on each other's wavelength at all, I went back the following day. I think Roger could be quite bombastic at times, he'd talk all over people, but he could be sensitive too. I said goodbye to Roger in Whaley Bridge and I flew back here to Ireland.

Bill Sykes: On occasion Roger would come up with the most inspired ideas, not always particularly practical but brilliant all the same. One of these was to have a classic Zen style garden with raked gravel, two or three large boulders carefully placed, maybe a couple of trees, a willow or a Japanese Maple whose leaves dramatically reflect the seasons with iridescent colours throughout the year. I seem to recall this garden would have only one seat, maybe something similar to a park bench.

But the killer detail that would set this garden apart would be as soon as you walked into this refined area of serenity your form would break a light sensor and set off the most incredible sound system. A thunderous crash of spring reverb, a roll on tight rotor toms and the bass kicks in, more to your solar plexus than your ears, the flying cymbals bounce across the stereo sound spectrum and the rimshot snare drum splinters into increasingly smaller fragments via the Roland Space Echo. The music you are hearing is that of the Dub master himself King Tubby, perhaps one of the greatest unsung musical talents of the 20th Century, a supreme innovator... the music is pure sound; minimal, meditational and all on just four tracks. This music is transcendental, enlightenment can be attained with this music.

Not quite the meditational silence required by traditional Zen practice but then again as Zen master Dogen Zenji said "Practice all that is good" and really – King Tubby is very good!

THE GREAT KING TUBBY
DUB MASTER, ZEN MASTER

Geoff Davis: I remember he came round to see me in the early mid 90's when I was on my arse financially, I was completely broke, and he knew this Roger. He turned up and said, "Right Geoffrey I've come to help you with your financial situation, let's have a look at your Reggae 12 inches."

He's saying "This stuff's wasted on you" he's pulling them off the shelves, I only let him have so many. As soon as he went out of the door I thought, you're gonna regret that. I only got £40, but it was a lot of money to me at the time. He took loads of stuff, there was some I thought 'I'm not parting with that'.

Brian Jackson: Anything you'd tell Roger about anything you produced, if you said to him it's a King Tubby – he'd say "Oh you need the Jamaican pressing with the extra tracks on it!" He said that to me when 'Heart Of The Congos' came out. He said "Oh that's the English pressing, you need the Jamaican one", he was right though, I got it.

Roger liked deflating people, it's like Steve Barker said on his tribute show he and I did, Roger was a very righteous man, you couldn't tell him very much, in fact you couldn't tell him anything. He knew his stuff, and he was usually right. He wasn't exactly the most diplomatic or tactful of people.

From an interview with the author in the spring of 1994, Roger speaks about having his beloved record collection stolen.

Roger Eagle: I got burned and burnt myself out at the age of 47, living the rest of my days in my dotage in the countryside, so as not to be burgled too often. Now it all depends how many people I kill next time I have a burglary Bill, it depends how many people are prepared to sort of allow me to shoot whole families that might be under vague suspicion.

I had them nicked three times, if you include Boxhead ripping off a load of records from the DJ booth, some of which were mine. I got burgled twice in Sefton Park in Liverpool. At The International I told Joe Strong over and over again, I had a load of twelves and

I said they'll get robbed, and they did get robbed, and I was really pissed off with him. They were early Sleng Teng things, and I was pissed off about that because he just kept leaving them lying about. It's just so obvious. But I'm planning on DATting them up; and I've got rid of a lot of stuff. I'll DAT them up and bury them in the bank.

Mick Baker: I can remember you'd walk in his front door and there was always a big pile of CD's stacked on the floor. That was the stuff he'd put aside to sell. He used to go to King Bee Records in Chorlton to sell his stuff, he'd always ask if you wanted any of the CD's he was selling. When he was skint he'd go there every week, a lot of the time hawking his precious vinyl. He'd come round and borrow stuff off us, you know teabags and stuff and he'd always have a tape.

Pete Dunn: He was a very thoughtful bloke, he'd work out what music you were into and tailor a tape to suit you.

Brian Smith: The last actual gig that he put on that I went to was an R&B singer called Tiger Lil, her name was Ayesha Khan, she did all Ruth Brown stuff and Roger put her on at a pub on Southport sea front. We went to the gig and there was about 20 people in and when they'd all come out at the end I'm stood on Southport front and you know how you get these little revelations. It was starting to rain and I turned to my friend Dave and said, "Do you realise I'm 53 years of age, got a wife and kids at home, it's 2 o'clock on a Tuesday morning in November and I'm getting pissed on?" Then he says "all because Roger Eagle said so" and that was it you know, Roger said come so we did.

Norman Killon: Funnily enough after Eric's and later The International he was doing Southport, Penny and I went four or five times. He had this night there in a hotel, it was a Roy Adams connection. He was playing his first love, which was rock 'n' roll and black R&B. He was bringing bands up from London, really good, they didn't play the bog standard 'Be Bop a Lula' stuff. He got Brian Rae doing Northern Soul in an upstairs room on the same night, there would be about 4 people in the Northern Soul room and less than a hundred downstairs.

Brian Jackson: I think the last gig I did with Roger would have been about 94/95 here in Colne. I asked him to do it because he'd been here and done a few gigs in the past. He'd done a gig for Hartley's Hospice and Friends Of The Earth and Greenpeace at the Union Hotel in Colne, as well as the Colne bowling club.

This gig was at a little place called the 'Rock Coven', it was called the coven because it's near Pendle. A guy called Frank was running this club; it was on two floors, a ground and an upper floor. It was upstairs where the bands played. It wasn't great but it had a late license.

Around this time we'd realised that the motorway that was threatening the town wasn't going to come through. So Friends Of The Earth and their helpers had succeeded. So I decided to organise a little celebration, the idea wasn't to make money, it was just to draw even and have a little party. I managed to persuade Pendle council to grant an all night licence, I don't know how I did it. I phoned Roger as well as a couple of other DJ's. I said to Roger, "We've finally beaten that road, we're having a little party, do you fancy coming up? I can only really pay expenses, it's just a private thing."

So he did, he came up, and to me it was a great honour to have Roger there. There's a few things I remember, I showed him the decks, he actually spoke to people over the microphone a couple of times which was unusual for him. At one point he said, "I understand that this is a special occasion, so this calls for a very special disco", and he immediately put an obscure Captain Beefheart track on. I thought, here we go, we're off! All the heads in the audience thought this was fantastic, after this he played some nice rockabilly and then some Studio One stuff. It was Roger doing his thing, he did two sets.

The sad thing was, and it didn't mean much to me at the time, it all came back to me later when I realised how ill he was. He said he was suffering from very bad indigestion and I gave him some peppermints. I knew his diet was crap and he ate too many curries.

*

Bill Sykes: By 1996 I'd moved to London. One evening Roger phoned me to tell me that he'd been diagnosed with cancer of the oesophagus, he'd also asked me if there was anything in his record collection I would like when he went. This really upset me and I said that no I didn't want any of his records. I travelled to Whaley Bridge the next day and went to see him, he was with Ron Taylor, Ron was helping him out with arrangements regarding moving to Stepping Hill hospital, and ultimately his later move to North Wales. He explained that the operation only had a 50/50 chance of success but he seemed in relatively good spirits. At the time I didn't see it, but regarding his record collection he wanted them to go to someone who'd play them, enjoy them, experience them and most of all let other people experience them.

Judy Williams: I found somebody for him to deal with his legal matters. The reason I helped him over the legal side of things, and got him hopefully, the right person, was because of how his condition had been missed. It was appallingly missed. He very clearly had symptoms that were extremely concerning and they were totally overlooked, he was diagnosed with anxiety. He couldn't swallow, his food was coming back and he was extremely distressed about it. I think really I'm a person who listens to people, I'm a person who sorts things out for people when they have their rights declined.

Val Randall: There were these two occasions that I hadn't heard from him for a long, long time, and I just knew there was something wrong, so I rang. He said, "How did you know? I've had the worst dental problems I've ever had in my life" and he proceeded to tell me all about that, because he had no time for doctors. That was the first strange thing that happened. Then I was on holiday in Durham and I just knew there was something wrong and I don't know why.

So I rang him when I got back, he said, "Oh hi, are you ringing because you've heard the radio?"

I went "What?"

He said, "So you've not heard the news on the radio?"

I went "No, what news?"

He said, "Oh I've got cancer."

I went, "No, I'm ringing because I was convinced there was something wrong."

He said, "I'm just having a bit of a clear out, I'm having a fire in the back yard."

I went, "Right", you know as you do.

Judy Williams: He did very well though in terms of the prognosis of such a cancer, he was very determined really. I thought the great sadness was of him not being able to eat, which had been one of his great joys in life. Every time I went to The International, after the show had finished, we'd always go to Rusholme, he'd always end his evening with a curry.

Pete Dunn: I went to see Roger in Stepping Hill hospital a couple of times. It was bizarre the way he announced his illness. He just came round one day, knocked on the door and gave me a big bowl of chicken chasseur that he'd made, he couldn't eat it. He said "Here you are Dunn, you can have this I can't eat it". I said "Why?" He said "I've got stomach cancer", that was it, he said "I'm going into hospital next week", that was his way of telling me something was wrong with him. When he was in hospital Jenny Downs and myself went to see him, he seemed quite cheerful, he looked like he was going to be alright. Not long after this he moved to Wales and a couple of years later he died.

Judy Williams: It was very sad, I was with him when he went down to theatre. The operation was at Wythenshawe, he was looked after at Stepping Hill then he was moved to Wythenshawe. He didn't want anybody else to see him in the state he was in. So I was with him when they took him down to theatre, I was also with him until they went into the sterile environment, and I was there when he came out. He wanted somebody there, but he didn't want people to see him in the condition he was in. They put him on a ward in the old part of Wythenshawe hospital, at the back, he was in a terrible state. They weren't monitoring the effects of the morphine and he was hallucinating and very paranoid. The morphine was on a drip but they weren't recognising he was in a paranoid state, so instead of understanding that plus the fear of what he'd just come through, they were dismissing him as difficult and agitated, they hadn't even picked up that he was hallucinating.

I think that I was somebody who, having worked in the NHS, understood the dynamics of it, and I was one of the people who could say "I want to speak to you, no I don't want to speak to you, now I want you to bring me this person, and I don't want this to happen to him. Go and get an X-ray machine and you X-ray him as he is now." Ron Taylor always laughs, he calls me the Rottweiller, it's hideous, but I do understand what he means. She'll go and sort it out.

Martin Eagle: The next time I saw him was at Wythenshawe hospital in Manchester, I was absolutely shocked at seeing this human skeleton in the hospital and that was within three years. Again he asked me for money. He said "Have you got any money you can let me have?" not borrow, have. So I gave him 4 or 500 pounds, then I went away; the whole thing was a bit sort of weird. I thought "Gosh, this shouldn't be". I took him in some CD's, my sort of halfway between classical and his sort of music. One was the composer Ibert, rather jolly stuff. I bought him that and some other things to listen to, I don't think he bothered to listen to them. I went over for the day and came back in the evening.

Judy Williams: When they discharged him from the hospital and he finally came home they hadn't got any of the aftercare sorted out, I was on the phone to the local authority and health services and by the time I'd finished everything was in place. I don't have a gentle style, I have an extremely direct and abrupt style.

Val Randall: After that he was still setting up the compensation case, he said "I won't benefit from it, but other people coming after me might" because of the negligence.

Jayne Casey: When he was ill we met up and talked a lot and that was kind of interesting. This was when he was living somewhere outside of Manchester. It was before he moved to Wales, and I used to go over and meet him in Manchester and we'd have a coffee. He'd got over the worst of the operations and he was just on his way. I spent quite a bit of time with him over that period, I had some really interesting reflective talks with him. Where he'd realised he'd been depressed all his life and he'd realised because he'd had this near death experience.

Over that period I got a different insight into him, as he was getting insights into himself really. Because his life had moved really fast and he wasn't a guy that was born with a silver spoon, he had to make a living. So he had to respond really quickly, so with a situation like Eric's he didn't have time to let it sink in. He couldn't deal with the disappointment of it, he just had to keep going, you know keep driving. He did a lot without having the time to understand it and the depression had become a kind of grey filter in his life. Over the years he'd not had time to stop and process it. He didn't get the recognition he deserved, if he'd got that, if he'd got the radio show etcetera it would have helped restore his personal pride. That scared him at the end of his life.

Judy Williams: When he'd had his op I'd also had a very serious neck injury and I'd ended up with my neck being fused and plated and what have you. We'd do ridiculous things together, y'know he was post-op, major hopeful recovering from his cancer and also very delicate and there was I with this fused and plated neck. His idea was that we should go and row on a lake in Wales, he said, "I know a great place to go Judy", so we did. I know we were mad in some respects to do that but it was something about living really.

11 - Llanfairfechan

Doreen Allen: When he went to Wales I remember him ringing me up and saying, "I want to move near to the Menai Bridge". I think he always thought I still worked for him, he thought of me as his personal secretary.

Dave Prosser: Ron mentioned that he was coming to Bangor, and I'd heard about him through Ron. I think we met one afternoon at Ron's. Ron invited him to come to Bangor because it would be a better environment for him.

Ron Taylor: He seemed to be alone a lot, I thought if we could get him to move down here we could keep an eye on him. At first he was ill, he wasn't desperately ill, but he needed to be looked after. As much as anything I felt he needed moral support, he seemed a bit isolated where he was.

Dave Prosser: I'll be honest with you, I don't think he regretted for one second coming here.

Ron Taylor: He seemed very down and also worried about his physical condition, here he'd be with people that cared about him, with a bit of social life. He never called me Taylor.

Dave Prosser: He did occasionally call me Prosser in an endearing way and it wasn't very often.

Ron Taylor: He was familiar with Dave in a way that he wasn't with me. Dave lived with him for all that time and went through a lot with him. Out of all of us it must have been emotionally hardest on Dave because he was there 24-7.

Dave Prosser: Honestly, and this is the truth, I didn't feel like that, I felt quite privileged that he trusted me enough to let me do that.

Ron Taylor: He was such a private person.

Dave Prosser: To be honest I think he liked having me around as a friend, and I was there to do things for him and I didn't mind in any way whatsoever, and it was the business. He never said to me "I want to be left alone" well maybe once when he was really knackered, it was all very laid back to be honest.

Ron Taylor: About the privacy thing, at the end he was morphined up to the eyeballs because he was in a lot of pain. He said to me once, "A lot of the time I don't know what's real and what's not" he was drifting in and out you know?

CD's

Dave Prosser: There was never a time that I remember thinking he's off his head, he's not in the land of the living kind of thing. I used to live in the lounge, it was my bedroom. So when he was taking morphine he would go to his room and he would instruct me on what needed doing, he'd say I'm going away for two hours. He used to leave me making bootleg CD's for him or something. The process was quite technical, after he'd made the DAT, we'd use the CDR to make copies. So while he was asleep I'd record six Burning Spear bootleg CD's and we'd have a little stock to flog off to people.

Ron Taylor: When he was bootlegging those CD's at first there was a moral dilemma over it, because nobody was getting any royalties. He had a feeling that he was ripping the artists off or something.

I said, "Roger, no, you've put your time in and you've done the right thing by this music. Now in your time of need you shouldn't feel guilty about making some money out of it, you've done so much to promote this music, you've bought these artists over here and they've had a fair crack of the whip, you don't owe anybody anything in this business."

Dave Prosser: I don't think it was about the money, to me the money was a healthy little sideline, money wasn't the reason he was doing it.

Ron Taylor: It was about getting the music out there.

Dave Prosser: Exactly, getting the music to the people.

Ron Taylor: Dave used to do the artwork for the CD's and the track listings and stuff, he was so fussy about it and rightly so, it wasn't just about sticking a bit of paper in the CD box, it was a properly put together artefact.

Dave Prosser: They were nicely produced with labels.

Brian Rae: When he moved to North Wales I spent many a night with him, I used to find things in his collection that he'd either forgotten or whatever. I found a brilliant album called 'Tangerine' by Percy Mayfield, I'd only heard his stuff prior to 'Tangerine', I didn't realise he'd done this mid-60's album, I've never been able to find the album, although I did find a few singles off it. There were one or two really good dance tracks on it that you could do as 'Northern' things you know? That's the sort of thing he would have in his collection.

Pete Fulwell: When I last saw him, which was when he'd moved to Wales, he said it was only a couple of weeks earlier that he'd finally conceded that Eric's was a punk club, because it wasn't what we'd set out to do at all and when you look at what we put on most of it wasn't punk. But punk came up and overwhelmed everything around, and the perception now is that it was a punk club. So for all of us really it was a kind of failure, because that wasn't what we set out to do. We'd originally set out to make the club more eclectic, and that's what we did, that's what was on. It's one of the reasons why the memory lingers because there were so many different people from so many genre interests who saw the club as part of their lives. He said he grudgingly admitted it, we both knew what he meant. It was a kind of failure.

Martin Eagle: The next I heard of him was that he'd moved to near Bangor and he was living in this flat. When I went to visit him there he came to pick me up at Hollyhead and drove me back in this car that the Simply Red chap had given him, it was a greyish Ford, Roger was delighted with it. But at this time he had a difference in his outlook; I was shocked to see him looking so thin. While I was there Roger drove me all over the place because he wanted me to buy a house on the Lleyn peninsular and we looked at several houses. But because at the end of the day we hadn't bought a house, he got really fed up and was treating me as a complete stranger and that was weird. On the last evening that I saw him I took him and his friend, a male friend, out to Capel Curig for a meal. When we got back Roger thought it would be rather nice if we went to a pub where there was lots of loud, live music, which I'm afraid is not my sort of thing. It was loud, almost a physical thing, by about half ten, eleven I had to leave. That was more or less the last time I saw Roger, because the following morning I was up early, I had to go to the station.

Ron Taylor: I went with him once or twice to this high powered lawyer in Manchester and I think it was decided that negligence couldn't be proven, so he didn't get anything out of that.

Tommy Smith: The last time I saw him he came in the shop, he'd put some of his tunes onto CD. It wasn't good to see him looking like that, I knew him as this larger than life, jolly, rambunctious figure and he'd turned into this frail person whose trousers didn't fit him. You could see you were looking at someone

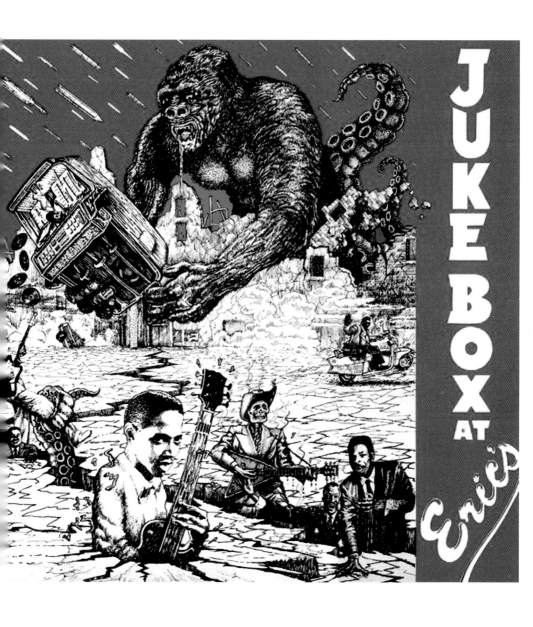

Jukebox at Eric's LP sleeve. Released in 1980 on the Crackin' Up label. Ostensibly a collection of extremely rare rockabilly tunes put together by Roger and Steve Hardstaff. Initially intended as the first in a series of many, the master tapes to this album were placed on Roger's coffin as he was interred - see page 226
Artwork by Steve Hardstaff.

Roger at the Lord Buckley restaurant. See page 228.

Roger with partner Maria and friends at the Lord Buckley restaurant, Clifton, nr Bristol, c. 1983. Both photos John Eagle.

Second left Nico, Alan Wise and Roger Eagle prior to Roger's promoting tenure at Manchester's International venue. c1985 - Photo Stephen Hopkins

(Left) Allan Frost at the International - Roger's chauffeur for the best part of 30 years.
(Above) Dougie James and Gareth Evans, who along with Matthew Cummins were the original co-owners of Manchester's International venue. - both photos John Eagle c1985

Roger at The International with unknown DJ's c1985

Roger at The International decks with unknown DJ. c1985 - both photos John Eagle

Roger with close friend Bruce Mitchell at The International c1985. Photo John Eagle.

Steve Barker, Lee 'Scratch' Perry and Roger Eagle at Radio Lancashire, recording Steve's 'On The Wire
radio show. - Photo Steve Barker

Roger with the author
Probe records Liverpe
c.199
Photo Norman Kil

Doreen Allen with Roger, recuperating in North Wales - Photo Martin Eagle

GOLDMINE RECORDS MANCHESTER PRESENT

soultime
4 SOCIAL
the R'n'B special

FEATURING NORTHERN SOUL ANTHEMS, R'N'B CLASSICS, CROSSOVER GEMS AND DEEP SOUL STIRRERS

SOMETHING FOR THE DANCEFLOOR AND THE CONNOISSEUR

th host dj TOM SMITH

is legendary first Twisted Wheel dj

OGER EAGLE

s guest spot from MIKE WARBURTON

turing rare and classic

's r-n-b and soul

SATURDAY 31ST JANUARY

THE MITRE HOTEL CATEATON STREET MANCHESTER 9PM-1AM

admission £3.00 on the night or tickets £2.50 from goldmine records, shambles square manchester

Poster for Roger's last DJ appearance at the Mitre Hotel, Manchester.

Roger's headstone in Bangor crematorium, the only one with red lettering.

who was close to death, it was uncomfortable for me to look at him.

Norman Killon: The last time I saw Roger was I think at a night Mike Warburton had put on. They were doing this Northern soul, rhythm & blues night in some pub, I think it became The Hideway. He played some records, he was really stick thin, but he was still saying "You must listen to this! You must listen to this!". It was at the Mitre hotel in the city centre, then I rang him a few times afterwards.

Tommy Smith: I was the person that put his last DJing gig on. I decided to get him on and get him to DJ there. The night was called 'Soultime Social' and it was at the Mitre hotel (31st January 1998). It was the precursor to what became The Hideway Club at The Twisted Wheel on Whitworth Street in Manchester, it celebrates the music Roger was playing at the original Twisted Wheel club. His work is being carried on in detail there every month.

Val Randall: Brian Smith sent me a photo of Roger, he sent me the last photo he ever took of him from the Band On The Wall in Manchester from the February before he died. He's all wasted but you can see in his eyes, he hated having his photo taken, his eyes are burning away saying 'Fuck off! Don't you dare take a picture of me'. Brian said he was cross, but he allowed it to be taken. When I look at the photo it makes me sad, in the sense that he's so ill, but in another way I love it because it's all still there in the eyes, he's not having any of it.

Brian Rae: He did a gig in Chester about a year or so before he died, I think he did two or three gigs in Chester and on the first one he invited me along and we got there for about 8 o'clock. There was no-one there at that time, just the bar staff. He was playing records and as soon as he spotted me he's quizzing me on the songs he's playing, "What's this one? What's that one?" I said to him, "It's years since I heard some of this stuff" he said "Forget all about that 'Northern' stuff, listen to some proper stuff" and he's having a go at me, and I looked round and the place is full now and he's still having a go at me.

Ron Taylor: I've got a photograph somewhere of him DJing at the Waterloo in Bangor with a tune in his hand.

Dave Prosser: We did a gig in Caernarvon, at least one, Owen from Cob Records organised it. It was at The Paradox, it was a great night, we did an R&B and blues set there. I played the tunes and he said what was to be played. It was really good fun. The way he saw me in a way was he was training me to help him carry on. I was perhaps his technician shall we say, he wanted me to learn as much as I could quickly. To Roger there was no such thing as Northern Soul, it was a load of bollocks.

Mark Thomas: In his later years when he moved back to North Wales I was working on one of the local newspapers and I was talking to him round at Ron's place and we came up with the idea of doing a regular column in the paper. It was basically a column about rare rock 'n' roll and rare soul.

*

Bill Sykes: I went to visit Roger in Llanfairfechan in 1998, it would be the last time I would see him. I travelled up on the train from London and he came to meet me in his car at Bangor station. Somehow, possibly because he had a different car, we seemed to miss each other. We eventually met up, a simple mistake, but he was extremely worried, his concern I think was a measure of the man. We spent time with Jillian Cowie travelling around the Lleyn peninsular and the hills around the Bangor area. He had a small flat over looking the sea and we also spent time listening to tunes – quite a bit of reggae. I remember his favourite tune from the time was 'Moonlight Bay' by the Champs. One evening I suggested we go to the local pub, Roger struggled to walk the short distance but he was determined to make it, he ordered a half pint of bitter but found that he couldn't drink it. I offered to walk back to the flat with him but he didn't want that, he left me to it and walked home. It was sad and it made me realise how ill he was.

The next day sat in his front room he showed me his word processor and said"You should get yourself one of these" and he passed me a page that he'd written to look at. It was well written and quite amusing. From what I remembered from when I had interviewed him in 1994, he said the book was going to be semi-autobiographical – stories connected to his time DJing and his experience of the dawn of rock 'n' roll. I seem to remember he was toying with the idea of calling the book 'Smoke and Mirrors'.

Dave Prosser: I don't know where it went, he had a small word processor and there were parts of the book in there but he didn't want me to look at it.

Ron Taylor: I never saw it either, in all his stuff after he died there was no sign of any manuscript.

Dave Prosser: It was all in the processor's memory as far as I'm aware. When I was with him he kept talking about the book but he never had the energy. To be honest it was about eating rather than hard work, I don't think he had the energy.

Ron Taylor: He did say to me he was struggling with it, kind of half to do with energy and half to do with writer's block kind of thing because his head was filled with what was happening to him.

Dave Prosser: What I remember him saying about the book was he was unsure about how to go about writing it. I got the impression it was definitely about him, if you listen to his tapes he used to make I think they were a great insight into his personality.

He used to make me play 'Moonlight Bay' virtually every night for him, before he went to bed sort of thing. There was a short period where he really got into that tune.

Ron Taylor: Music can be like that, sometimes you've got to play certain things everyday until you've got it into your system.

Dave Prosser: I remember one time Roger made me drive up to Manchester on a New Year's Eve, I said, "Ok, on condition that we get back at a reasonable time, like 8 o'clock so I can go out with my mates." He said "Oh yeah, you'll be fine." I'm not sure what we did in the afternoon, but early evening we'd done some business in Manchester and on the way back we went to pick up a record deck that was meant to be the bollocks of record decks. I saw it and I thought what a heap of shite. It was really old and it had counter weights and all this kind of stuff on it, it looked 70's maybe 60's. When we saw it he said "We're buying this." I actually thought the guy was charging too much for it, the guy was saying "You won't get better than this." It may have been Dave Lunt. I remember looking at it and thinking if it's got all these counter weights on it, and we're moving it we'll never get it to work again.

Anyway on the way home something happened and we got lost and we didn't get back until virtually midnight and I was fuming with Roger. He only had a few weeks to live, anyway I dropped him off, put him to bed and I said "Do you mind if I go out partying?" he said "No not at all, you deserve it – it's the only time you'll deserve anything in your life." He said "Don't worry Dave, I'm just gonna do a load of drugs and go straight to bed, just shut me in my room." It was just strange driving this car in the dark with Roger, with this silly little record deck in the back, on New Year's Eve. I thought to myself 'I wouldn't do this for anyone else on earth'.

But do you know what? He managed to get the deck working, but it did have some peculiarity, on 45's it wouldn't play up towards the end, so we couldn't record the whole of a 45. But he was quite happy with that, he said "It's so close to the end, I'll just fade it out". I wasn't very happy you know? You've bought this deck and paid a lot of money for it, the guy ripped us off and you can't even hear the end of the tune, but he was quite philosophical about it, it was funny.

Ron Taylor: Unfortunately towards the end I think he sold some of his best tunes, he needed the money.

Val Randall: I remember saying to him on the phone when he was dying, before he lost his voice, "You used to scare the crap out of me sometimes", he said, "Well let's face it Val, somebody had to, it had to be me didn't it?"

Steve Hardstaff: Apparently he was still buying box sets right up until the end. I went to see him about three weeks before he died. Geoff and I went over to his little house in Wales and he was still doing compilations and writing pieces for the local newspaper. It was shocking because he was so weak. But he was still enthusiastic, it was still "Steve listen to this!", I was thinking "how do you cope?"

Geoff Davis: I went to see him in Llanfairfechan a few months before he died, I think I went twice, I went with Steve Hardstaff and I went on my own. I bought a dub compilation on CDR off him, and do you know I lent it to somebody, I can't remember who it was.

Dave Prosser: Smoking, he wouldn't give up smoking right until the end. I went to see him with this guy called Chaz who was his carer, whom he would have to go and visit, he was from the hospital. I remember Roger telling me that he'd been to see this guy Chaz and he'd said to Roger "You're silly not to stop smoking" he reckoned Roger would live longer. I had a go at him about it and he said "Listen, the damage has been done and the truth is it's one of the only joys I have left." He was also very particular about his ganja. I used to have to go and search out black for him. It was strange because I'd stopped smoking draw years before. I think because we'd had chats about ganja making your hearing better, and helping you appreciate music more, but I totally disagree with that.

Judy Williams: I think he really wanted someone to carry on the legacy, I think he wanted someone to carry on Roger Eagle, not to be Roger Eagle but to carry on the knowledge, he dedicated his life to it, it was the blood in him really.

Dave Prosser: Even when he was really ill, the energy he got when I made enquiries about certain tunes, "What's this?" sort of thing, it was just phenomenal. I don't know if Ronnie's aware of this but he used to make me do homework. He used to write down questions for me and I'd have to answer them. Mine wasn't just about reggae music it was about everything, it was rock 'n' roll, everything, it was hard do you know what I mean? I did well you know? 18 out of 20, and I used to be shit scared, it was like "Oh no it's homework tonight!" it's true, oh it was funny.

Ron Taylor: I can verify that, he did used to get given homework.

Judy Williams: When I last saw him he couldn't get out of bed and it was at that time that he was doing the lessons and tests with Dave Prosser, and he asked me what I wanted of his, and I just really didn't know. I left it to him to decide because he knew what was right for me. He left me the most lovely gift really, it was 'Live at the Apollo', Otis Redding with Rufus Thomas and Ben E King, and it's signed, not by Otis Redding but by nearly all the others, and it's a lovely gift.

'Saturday Night At The Apollo' was recorded on 16th November 1963 at the Apollo Theatre, Harlem, New York City.

Appearing on the record are Ben E King, The Coasters, Doris Troy, Otis Redding, Rufus Thomas, The Falcons, Wilson Pickett and Eddie Floyd.

Judy Williams: He left me what I would really appreciate and that was the music that I couldn't describe to him but he worked it out.

Dave Prosser:He died a few hours after I left him. Like Ronnie mentioned about his dignity, I didn't quite know what to do, because... I took him to the hospital supposedly for another blood transfusion, but we were both aware that this wasn't good news at all. He was lying in this sit up bed and we looked at each other, I don't know what it was but I knew that was going to be the last time I was going to see him alive, and he knew that as well. There was something in his eyes that said that to me.

Ron Taylor: Resignation.

Dave Prosser: Yes. I felt quite bad because I don't think he particularly wanted me there, which I didn't mind, I respected that. But also the authoritarian nature of the hospital, they were kind of barring me from even having a choice. I think what they kind of said was "You'll see him later" we both knew damn well that I wouldn't be seeing him later. It wasn't really until we actually got into the hospital and actually started putting him into the room that I realised this guy is not coming out of this room. So I just wanted to make sure that I was doing everything I could for him.

Ron Taylor: For his tombstone, we talked about it before he died, towards the end he knew what was happening and he told me what he wanted on it. You know how he always wore red and black? That was his thing. Well I had to get special permission from the cemetery because he wanted a black stone with red lettering. It's like Hammer horror.

Roger Eagle passed away in Bangor Hospital on May 4th, 1999.

Epilogue - Roger's Legacy

"I'm thrilled to bits that I was alive in this century, I've seen most of the major artists of the century, obviously since the fifties. It has been a phenomenal century really, but it's over now, in fact musically the 20th century finished in about '77."

ROGER EAGLE

Bill Drummond: I know there's a whole generation of people in Liverpool who had a chance to do stuff that wouldn't have done anything if it wasn't for what Roger had bought or made available.

Steve Hopkins: The important thing about Roger is how he influenced a whole generation of Manchester musicians, he influenced their taste and was responsible for educating them.

Bernie Connor: I've been a DJ all my life, when my mates were in bands I couldn't see the point in it. I wanted to be a DJ I wanted to play records, I picked that up from Roger. Being a DJ is much more fun, it saves a lot of heartache and you don't have to sign to a major record label. It's that pioneering spirit and it's not just me, I know shitloads of people who got into that pioneering thing because of Roger.

Pete Burns: Roger Eagle just decided I should be in a group because I dressed up freaky.

Judy Williams: He was always very clear that he wanted to give people something good, that they could enjoy and that would be safe, and whilst he could look at the risque side of the music world, like what went on and what young people got up to, he was very clear about things being safe and enjoyable.

John Robb: There would be no Manchester music scene without Roger Eagle.

Henry Priestman: He was very influential in turning me on to music I wouldn't otherwise have heard.

Steve Hardstaff: He's an unsung hero of rock 'n' roll, he was big enough to get a decent obituary in *The Guardian* and that was because the people that knew him pushed on that.

Zane Branson: It's remarkable, if you're a music fan you can't not appreciate what Roger did.

Brian Rae: To me he was my mentor.

Val Randall: The music and entertaining were very important to Roger as well as educating people, he was relentless, he'd pin you down. At the cost of his own health, at the cost of his own career, what he could have been and could have done. He was one of the most intelligent men I've ever known.

Ron Taylor: There's not many days when I don't think about Roger Eagle one way or another, I'm not saying I sit there dwelling or anything, he'll pass through my head, picking a tune up. It seems strange that he's been dead as long as he has. In my own personal way I've kept him alive in my head through the music, he was it and it was him, and while that's there...

CP Lee: Up until his dying day he educated people in music, he literally would say, "Right, sit down!" he'd sit you in a chair and say "Now listen to this!". To Roger it wasn't just about music, it was a way of life, a massive undertaking. He was a very kind bloke, but the kindness of Roger was his university of music.

Mick Hucknall: 'Farther Up The Road' was the first song I heard by Bobby Bland. I heard this song in Liverpool in a club called Eric's and the manager of the club was a guy called Roger

Eagle who was a huge Bobby Bland fan and he in fact managed my first band The Frantic Elevators for two years. Roger was probably my biggest musical mentor and I discovered a lot of music through Roger.

Tony Wilson: The origin of Factory Records is a falling out over the format of this Manchester/Liverpool collaboration. Who knows, if Roger Eagle hadn't rung me at home saying will you do it (Work as A&R man for Roger's record label – Eric's Factory), I might have been just a TV presenter.

I think Roger represents something very odd which is a connection between the two cities, normally everybody's story is about the disconnections, and I'm probably one of the prime symbols of the disconnection because I'm a Manchester lad.

Jayne Casey: The teaching side of things was very important to Roger and he continued that until his dying day. It was a big part of who Roger was. There was Roger the promoter and Roger the teacher and not everybody got to know Roger the teacher. You were privileged if you sat at the teacher's feet, I always felt privileged.

Pete Fulwell: If anything that's what I remember him most for, the passion and the wanting to educate people.

Martin Dempsey: In his own way, to me he was more influential than the likes of John Peel.

Mike Badger: If you're a music lover you don't covet music, if you do you're not a real music lover. Because you want to spread the joy and pass on the knowledge, that was very much what Roger Eagle was about.

Roger Eagle: Having been a fanatical fan myself of many different artists I will tell you that what really counts is when you get across to the ordinary punter who doesn't know anything, but just enjoys stuff in an honest, open sort of way. If you can hit those people, then you can earn money for the artist or his estate.

*

As a cultural commentator and observer, Eagle would constantly refer to the 'ordinary guy', the 'ordinary punter', the 'man on the street', the 'average punter' and the 'wider public' – to Roger these people were the most important people in the world. His ideal demographic was made up of these people. In his world, if you appealed to those people, half the battle was won.

His ability also to judge and take advantage of the zeitgeist of the different eras he worked in gave him, and the clubs he was involved with, a huge advantage. It could be said that his knowledge and experience was something that was never exploited to it's full potential, whether as radio DJ, club DJ, promoter or club owner.

Bernie Connor: Roger could have been a millionaire a billion times over. Try to explain that to some people, they'll think you're mad. It's not about money it's about that piece of plastic. He must have had a million opportunities to go "Yeah, fuckin' 'ell I'll have that, see yer I'm off, you put the numbers on the cheque for me an' I'll sell out", because that's what people do. It's not even about integrity, it's about doing what you believe. If you believe that music doesn't necessarily have to be a global concern then you're seen as some kind of freak.

Elliot Rashman: He had times when he was on the cusp of making big money but something within himself made him not do that, otherwise he would've been Harvey Goldsmith, he would've been in an office and it wouldn't have been about music.

As Mancunian music authority Elliot Rashman points out, Roger should, by rights, have been a high powered music business executive – but there was always something that got in the way and prevented this. It would seem that Roger needed to be at the grass roots level where he was always in touch with the music. His precious music. That was literally where he got his energy from. As the man himself explains:

Roger Eagle: I crave excitement, I must have excitement in my music, it has to do something for me, otherwise I'm not interested. It's very rare that I'll play anything relaxing, if I do it'll be very high quality piano jazz, or something like that, you know what I mean? I crave excitement, and if I get it from a Charlie Parker alto solo, or Little Richard or King Tubby or whatever I've gotta have that excitement. It's gotta have an edge, a tension, because it's what keeps me going you know, it's fuel to me, it's what you need immediately after food (laughs). I'm one of the very few people that has that depth and range of taste that goes right the way back, which is a very precious thing. It's almost unnecessary to clutter yourself up with modern stuff, I mean if it was necessary for me to do so then I would. But I haven't got time for anything that isn't what I regard as being really good, I haven't got time to listen to it.

Eagle's opinions on the roots of modern music were, and still are, so important because they were borne of years of research for his DJing and promoting – for his students and for his own interest. There were so few knowledgeable public music devotees, who had not only witnessed the birth of rock 'n' roll but all the subsequent pop/rock explosions up until the end of the twentieth century. He didn't just witness these massive cultural shifts, he participated in and experienced each evolutionary revision and was able to speak about them with passion and authority. If one looks at the modern music press or pop radio in general as a comparison, there are no experts on the historical background of what came previous to current trends – there is no context. He was extremely concerned that his work and knowledge be carried on – with hindsight it's understandable as this expertise is slowly being lost to the internet and the digital age.

Finally, from an interview published in *The Guardian* in 1993 the last words are from Mr Roger Eagle:

> *"I don't like to analyse it too much. It's the rhythm probably. All I know is that when I put a record on if it hits, it hits, if it doesn't, it doesn't. I put all that down to the fact that Hank Williams was taught to play guitar by a black man. Instead of just strumming, he put the accent on the second and fourth beat."*

OBITUARY

The energy and enthusiasm behind northern soul

By Bob Dickinson, The Guardian, Saturday 15 May 1999

Roger Eagle, who has died of cancer aged 56, was an influential DJ, record collector, club promoter, and musical mentor. Without him, performers like Mick Hucknall of Simply Red, would have missed a vital element in their musical education and their vocal approach – when Hucknall's punk band, the Frantic Elevators, split, the singer spent weeks in Liverpool with Roger absorbing his knowledge of Afro-American and Afro-Caribbean music.

Roger was born in Oxford. Distantly related to George Bernard Shaw, his mother, Dorothy, edited the Oxford Literary Guide To The British Isles. But like many teenagers in 1950s Britain, Roger was captivated by black American rock 'n' roll and blues. The beat group scene lured him on a weekend motorbike jaunt to Manchester. He stayed, and had his mother send his clothes by post. Surrounded by his record collection, he edited the magazine R&B Scene – unsold copies propped up his bed.

In 1965 Roger was hired as a DJ by Ivor Abadi, owner of a coffee-shop-cum-nightclub called the Twisted Wheel. Here he pumped out a repertoire of R&B and soul, on discs by artists such as Bobby Bland, Ike and Tina Turner and James Carr. All-night sessions gave rise to a demand for increasingly fast-tempo dance tracks to satisfy the amphetamine-fuelled clientele. The musical genre and sub-cultural lifestyle subsequently known as northern soul was born.

But Roger didn't approve. In his last interview, to be seen in Ian Levine's forthcoming documentary The Strange World Of Northern Soul, he recalled: 'I got very, very fed up having to call ambulances . . . and not being allowed to play the full range of music.'

By 1967, Roger was becoming interested in Manchester's underground music scene, for which he supplied a focal point in the form of the Magic Village, staging light shows, films and happenings, as well as concerts by blues-derived American west coast acts, including Country Joe Macdonald, and Big Brother and the Holding Company. He also brought together Manchester's first psychedelic band, Greasy Bear, which became the more satirical Alberto Y Lost Trios Paranoias.

In the early 1970s, Roger moved to Merseyside and took over Liverpool stadium, an old boxing venue, which played host to Lou Reed, David Bowie, Mott the Hoople and Captain Beefheart. With Geoff Davis, he was involved in setting up Probe Records shop, which became a meeting place for Liverpool's next generation of musicians, motivated by punk rock.

In October 1976, in a basement opposite the site of the Cavern, he opened his most fondly-remembered club, Eric's, where musicians, who included the nascent line-ups of groups like the Teardrop Explodes, Echo & The Bunnymen, and Frankie Goes To Hollywood, could cut their teeth alongside Roger's eclectic headline billings, bringing together anything from dub reggae to Louisiana zydeco to the Clash.

The early 1980s saw Roger's return to Manchester, where he set up the International Club, securing early performances from bands like REM, as well as local unknowns the Stone Roses. Regularly to be seen in the foyer, attired in one of his characteristic

Hawaiian shirts, Roger always responded to inquiries about the music he championed with a barrage of information and frequently a compilation tape. His enthusiasm never let up. I remember him crying with joy when he secured a booking for his Tamla Motown hero, Junior Walker.

Since the mid 1990s, Roger had been living at Llanfairfechan, north Wales, where he could be close to friends and the landscape he loved. He leaves two brothers, Martin and John.

Roger Eagle, DJ, born July 15, 1942; died May 4, 1999

Roger Eagle: A Gigography

ALL-NIGHTERS, TWISTED WHEEL, BRAZENNOSE STREET, MANCHESTER

All gigs took place on a Saturday night/Sunday morning. All gigs DJ'd by Roger Eagle

1963

28th September	Graham Bond Quartet + Spencer Davis
5th October	John Mayall's Blues Breakers
12th October	Jimmy Powell and the Dimensions
19th October	Graham Bond Quartet + Spencer Davis
26th October	Spencer Davis Quartet
2nd November	John Mayall's Blues Breakers
9th November	Roadrunners
16th November	Hogsnort Rupert
23rd November	Spencer Davis Quartet
30th November	Graham Bond Quartet
7th December	Jimmy Powell and the Dimensions
14th December	Rocking Berries
21st December	John Mayall's Blues Breakers
28th December	Graham Bond Quartet

1964

4th January	Downliners Sect
11th January	Long John Baldry + Cyril Davis All Stars
18th January	Jimmy Powell and the Dimensions
25th January	Graham Bond Quartet
1st February	John Mayall and the Bluesbreakers
8th February	Manfred Mann
15th February	Sonny Boy Williamson + The Animals
22nd February	Graham Bond Quartet
29th February	Long John Baldry and the Hoochie Coochie Men
7th March	Jimmy Powell and the Dimensions
14th March	Spencer Davis Quartet
21st March	John Mayall and the Bluesbreakers

28th March	Graham Bond Quartet
4th April	Long John Baldry and the Hoochie Coochie Men
11th April	Alex Harvey and his Soul Band
18th April	The Animals
25th April	Georgie Fame and the Blue Flames
2nd May	Graham Bond Quartet
9th May	Memphis Slim
16th May	Spencer Davis Quartet
23rd May	Long John Baldry and the Hoochie Coochie Men
30th May	Georgie Fame and the Blue Flames
6th June	The Cheynes
13th June	John Lee Hooker & John Mayall
20th June	Jimmy Powell
27th June	Graham Bond
4th July	Long John Baldry and the Hoochie Coochie Men
11th July	Georgie Fame and the Blue Flames
18th July	Spencer Davis Group
25th July	Charlesworth Big Blues with Bobby Breen
1st August	Graham Bond Organisation
8th August	The T-Bones
15th August	Long John Baldry and the Hoochie Coochie Men
22nd August	Alexis Korner's Blues Incorporated
29th August	John Lee Hooker + The Groundhogs
5th September	Memphis Slim + Georgie Fame + The Sheffields
12th September	Jimmy Powell and the Dimensions
19th September	Alexis Korner and the Soul Seekers
26th September	Spencer Davis Group
3rd October	Little Walter + Alexis Korner
10th October	John Lee Hooker + The Groundhogs
17th October	Alex Harvey and the Soul Band + The Plebs
24th October	The T-Bones
31st October	Long John Baldry and the Hoochie Coochie Men
7th November	Sonny Boy Williamson + The Moody Blues
14th November	The Yardbirds + Clayton Squares
21st November	Jimmy Reed
28th November	Spencer Davis Group + Beat Boys
5th December	Georgie Fame + Blues Giants
12th December 1964	John Mayall and the Bluesbreakers + Night Style
19th December 1964	John Lee's Groundhogs + Joe Cocker Big Blues
26th December 1964	Sonny Boy Williamson + Spencer Davis Group

1965

2nd January	Impullsions

9th January	Crusaiders
16th January	John Mayall + The Falling Leaves
23rd January	The T–Bones + The Fairies
30th January	Duffy Powell and the Sorrows
6th February	Spencer Davis
13th February	Rod Stewart and the Soul Agents + 5 Dimensions
20th February	Screaming Jay Hawkins and the Falling Leaves
27th February	Zoot Money's Big Roll Band + Brian Auger Trinity
6th March	Buddy Guy + Rod Stewart and the Soul Agents
13th March	Alexis Korner + 5 Dimensions
20th March	Champion Jack Dupree + The Sheffields
27th March	T–Bone Walker + John Mayall
3rd April	Larry Williams + Johnny Guitar Watson
10th April	Jimmy Powell 5 Dimensions + John Lee's Groundhogs
17th April	Graham Bond
24th April	Long John Baldry + Blues Giants
1st May	Spencer Davis Group
8th May	John Mayall's Blues Breakers + Tea Time 4
15th May	5 Dimensions + Blues Giants
22nd May	Brian Auger Trinity + Fetish Crowd
29th May	Champion Jack Dupree + The Action + Blues Set
5th June	John Lee Hooker + Blues Giants
12th June	Rod Stewart + St Louis Union
19th June	Brian Auger Trinity + Soul Sisters
26th June	Jimmy Powell 5 Dimensions
3rd July	John Lee's Groundhogs
10th July	Georgie Fame and the Blue Flames
17th July	5 Dimensions
24th July	Inez and Charles Foxx + The Ram Jam Band
31st July	Spencer Davis
7th August	Jimmy Powell and the 5 Dimensions
14th August	5 Divisions
21st August	Graham Bond Organisation
28th August	John Lee's Groundhogs
4th September	St Louis Union
11th September	John Mayall and the Bluesbreakers

And that was it, the last gig at the Brazennose Street Twisted Wheel, Saturday night was the night Roger Eagle DJ'd, but it wasn't the only night to feature live bands. As the Brazennose Street Wheel's reputation grew, so did the standard of artists booked throughout the week. Below are some of the better known acts that appeared at the Brazennose Street venue during the week. It should also be noted that from the very first All–Nighter there were two separate live performances, either from separate bands or the same band would play an early and a later set.

ALL-NIGHTERS, TWISTED WHEEL,
WHITWORTH STREET, MANCHESTER
All gigs took place on a Saturday night / Sunday morning. All gigs DJ'd by Roger Eagle

1965

18th September	Spencer Davis Group
25th September	The Action
2nd October	Graham Bond Organisation
9th October	The Steam Packet
16th October	T-Bone Walker
23rd October	Georgie Fame
30th October	Spencer Davis Group
6th November	The Action
13th November	CLUB CLOSED
20th November	Steam Packet
27th November	Graham Bond
4th December	Spencer Davis Group
11th December	Champion Jack Dupree
18th December	John Mayall
25th December	All-Nighter

1966

1st January	Spencer Davis Group
8th January	Zoot Money's Big Roll Band
15th January	Drifters + Ram Jam Band
22nd January	Steampacket
29th January	Graham Bond Organisation
5th February	Georgie Fame & The Blue Flames
12th February	Doris Troy / Alan Bown Set & Bluesology
19th February	Charles & Inez Foxx
26th February	John Mayall
5th March	Spencer Davis Group
12th March	Steampacket
19th March	Therma Thomas & Wilson Picket
26th March	St. Louis Union
2nd April	Don Covay
9th April	Vibrations
16th April	John Mayall
23rd April	Lee Dorsey
30th April	Chris Farlowe
7th May	Zoot Money

14th May	Ram Jam Band & Patti LaBelle
21st May	The Drifters
28th May	Georgie Fame & The Blue Flames
4th June	Ben E. King
11th June	Alan Bown Set & The Inkspots
18th June	Mike Cotton Sound
25th June	Roy C
2nd July	Orlons
9th July	Rufus Thomas
16th July	Jimmy Cliff & the Explosive Sound
23rd July	Solomon Burke
30th July	Joe Tex (Postponed) replaced by The Cream
4th August	Mike Cotton Sound
13th August	John Mayall & The Blues Breakers
20th August	Geno Washington & The Ram Jam Band
27th August	Zoot Money's Big Roll Band

MAGIC VILLAGE
CROMFORD COURT,, MANCHESTER

1968

Sat 9th March	Jacko Ogg + Gemini Zent
Fri 15th March	John Senior's Blues Band
Sat 16th March	Tyrannosaurus Rex
Fri 21st March	John Senior's Blues Band
Sat 22nd March	Doc K's Blues Band
Fri 29th March	Gulf Stream Drift
Sat 30th March	Spirit of John Morgan
Fri 5th April	John Senior's Blues Band
Sat 6th April	Jethro Tull
Sat 20th April	Liverpool Scene
Sunday 21st April	Mark Stone's Witchcraft + Passion
Sat 27th April	Modes Codes + Jack Lancaster Quartet featuring Bruce Mitchell
Sunday 28th April	Van Der Graaf Generator
Sat 4th May	The New Religion (Early session) Bruce Mitchell's Group feat. J.J. Denson (Late)
Fri 10th May	John Senior's Blues Band
Sat 11th May	Gulf Stream Drift + Psycho Blues + The Inner Light Show
Sat 18th May	Tyrannosaurus Rex + John Peel + Bruce Mitchell Quartet
Fri 24th May	Gulfstream Drift
Sat 25th May	Tomorrow's World

Sat 1st June	John Senior's Blues Band
Sat 8th June	John Mayall
Sat 15th June	Clouds

(Pink Floyd will not be playing tonight owing to the fact
that they will only play half an hour on each session)

Sat 22nd June	12 Hour Happening + The Liverpool Scene
Fri 28th June	The Living Tribunal ft. Mark Stone & Peter Firth
Sat 29th June	Fairport Convention
Sat 6th July	Eclection + Bruce Mitchell & Mike King
Sat 13th July	The Nice
Fri 19th July	Lennox Avenue
Sat 20th July	Jethro Tull + Edgar Broughton Band + The Dawn Rain Band
Sat 27th July	Chicken Shack + Shape of the Rain + Purple Stone + The Dawn Rain Band
Fri 2nd August	Gobi Desert
Sat 3rd August	Liverpool Scene + Climax Farm
Fri 9th August	The Dawn Rain Rain Band
Sat 10th August	Edgar Broughton Band + The Dawn Rain Band
Fri 16th August	Lennox Avenue
Sat 17th August	Shape of the Rain + The Dawn Rain Band
Fri 23rd August	Lennox Avenue
Sat 24th August	CKreed Blues Band + Lennox Avenue + Blue Pig
Fri 30st August	Brownsville Jug band
Sat 31st August	Edgar Broughton Band + The Dawn Rain Band
Fri 6th September	Lennox Avenue
Sat 7th September	Jethro Tull + Climax Farm
Fri 13th September	Brownsville Jug Band
Sat 14th September	Glass Menagerie + Elmer Gantry's Velvet Opera
Fri 20th September	Brownsville Jug Band
Sat 21st September	Blossom Toes + Gary Farr + Andy Leigh
Fri 27th September	The Dawn Rain Band
Sat 28th September	Tim Rose
Fri 4th October	Neil Mclean + Mark Stone
Sat 5th October	Roy Harper + Purple Stone & the Alchemist
Fri 11th October	Chris Lee & Mark Stone
Sat 12th October	Liverpool Scene + The Sponge
Fri 18th October	Brownsville Jug Band
Sat 19th October	Edgar Broughton Band + Chris Lee & Tony Cane
Fri 25th October	Lennox Avenue
Sat 26th October	Climax Farm + Chris Lee & Tony Cane
Fri 1st November	Lennox Avenue
Sat 2nd November	The Nice + Purple Stone & the Alchemist + Mark Stone

Fri 8th November	Chris Lee & Tony Cane
Sat 9th November	Savoy Brown + The NSU
Fri 15th November	Skidmore Row Blues Band
Sat 16th November	Joe Cocker + The Grease Band + The King Mob Echo
Fri 22nd November	The NSU
Sat 23rd November	Jethro Tull + The NSU
Fri 29th November	The NSU
Sat 30th November	Duster Bennett
Fri 6th December	John Senior's Blues Band + Mark Stone & Patrick Mullen
Sat 7th December	Pete Brown's Battered Ornaments + Chris Lee + Tony Cane
Fri 13th December	Lennox Avenue + The Pleasure Machine
Sat 14th December	Bobby Parker
Fri 20th December	Bruce Mitchell & his mind expanding group)
Fri 21st December	Bridget St. John + Mark Stone & Patrick Mullen
Tue 24th December	Edgar Broughton Band
Fri 27th December	The Puritans
Sat 28th December	Bakerloo Blues Line
Tue 31st December	The Puritans

1969

Fri 3rd January	Axis + Chris Lee, Tony Cane & Mark Stone
Sat 4th January	Junior's Eyes
Fri 10th January	Mark Stone
Sat 11th January	Duster Bennett
Fri 17th January	The Puritans
Sat 18th January	Third Ear Band
Fri 24th January	Jo-Ann Kelly
Sat 25th January	The Liverpool Scene
Fri 31st January	Mark Stone
Sat 1st February	Third Ear Band
Fri 7th February	Greasy Bear
Sat 8th February	Clouds
Sat 15th February	Glass Menagerie
Fri 21st February	Greasy Bear
Sat 22nd February	Van Der Graaf Generator
Fri 28th February	St. Louis Union
Sat 1st March	Edgar Broughton Blues Band
Fri 7th March	Lennox Avenue + Mark Stone & Allan Prior
Sat 8th March	Mick Abraham's Blues Band + Greasy Bear + Mark Stone
Fri 14th March	Mark Stone
Sat 15th March	Groundhogs
Fri 21st March	Lennox Avenue

Fri 28th March	Mark Stone
Sat 29th March	Third Ear Band
Fri 11th April	Greasy Bear
Sat 12th April	Mick Abrahams + Blodwyn Pig
Fri 18th April	Anton Farmer
Sat 19th April	Jo-Ann Kelly
Fri 25th April	Roy Harper
Sat 26th April	Roy Harper
Fri 9th May	Greasy Bear
Sat 10th May	Gordon Giltrap + Mark Stone
Fri 16th May	Sweet Marriage
Sat 17th May	Black Cat Bones
Fri 23rd May	The Puritans
Sat 24th May	Duster Bennett
Fri 30th May	Kinetic Living + Sculpture
Sat 31st May	Greasy Bear
Fri 6th June	Dunbar's Magic Machine + The Electric Hat
Sat 7th June	The Glass Menagerie
Fri 13th June	The Grit Band
Sat 14th June	The Misunderstood
Fri 20th June	James Valentine + Ex Electric Hat + Iain Mclean
Sat 21st June	Ace Kefford
Fri 27th June	Delta String Band + Mike King & Paul Frost
Sat 28th June	The Zap Band
Fri 4th July	The Zap Band
Sat 5th July	The NSU + Gordon Smith
Fri 11th July	Strawberry Blues
Sat 12th July	Duster Bennett
Fri 18th July	Spider King
Sat 19th July	Edgar Broughton
Fri 25th July	The Burning Bush
Sat 26th July	The Third Ear Band
Fri 1st August	Anton Farmer
Sat 2nd August	Mike Absolam
Fri 8th August	J.C. Heavy
Sat 9th August	The Deviants
Sun 10th August	Pete Brown
Fri 15th August	Gordon Smith
Sat 16th August	Gordon Smith
Fri 22nd August	J.C. Heavy
Sat 23rd August	The Burning Bush
Fri 29th August	David Lear
Sat 30th August	The Glass Menagerie

Sat 13th September	Atomic Rooster
Fri 3rd October	Strawberry Blues
Sat 4th October	Blossom Toes
Fri 10th October	Urban Guerilla Blues Band
Sat 11th October	Third Ear Band
Sat 18th October	Forest
Fri 24th October	James Valentine
Sat 25th October	Al Stewart
Fri 31st October	Anton Farmer
Sat 1st November	Groundhogs
Fri 7th November	Greasy Bear
Sat 8th November	Jody Grind
Fri 14th November	Dave Lear
Sat 15th November	The Strawbs
Fri 21st November	The Puritans
Sat 22nd November	Barefoot
Fri 28th November	J.C. Heavy
Sat 29th November	Caravan
Fri 5th December	Symbion
Sat 6th December	Flaming Youth
Sat 13th December	Skin Alley
Fri 19th December	Axis
Sat 20th December	Sam Gopal
Wed 31st December	Barefoot

1970

Sat 3rd January	Jo-Ann Kelly

As well as booking acts for the Magic Village, Roger would also put gigs on at other venues. The Houldsworth Hall on Deansgate in Manchester was a larger capacity venue than the Magic Village, this would have made it possible to put on bigger name bands. Some of these shows were benefit gigs.

HOULDSWORTH HALL, DEANSGATE, MANCHESTER

Sat 19th January	Family + Roy Harper + Bridget St. John + John Peel
Sat 22nd March	Country Joe & the Fish + Principal Edwards + Liverpool Scene
Sat 28th June	Fleetwood Mac + Glass Menagerie
Sat 5th September	Family + Caravan + Bridget St. John

LIVERPOOL STADIUM

1970

30th May	Edgar Broughton Band + Third Ear Band + Kevin Ayres + Michael Chapman
19th September	Free + Fotheringay + Mott the Hoople + Bronco
5th December	Yes + East of Eden + Stray
19th December	Mott the Hoople + If + Bronco + Dhyani

1971

6th February	Free
2nd March	Hawkwind + High Tide + Cochise
4th March	Yes + Bonzo Dog Band + Argent + Jonathan Swift
20th March	Hawkwind
27th March	Incredible String Band
3rd April	Mott the Hoople + Greasy Bear + Stoned Rose
22nd May	Faces
3rd July	Sha Na Na + Juicy Lucy + Uriah Heep + Paladin
9th October	Mott the Hoople + Peace
14th October	Canned Heat + Terry Reid + Stone the Crows
26th October	Yes + Jonathon Swift
11th November	T. Rex
29th November	Led Zepellin

1972

31st January	Black Sabbath + Wild Turkey
19th February	Mott the Hoople
25th March	Chuck Berry
27th March	Jethro Tull + Tir na nog
1st April	Hawkwind
3rd April	Captain Beefheart & the Magic Band
8th April	Mott the Hoople + Max Wall + Hackensack
10th May	Edgar Broughton Band + Flying Hat Band
24th May	Camel + Lindisfarne + Khan
3rd June	David Bowie and the Spiders From Mars
7th June	Kingdom Come
14th June	Rory Gallagher + Roxy Music + Nazareth
17th June	Paladin + Sha Na Na
20th July	Argent
2nd September	Mountain
16th September	Status Quo

22nd September	The Everly Brothers
23rd September	Mott the Hoople + Home
24th September	Procul Harem
30th September	Hawkwind + Brinsley Schwartz + Sutherland Brothers + Spider Mike King
4th October	Ten Years After + Brinsley Schwartz
11th October	Curved Air + Greasy Bear
12th October	Fanny
14th October	The Kinks + Victor Brox
16th October	Vinegar Joe
18th October	Slade
19th October	Lou Reed + Phillip Goodhand Tait + Amsterdam Lil
21st October	Steeleye Span + Amazing Blondel
8th November	Roxy Music + Supertramp + Sunrise
19th November	Thin Lizzy + Slade
25th November	Argent + Greasy Bear
30th November	Wishbone Ash
9th December	Quintessence
10th December	Faces
16th December	Groundhogs + Gentle Giant + Stray
23rd December	Hawkwind + Greasy Bear

1973

21st January	Focus
27th January	Uriah Heep
17th February	Kinks + Hackensack
28th February	Deep Purple + Nazareth
1st March	Rory Gallagher + Greenslade
10th March	Black Sabbath + Badger + Nutz
17th March	Can + Gunner Cade
19th March	Jethro Tull
7th April	Captain Beefheart & the Magic Band
12th April	Curved Air + Nick Pickett
28th April	Arthur Brown's Kingdom Come + Kala + Ange
26th May	Amon Duul II + Zoe
2nd June	Sha Na Na + Esperanto
9th June	Fancy + Moonstone + Amsterdam Lil
26th June	Wishbone Ash
14th July	Hawkwind + Swan Revived + Clancy
11th September	Frank Zappa & the Mothers of Invention
22nd September	The Kinks + March Hare + Bloodstone
6th October	Argent + Glencoe
11th October	Status Quo + Savoy Brown

27th October	Faust + Henry Cow
15th November	Uriah Heep + Heavy Metal Kids
17th November	Mott the Hoople + Queen
15th December	Golden Earring + Caravan

1974

12th January	Hawkwind + Fruup
2nd February	Can + Keith Christmas
14th February	Barclay James Harvest + Tom Mcmasters
23rd March	Golden Earring + Alquin
13th April	Bad Company + Darian Spirit
27th April	Global Village Trucking Co. + Hatfield & the North + Gong + Tubular Bells (Film)
11th May	Sensational Alex Harvey Band + Stryder
18th May	Nazareth + Heavy Metal Kids
8th June	Budgie + Judas Priest
13th June	Alquin + Blue
15th June	Captain Beefheart & the Magic Band + Henrý Cow
22nd June	Cockney Rebel + Be Bop de Luxe
29th June	Barclay James Harvest
13th July	Brinsley Schwartz + Ducks Deluxe + Jon Dummer Band + John Gladwin
27th July	P. Bardens Camel + Supercharge + Keith Christmas
3rd August	Alberto Y Los Trios Paranoias + Jonathon Kelly's Outside + Strider
10th August	Greasy Bear + Pete Atkin + Clive James + J.S.D. Band
17th August	Stackridge + Amsterdam Lil + Renegade
31st August	Rare Bird + Barclay James Harvest
14th September	Sutherland Brothers and Quiver + Jess Roden + Rinky Dink + Crystal Set
28th September	Edgar Broughton Band + Lol Coxhill + Still Life
5th October	Thin Lizzy
9th October	Thin Lizzy
10th October	Gong + Isotope
19th October	Supertramp + Global Village Trucking Co. + Steve Ashley
26th October	Strife + Supercharge + Flag + Hamster
27th October	Faust
2nd November	Tangerine Dream
9th November	Thin Lizzy + Slack Alice
24th November	Curved Air + Watt Roy Turner + Sassafras

4th December	Rory Gallagher + Jackie Lynton Band
11th December	Argent + Clancy
12th December	Budgie + Skyfall
14th December	A Band Called O + Neutrons

1975

18th January	Hawkwind + Al Mathews
8th February	Robin Trower + Mandala Band
15th February	Barclay James Harvest
16th February	Black Oak Arkansas + Sassafras
8th March	Edgar Broughton Band + Ellis
25th March	Cockney Rebel + Sailor
5th April	Fruup
26th April	Gong
3rd May	Can
10th May	Camel + Nick Pickett
11th May	Love
17th May	The Nuetrons + Curly + Socrates
20th May	Uriah Heep
24th May	Snafu + Nutz + Shanghai
31st May	Stackridge + Zzebra
7th June	Be Bop De Luxe + Skyfall + Filthy McNasty
14th June	Blythe Spirit + Supercharge + Sassafrass
21st June	The Jess Roden Band + Jack the Lad + Silk
28th June	Ronnie Lane's Slim Chance + Upp
26th July	Hawkwind + Stonehenge
20th September	Budgie + Hobo
4th October	Pink Fairies + Thunderpuss
5th October	Van Der Graaf Generator
11th October	Thin Lizzy
19th October	Dr Feelgood + GT Moore and the Reggae Guitars
1st November	Heavy Metal Kids
16th November	Andy Fraser Band
13th December	Gentle Giant
22nd December	Heavy Metal Kids + Supercharge + Sassafras
26th December	Osibisa

1976

22nd January	Dr Feelgood + Roogalator
28th February	Be Bop Deluxe + Doctors of Madness
20th March	Thin Lizzy + Graham Parker & the Rumour
17th July	Sad Cafe + Sassafras
6th November	AC/DC
18th December	Ultravox + Eddie & the Hot Rods

Thanks to the Liverpool Stadium website for gig information.

★

ERIC'S,
MATHEW STREET, LIVERPOOL

1976

24th September	CLUB OPENS
1st October	The Stranglers
8th October	The Runaways
15th October	Sex Pistols
22nd October	Count Bishops
29th October	Racing Cars
5th November	Roogalator
12th November	Flamin' Groovies
26th November	The Damned

1977

11th February	Little Bob Story
10th March	The Heartbreakers + Cherry Vanilla + The Police
11th March	Darts
12th March	Dave Edmunds Rockpile
18th March	Buzzcocks
19th March	Frankie Miller
4th April	The Western Kirkby Cowboy
5th April	The Western Kirkby Cowboy
6th April	The Western Kirkby Cowboy
23rd April	The Pirates
5th May	The Clash
11th May	Johnny Griffin & Carmel Jones + The Joe Palin Trio

14th May	Siouxsie & the Banshees
19th May	The Ramones + Talking Heads
25th May	Red Brass
28th May	The Damned
1st June	Barbara Thompson Paraphernalia
6th July	Liverpool Jam
8th July	The Darts
9th July	The Saints
12th July	World Premier of 'Sleak' starring Alberto Y Los Trios Paranoias
13th July	'Sleak'
14th July	'Sleak'
15th July	'Sleak'
16th July	The Spitfire Boys + Radio Blank
18th July	Deaf School
19th July	Deaf School
20th July	Liverpool Jam
22nd July	The Spitfire Boys
23rd July	The Vibrators
27th July	Liverpool Jam
30th July	Elvis Costello & the Attractions
2nd August	Elvis Costello & the Attractions
3rd August	Liverpool Jam
5th August	'Murder at Eric's'– The Everyman Theatre Company'
6th August	Buzzcocks
10th August	Liverpool Jam
12th August	Flying Saucers
13th August	XTC + The Table
20th August	The Slits + The Prefects + The Spitfire Boys
22nd August	Slaughter & the Dogs + Wire + Fast Breeder
27th August	X-Ray Spex + Warsaw + Afternoon Matinee Show
27th August	Generation X + Big In Japan
3rd September	Buzzcocks + The Worst + Rage
16th September	The Adverts
15th October	Adam & the Ants
21st October	Boomtown Rats
22nd October	The Clash + The Toilets
26th October	Siouxsie & the Banshees
29th October	Eater + The Crabs
18th November	Buzzcocks + The Fall + The Toilets
23rd November	Wayne County & the Electric Chairs
10th December	The Clash
11th December	Ian Dury

17th December	The Fall + Penetration
24th December	Sausages From Mars + Radio Doom + Fast Breeder

1978

5th January	Stiff Records Talent Contest with The Smirks,
27th January	Magazine
28th January	Radiators from Space
29th January	Robert Gordon + Link Wray
31st January	The Bothy Band
1st February	Dillinger + Zabandis + Hortense Ellis
3rd February	Wire
4th February	Rich Kids
5th February	Deke Leonard's Iceberg
10th February	Ultravox
11th February	XTC
15th February	Colosseum
17th February	Sham 69
19th February	John Otway & Wild Willy Barratt
22nd February	Earthquake
24th February	The Rezillos
25th February	The Boys
28th February	Albion Dance Band
3rd March	Siouxsie & the Banshees
4th March	Electric Chairs
5th March	Richie Havens
24th March	Elvis Costello & the Attractions
25th March	Elvis Costello & the Attractions
27th March	Psalms
28th March	Buzzcocks
29th March	Rubinoos
30th March	Gloria Mundi
31st March	Greg Kihn Band + The Smirks
1st April	X-Ray Spex
3rd April	Tapper Zukie
5th April	Planet Gong
6th April	Clayson & the Argonauts
7th April	The Fall
8th April	The Saints
10th April	British Lions
11th April	Marseilles
13th April	Bernie Torme
15th April	Tradition
17th April	Supercharge + 29th & Dearborn + Fun

18th April	Everyman Theatre Production – Venus Flytrap
20th April	The Young Ones
21st April	Siouxsie & the Banshees + Spizz Oil
22nd April	Wreckless Eric
24th April	The Gladiators
25th April	Magazine
27th April	The Young Bucks
28th April	Doctors of Madness
29th April	Pere Ubu + The Pop Group
1st May	Aswad
4th May	Dead Fingers Talk
5th May	Cherry Vanilla
6th May	Wire
8th May	Johnny Moped
9th May	Slaughter & the Dogs + Eater + Blitzkrieg Bop
11th May	The Records
12th May	Rabid Records Show – John Cooper Clarke + Gyro + Jilted John + Ed Banger + Prime Time Suckers + Nose Bleeds
13th May	Radio Stars
15th May	Van Der Graaf
18th May	Gruppo Sportivo
19th May	The Pirates
20th May	The Motors + Marseilles
22nd May	Flaming Groovies + Radio Birdman
23rd May	Planet Gong + Steve Hillage + National Health
24th May	Planet Gong + Steve Hillage + National Health
25th May	Stadium Dogs
26th May	Alternative TV
27th May	The Rezillos
30th May	John Otway and Wild Willy Barrett
31st May	John Otway and Wild Willy Barrett + The Smirks
30th June	The Cramps + Pink Military
8th July	Magazine + The Zones
14th July	The Dickies + The Edge
15th July	Rich Kids + Joy Division
17th July	The Shirts
21st July	The Clash + The Specials
22nd July	The Clash + The Specials + Suicide + Afternoon Matinee Show
28th July	The Fall + John Cooper Clarke
29th July	Suicide
10th August	Orchestral Manoeuvres in the Dark + A Certain Ratio

11th August	The Movies + Dead Trout
12th August	The Rezillos + Gang of Four
17th August	The Germs + Mainline Junction
18th August	Punishment of Luxury + Dalek I Love You
19th August	Rabid Records Show - John Cooper Clarke
	+ Jilted John + Giro + Ed Banger
	+ Prime Time Suckers + Gordon the Moron
25th August	Doll By Doll + Manicured Noise
26th August	Big In Japan + The Durutti Column
1st September	The Human League
2nd September	C-Gas 5
8th September	The Specials
9th September	Tanz Der Youth + Joy Division
15th September	Sore Throat + Spherical Objects
16th September	The Lurkers + Gang Of Four
	+ Afternoon Matinee Show
21st September	The Second Thought Band
22nd September	Johnny Moped
23rd September	Ultravox + Ded Byrds + Afternoon Matinee Show
28th September	Stevie & The Secrets
29th September	The Edge
30th September	999 + The Razars + Afternoon Matinee Show
3rd October	Crawler
6th October	Prince Far I + Creation Rebel
7th October	Split Enz
13th October	The Electric Chairs with Wayne County
14th October	The Pirates
20th October	Matumbi
21st October	Wire
27th October	Yachts
28th October	Penetration
2nd November	Ludus
3rd November	The Fall + The Prefects
4th November	John Cooper Clarke + Joy Division + Ded Byrds
9th November	Nancy Pallones
10th November	The Shirts + Hot Water
11th November	Rabid Records Show - Ed Banger + Giro
	+ Gordon The Moron + Bulldog Clips
15th November	Teardrop Explodes + Echo & the Bunnymen
16th November	Crash Course
17th November	X-Ray Spex + The Invaders
18th November	The Skids + Gang Of Four
20th November	John Martyn

23rd November	The Teardrop Explodes + Orchestral Manoeuvres In The Dark
24th November	David Johannsen
25th November	Pere Ubu + The Soft Boys
7th December	Pink Military Stand Alone
8th December	The Doomed
15th December	Essential Logic + Razar
16th December	Generation X + Stevie & the Stopouts + Afternoon Matinee Show
21st December	The Moderates + Phil Jazz
22nd December	Crash Course
23rd December	Wayne County & The Electric Chairs + Sausages From Mars + Glass Torpedos
26th December	Supercharge + Azania
29th December	Ded Byrds
30th December	999 + Afternoon Matinee Show

1979

5th January	Hot Water
6th January	The Slits + Afternoon Matinee Show
20th January	The Damned + Afternoon Matinee Show
26th January	Bette Bright & the Illuminations
27th January	Adam & the Ants
10th February	The Police
16th February	Joy Division + Cabaret Voltaire
23rd February	National Health + Inside Out
24th February	Stiff Little Fingers + Teardrop Explodes + Prag Vec
28th February	Roger Chapman
1st March	RAAW
2nd March	Cabaret Voltaire + Frantic Elevators
3rd March	The Undertones + Afternoon Matinee Show
8th March	The Smirks – John Dowie
9th March	Joe Jackson
10th March	Punishment of Luxury
15th March	Those Naughty Lumps + S.P.G.
16th March	Jonathan Richman
17th March	The Skids + Afternoon Matinee Show
22nd March	Pink Military Stand Alone + A.D.T.
23rd March	Patrick Fitzgerald + The Molesters + Ed Banger
24th March	The Pretenders + Afternoon Matinee Show
30th March	The Fall
31st March	The Cure + Frantic Elevators
2nd April	Supercharge + C.P. Lee

5th April	Ded Byrds
6th April	Prince Far I + Bim Sherman + Prince Hammer + Creation Rebel
7th April	UK Subs + The Distractions
9th April	Supercharge
12th April	Doll by Doll
13th April	Crass + Poison Girls
14th April	The Damned + Toyah
16th April	Supercharge
17th April	Jean Jacques Burnell
18th April	XTC
20th April	The B52's
21st April	Iggy Pop + The Zones
22nd April	Supercharge
26th April	Prag Vec
27th April	Inner Circle + Hot Water
28th April	The Specials + Swell Maps
1st May	Margox & the Passions
2nd May	Here & Now
3rd May	Joy Division + The Passage + Fireplace
4th May	Wayne County & the Electric Chairs
5th May	Members + Pinpoint
7th May	Next
10th May	The Glass Torpedos
11th May	John Otway + The Head Boys
12th May	The Undertones
14th May	Next
17th May	Sore Throat
18th May	Cool Notes and Vhybes
19th May	The Dickies
21st May	Next
24th May	The Knack
25th May	Kleenex + The Raincoats + Spizz Energy
26th May	Gang of Four + Delta Five
28th May	Next
31st May	Orchestral Manoeuvres in the Dark + Angletrax
1st June	Clint Eastwood + Bongo Danny + Freedom Fighters
2nd June	The Pop Group + A.T.V.
7th June	The Cure + Modern Eon
8th June	The Human League + The Flowers
9th June	The Skids + The Edge
14th June	The Moondogs + The Frantic Elevators
15th June	John Cooper Clarke + Fashion

16th June	The Lurkers + Essential Logic
21st June	Patrick Fitzgerald + Teardrop Explodes + Pinpoint
22nd June	Yachts
23rd June	Original Mirrors + The Mekons
28th June	The Tourists
29th June	Joe Jackson + Comsat Angels
30th June	Bette Bright + Clive Langer & the Boxes
2nd July	The Tunes + The Donkeys + C.P. Lee + Gordon The Moron
5th July	Dexy's Midnight Runners + The Upsets
6th July	B52's + The Fall + Fashion
7th July	Wire + Manicured Noise
12th July	Activity Minimal + Modern Eon + Chink & The Drills
13th July	Chelsea + Vermillion
14th July	The Specials + Madness
19th July	Albertos Y Los Trios Parasnoias + John Dowie
20th July	The Pretenders
21st July	The Adverts
26th July	Adam & the Ants + Protex
27th July	Simple Minds + The Pictures
28th July	The Merton Parkas + Dexy's Midnight Runners
30th July	Rockin' Dopsie & The Twisters + The Opposition
2nd August	Ed Banger + Chris Sievey & the Freshies
4th August	Stiff Little Fingers + The Starjets
10th August	Orchestral Manoeuvres in the Dark + A Certain Ratio
11th August	Joy Division + Swell Maps + Afternoon Matinee Show
17th August	The Selector
18th August	The Adverts + Local Operator
23rd August	Toyah + The Allumettes
24th August	Madness + Clive Langer's Big Boxes
1st September	Secret Affair + Purple Hearts + Back To Zero + Afternoon Matinee Show
3rd September	Here & Now
6th September	The Not Sensibles + Vibrant Thigh + Property Of + Manchester Mekons
7th September	Tribesmen + Exodus
8th September	Shake + Nightmare in Wax + Afternoon Matinee Show
13th September	Protex + The Drills
15th September	Teardrop Explodes + Echo & the Bunnymen + Expelaires + Afternoon Matinee Show

20th September	The Astronauts + The Mob + Androids of Mu
21st September	The Chords
22nd September	The Revillos
27th September	Phil Rambo
28th September	The Royal Rasses + Jennifer Laur + Pablove Black
29th September	The Ruts + Afternoon Matinee Show
4th October	Dangerous Girls + The Denizens
5th October	The Walkie Talkies + Running Voices
6th October	Crass + Poison Girls + Afternoon Matinee Show
8th October	The Selector + The Fall + The Cheaters
11th October	Destroy All Monsters + Viva
12th October	The Mekons
13th October	Slaughter & the Dogs + Victim + Afternoon Matinee Show
15th October	The Little Roosters + The Mods
18th October	Sore Throat + The Inmates
20th October	Spizz Energi + Swell Maps + Red Crayola + Afternoon Matinee Show
22nd October	Back To Zero + Stay Press
26th October	The Motels
27th October	Pink Military
29th October	Eddie C. Campbell + Good Rockin' Charles + Billy the Kid Emerson + Lester Davenport + Chico Chism + Little Smokey Smothers
3rd November	Merton Parkas + Two Tone Pinks
8th November	The Fall
16th November	The Cure
22nd November	Landscape + Inside Out
23rd November	The Distractions + Art Failure
24th November	Generation X + Algiers
29th November	Tours
30th November	Simple Minds + Nightmares in Wax + The Portraits
1st December	The Pop Group + Delta Five
6th December	Junk Art
7th December	The Modettes + Wah ! Heat
8th December	Joy Division + Section 25 + Afternoon Matinee Show
13th December	Steel Pulse
14th December	The Pirates + The Nice Men
15th December	Eddie & the Hot Rods
17th December	The Damned + The Victims
18th December	Neuklon + Gothons
19th December	The Beat + God's Toys
20th December	Those Naughty Lumps + The Moderates

	+ Roy White & Steve Torch
21st December	The Mighty Vhybes + I Society + The People's Sound System
22nd December	The Teardrop Explodes + Echo & the Bunnymen
27th December	The Zorkie Twins + Junk Art + Attempted Mustache + The Posers + Tim Byers
28th December	Featuring members of Orchestral Manoeuvres in the Dark + Dalek I love you
29th December	Bad Manners + Lew Lewis

1980

10th January	The Modettes + The Passions
11th January	Tom Robinson Band + Modern Eon
12th January	Killing Joke + The Moth Men
15th January	Alexis Korner & the Moondogs
18th January	Red Beans & Rice + Eat at Joes
19th January	The Modettes + The Passions
24th January	999 + Pinpoint
25th January	The Bogey Boys + Cadenza
26th January	Bad Manners + The Bodysnatchers
1st February	The Boys + Red Line
2nd February	Spizz Energi
8th February	Splodgenessabounds + The Sex Beatles + The Lone Groover
9th February	Wreckless Eric + Red Line
11th February	Inside Out
14th February	Nightmares In Wax + Shattered Dolls + Think Of The Winter
15th February	Orchestral Manoeuvres in the Dark + Nueklon
16th February	The Pop Group + The Raincoats
18th February	Inside Out
20th February	After the Fire
21st February	The Movies
22nd February	The Vibrators + The Nice Men
23rd February	Killing Joke + Dr Mix
28th February	Albertos Y Los Trios Paranoias
29th February	The Planets + The Room
1st March	The Inmates + Mark Andrews and the Ghosts
3rd March	Rockin Dopsie & the Twisters
6th March	Eddie & the Hotrods
8th March	The Cramps + The Fall
14th March	Psychedelic Furs + A Certain Ratio + Wah! Heat

THE INTERNATIONAL 1,
ANSON ROAD,
LONGSIGHT, MANCHESTER

1985

Sunday 5th May	Somo Somo
Friday 10th May	It's Immaterial + The Stone Roses
Friday 14th June	Kalima
Saturday 15th June	Simply Red
Wedneday 19th June	The Fall
Friday 21st June	Echo & the Bunnymen
Saturday 22nd June	Hugh Masekela
Monday 24th June	REM
Thursday 27th June	Restless
Saturday 6th July	The Last Poets
Thursday 11th July	The Blasters
Friday 12th July	Thomas Mapfumo & Orchestra
Friday 19th July	Al Rapone & Zydeco Express
Monday 22nd July	Toots & the Maytals
Saturday 27th July	Happy Mondays
Friday 4th October	The Waterboys + Ten Ten
Friday 11th October	That Petrol Emotion
Friday 15th November	The June Brides + The Brothers Kirk
Saturday 23rd November	The Rain Parade
Friday 20th December	The Damned
Saturday 21st December	The Damned

1986

Saturday 11th January	The Jazz Butcher
Thursday 16th January	Fairport Convention
Saturday 15th February	Psychic TV
Friday 28th February	Shop Assistants + T'challa Grid
Friday 14th March	The Men They Couldn't Hang + First Circle
Friday 21st March	Husker Du
Thursday 27th March	The Mission + Pauline Murray & the Storm
Saturday 29th March	The Jazz Butcher
Friday 11th April	The Go-Betweens
Thursday 17th April	The Three Johns + Dust Devils
Saturday 10th May	That Petrol Emotions
Monday 19th May	The Risk + The Cage + Spiro Spira
Saturday 5th July	The Triffids
Saturday 12th July	We've Got A Fuzzbox + Ted Chippington

Friday 5th September	Ministers of the Groove
Thursday 11th September	Balaam and the Angel
Friday 12th September	The Chameleons
Thursday 25th September	It Bites + 5.T.A.
Friday 26th September	Xmal Deutschland + All Fall Down
Saturday 27th September	Bloodfire Posse
Monday 30th September	Freshers Dance Night
Friday 3rd October	Love And Rockets + Spacemen 3
Saturday 4th October	World Party
Monday 6th October	Passmore Sisters + Third Spain + I'll Show Harry
Tuesday 7th October	Robin Hytchcock And The Egyptians
Wednesday 8th October	Weather Prophets + Andy White
Thursday 9th October	Roger McGuinn + Distant Cousins
Friday 10th October	Mighty Lemon Drops + Vee V. V.
Saturday 11th October	Tom Robinson And His Band
Monday 13th October	Naughty Boys + Black & White Lovers
Tuesday 14th October	Dance Night
Thursday 16th October	Women Only Dance Night
Friday 17th October	Peter Case
Saturday 18th October	Zoot And The Roots + The Lawnmower
Monday 20th October	Gift Shop + Knowing Irene + Paperboys
Wednesday 22nd October	Ruby Turner And Her Band
Thursday 23rd October	Soup Dragons + The Shamen
Friday 24th October	Loudon Wainwright III
Saturday 25th October	Robert Calvert's Crankshaft
Monday 27th October	New Morning + Danny Boys + Walter Mitty
Tuesday 28th October	Dance Night
Thursday 30th October	Shop Assistants
Friday 31st October	Robert Cray Band
Saturday 1st November	Jimmy Smith
Monday 3rd November	Lone Justice + Maria McKee
Tuesday 4th November	Hugh Masekela
Thursday 6th November	Chakk
Saturday 8th November	Curtis Mayfield
Friday 14th November	Jazz Defectors + Yargo
Saturday 15th November	The Men They Couldn't Hang + Skol Bandeleros
Monday 17th November	The Train Set + Dance Hall Daze + Eskimos & Egypt
Wednesday 19th November	Marc Almond
Thursday 20th November	Wedding Present + Blyth Power
Friday 21st November	Courtney Pine + The Flying Viaducts
Saturday 22nd November	Freddie Mcgregor + The Scottsman
Monday 24th November	The Raw Herbs + Enormous Room

	+ Dutch by Birth
Wednesday 26th November	Commander Cody and his Lost Planet Airmen
Thursday 27th November	Bloodfire Posse + The Scottsman
Friday 28th November	The Primitives + Dave Howard Singers
Saturday 29th November	Roy Harper
Monday 1st December	Young Mark Twains + Pure + Patio Decorum
Wednesday 3rd December	We've Got A Fuzzbox And We're Gonna Use It
Thursday 4th December	Martin Stephenson And The Daintees
Friday 5th December	The Woodentops + Miaow
Saturday 6th December	Katrina & The Waves + John Otway
Monday 8th December	Last Word + Dum Spero Spero + DavincisMonday
15th December	The Pogues

1987

Friday 30th January	The Stone Roses
Thursday 19th February	The Icicle Works
Friday 20th February	Lone Justice + Maria McKee
Thursday 26th February	Big Audio Dynamite
Saturday 21st March	Michelle Shocked
Friday 27th March	Steve Earle
Friday 1st May	The Go-Betweens
Saturday 9th May	Weather Prophets + Blow Up + David Westlake
Monday 11th May	Heatwave
Friday 15th May	That Petrol Emotion + Voice Of The Beehive
Saturday 16th May	Paul Brady Band
Saturday 23rd May	Band Of Holy Joy + The Man From Del Monte
Wednesday 27th May	I.Q. + Jadis
Thursday 28th May	Latin Quarter
Friday 29th May	Richard Thompson + Sally Barker
Saturday 30th May	Zoot And The Roots
Monday 1st June	The Long Ryders
Friday 5th June	The Primitives + Apple Mosaic
Saturday 6th June	Dr Feelgood + Ministers Of The Groove
Monday 8th June	Pop Will Eat Itself
Friday 26th June	The Stone Roses + The Waltones
Saturday 8th August	Gil Scott-Heron + Amere Facade + Rhonda
Thursday 13th August	Albert King Band + Bare Wires
Saturday 22nd August	Zoot & The Roots + Brendan Croker
	& The Five O'clock Shadows
Thursday 27th August	David Rudder & Charlie's Roots
Thursday 17th September	Hue & Cry
Friday 18th September	The Meat Puppets + The Inca Babies
Saturday 19th September	Virginia Wolf
Saturday 26th September	Rockin' Sidney + Jukebox Johnson

Friday 9th October	That Petrol Emotion
Saturday 17th October	Buddy Curtess & The Grasshoppers
Thursday 22nd October	The Ramones
Friday 23rd October	The Gun Club
Wednesday 28th October	Soup Dragons
Saturday 31st October	Gaye Bykers On Acid
Monday 2nd November	Expanding Men + Ministers Of The Groove + Shine + Side FX
Wednesday 4th November	Distant Cousins + Devilfishhornclub + Sonja
Thursday 5th November	The Proclaimers + James King & The Fun Patrol
Friday 6th November	The Cardiacs + The Tractors + Slum Turkeys
Saturday 7th November	Mary Coughlan
Thursday 12th November	Fields Of Nephilim
Friday 13th November	Stone Roses + Inspiral Carpets
Saturday 14th November	10 000 Maniacs + The Wallflowers
Wednesday 18th November	Super Diamano De Dakar
Friday 20th November	Loudon Wainwright III + The Eternals
Saturday 21st November	Working Week
Monday 23rd November	Rumillajta
Wednesday 25th November	Tease By Touch
Friday 27th November	Twang + The Great Leap Forward + A Witness
Saturday 28th November	Jive Alive + Ministers Of The Groove + Jukebox Johnson
Monday 30th November	Wire + Dub Sex
Wednesday 2nd December	Andrew Williams
Saturday 5th December	The Bhundu Boys
Thursday 10th December	Here And Now + John Cooper Clarke
Friday 11th December	The Primitives
Saturday 12th December	The Sugarcubes
Monday 14th December	Harry Wharton & Co + Hands Up For Batman + The Light Brigade + Western Dance
Friday 18th December	Stiff Little Fingers
Saturday 19th December	Dr Feelgood
Thursday 24th December	Zoot & The Roots + Bernie Hot Hot
Thursday 31st December	52nd Street

1988

Wednesday 20th January	The Waltones + Parade
Friday 19th February	Yargo
Friday 26th February	The Stone Roses + The Monkey Run
Wednesday 16th March	The Primitives + Ten Ten

Thursday 17th March	Hothouse Flowers
Friday 18th March	Lick The Tins
	+ The Lonesome & Penniless Cowboys
Saturday 19th March	Aslan + M.D.M.A.
Friday 25th March	Pere Ubu + The Mekons
Saturday 26th March	John Martyn
Thursday 31st March	Outside London + The Very Fellows
	+ New Morning
Thursday 7th April	Wayne Shorter Quartet
Saturday 9th April	Gone To Earth + Skol Bandeleros + After The Fox
Saturday 16th April	Zoot & The Roots + Andrew Williams
Wednesday 20th April	Roy Harper + James Varda
Friday 22nd April	Soup Dragons + Something Happens
Saturday 23rd April	Microdisney
Friday 29th April	Throwing Muses + The Pixies
Saturday 30th April	Bradford + Eskimos In Egypt + The Volunteers
	+ John Cooper Clarke
Friday 13th May	Toss The Feathers + Playing At Trains
Saturday 14th May	Bhundu Boys
Wednesday 18th May	The Shamen + King Of The Slums + Kit
Thursday 19th May	The Red Hot Chilli Peppers + The Seers
Friday 20th May	Fairground Attraction + Craig Davies
Saturday 21st May	Wilko Johnson + Switch Doctor
Thursday 26th May	Runrig
Friday 27th May	The Membranes + My Bloody Valentine
	+ Dog Faced Hermans
Saturday 28th May	Frank Sidebotham & The Oh Blimey Band
Monday 30th May	James
Friday 3rd June	Mirrors Over Kiev + Inspiral Carpets
	+ Hollow Sunday
Saturday 4th June	Samson + Tokyo
Wednesday 8th June	Hothouse Flowers + John Wesley Harding
Thursday 9th June	The Bible
Monday 13th June	Lester Bowie's Brass Fantasy
Thursday 16th June	Ali Farka Toure
Friday 17th June	The Beat Farmers
Saturday 18th June	Matraca
Wednesday 22nd June	The Quire Boys + Wolfsbane
Thursday 23rd June	Balkana
Friday 24th June	Ghost Dance
Saturday 25th June	Curtis Mayfield & His Band
Thursday 30th June	Green On Red
Saturday 2nd July	The Wonderstuff

Saturday 16th July	Voice Of The Beehive + A House
Monday 18th July	The Georgia Satellites + Bare Wires
Thursday 21st July	Amayenge
Friday 22nd July	David Rudder & Charlie's Roots
Saturday 23rd July	Robert Calvert
	& His Cyberdelic Ensemble
	+ George Borowski Band + The Serpents
Thursday 28th July	The Sun And The Moon
	+ Eskimos And Egypt
Saturday 30th July	Goodbye Mr Mckenzie
	+ The Creature Comforts
	+ Everything Change
Friday 12th August	The Lloyd-Langton Group
Saturday 13th August	In Tua Nua + Toss The Feathers
Friday 19th August	Sham 69
Saturday 20th August	The Wee Papa Girl Rappers
	+ The London Rhyme Syndicate
Monday 22nd August	Julia Fordham
Thursday 25th August	Broken English
Wednesday 31st August	The Triffids + Inspiral Carpets
Saturday 17th September	Tanita Tikaram
Thursday 20th October	Tom Tom Club
Friday 11th November	Frank Chickens
Monday 28th November	Suicidal Tendencies
Wednesday 30th November	Willum Wozzum Bullum Buzzom
	+ Knowing Irene + Bounce The Mouse
Thursday 1st December	Green On Red
Wednesday 7th December	Suicide
Thursday 8th December	Psychic TV
Saturday 17th December	Dr Feelgood

1989

Friday 20th January	Nitzer Ebb
Wednesday 25th January	Jane's Addiction + Birdland
Wednesday 15th February	Lords Of The New Church
Friday 24th February	Throwing Muses + The Sundays
Saturday 4th March	The Man From Delmonte
Saturday 11th March	The Silencers
Monday 13th March	Diesel Park West
Thursday 16th March	Rose Of Avalanche
Monday 20th March	The Toll
Wednesday 29th March	Wrathchild
Thursday 30th March	American Music Club
Saturday 1st April	Gregson Collister Band

Monday 3rd April	Fishbone + What? Noise
Wednesday 5th April	The La's
Saturday 8th April	Green On Red + Harbour Kings
Thursday 13th April	Front 242
Wednesday 26th April	Wolfsbane
Monday 1st May	Jesus Jones
Friday 16th June	Psychic TV
Wednesday 5th July	Faith No More + Slum Turkeys
Saturday 16th September	Big Audio Dynamite + Havana 3AM
Monday 13th November	The Psychedelic Furs
Thursday 23rd November	Nitzer Ebb
Sunday 26th November	Deborah Harry
Wednesday 29th November	Screaming Blue Messiahs
Monday 4th December	Loop + World Domination Enterprises
Monday 11th December	Melissa Etheridge

1990

Friday 2nd March	Pale Saints
Thursday 26th April	The Charlatans
Friday 1st June	Kitchens Of Distinction
Friday 15th June	Carter the Unstoppable Sex Machine
Thursday 28th June	Lush
Saturday 7th July	The Lemonheads + Buffalo Tom
Wednesday 18th July	Flowered Up + Manic Street Preachers
Friday 27th July	The Mock Turtles
Saturday 11th August	World of Twist
Monday 17th September	Mark Stewart & the Mafia
	+ Gary Clail & On U Sound
Thurday 4th October	African Headcharge + Steve Barker
Saturday 6th October	Haji JB + Funk Ambassadors
Monday 8th October	Mad Jacks + Motion Incorporated
Wednesday 10th October	24-7 Spyz + Stevie Salas Color Code
Thursday 11th October	The Darling Buds
Friday 12th October	The Heart Throbs
Saturday 13th October	Le Rue + Paye
Monday 15th October	Ashley & Jackson
Wednesday 17th October	Sacred Reich + Xentrix + Atrophy
Thursday 18th October	The Blue Aeroplanes
Friday 19th October	Ambitious Beggars + Wax Tablets
Saturday 20th October	Jesse 'Guitar' Taylor
Monday 22nd October	Levellers 5
Wednesday 24th October	Thee Hypnotics + Metal Monkey Machine
Thursday 25th October	Ned's Atomic Dustbin
Friday 26th October	Gary Clail's On-U Sound System

Saturday 27th October	James Taylor Quartet
Monday 29th October	Rig + Joanna
Wednesday 31st October	Jah Wobble + Andy Wetherall
Thursday 1st November	Lush + Faith Over Reason
Friday 2nd November	Frank Sidebottom + Edward Barton
Saturday 3rd November	Wilko Johnson + Jukebox Johnson
Friday 9th November	Revenge
Saturday 10th November	The Big Town Playboys
Wednesday 14th November	Galaxie 500
Wednesday 28th November	Echo & the Bunnymen + Noel Burke
Saturday 22nd December	A Certain Ratio

1991

Saturday 26th January	Revolting Cocks + Minister of Noise
Saturday 9th Feb	Chumbawamba
Wednesday 6th March	Throwing Muses
Wednesday 18th April	Kitchens of Distinction + Kit
Saturday 20th April	Mark Stewart + Dub Syndicate + African Headcharge + Bim Sherman
Monday 22nd April	Gangstar + MC Nikke
Friday 26th April	Sonic Boom
Monday 13th May	Julian Cope
Friday 24th May	Ozric Tentacles
Saturday 25th May	Spiritualised
Saturday 15th June	Psychic TV
Wednesday 7th August	Steve Earle

THE INTERNATIONAL 2, PLYMOUTH GROVE, LONGSIGHT, MANCHESTER

1987

Monday 20th April 1987	The Fall
Friday 29th August 1987	Byron Lee & The Dragonaires
Monday 31st August 1987	Berres Hammond & his All Star Band
Saturday 12th September 1987	Jesus And Mary Chain
Wednesday 23rd September 1987	New Model Army
Thursday 8th October 1987	Rory Gallagher
Thursday 15th October 1987	Christy Moore
Friday October 1987	Maxi Priest
Saturday 21st November 1987	Augustus Pablo + Junior Delgado & The Rockers Band

Thursday 26th November 1987	Odyssey + Uthingo + Kabbala
Friday 27th November 1987	Jim Silk +
Monday 30th November 1987	Johnny Thunders + The Quire Boys
Tuesday 1st December 1987	The Woodentops + The Man From Delmon-

te+ Gone To Earth + The Poors Of Reign + Frank Sidebottom

Thursday 3rd December 1987	Frankie Paul + Dennis Brown
Friday 11th December 1987	Happy Mondays + Dudu Pukwana's Zila
	+ The Poors Of Reign
Friday 18th December 1987	Maxi Priest & The Select Committee

1988

Monday 30th May 1988	Stone Roses
Saturday 2nd July 1988	Audio Two + M.C. Lyte + Wrecks 'N' Effect
	+ M.C. Buzz B
Thursday 21st July 1988	Dennis Brown & His Band
Friday 5th August 1988	Joe Strummer & The Latino Rockabilly War
	+ One Style + Bradford
Friday 12th August 1988	Trevor Sparks + Admiral Sparks
	+ Shaka Demus + Tinga Stewart
	+ Patrick Rose & Band
Saturday 27th August 1988	The Mighty Diamonds
Saturday 17th September 1988	The Wolfetones
Saturday 22nd October 1988	The Wolfetones
Saturday 29th October 1988	Josey Wales
	+ Johnny Osbourne & The Instigators
Saturday 5th November 1988	Rick Clarke + Soul to Soul
Friday 11th November 1988	The Men They Couldn't Hang + Mayo Youth
Friday 18th November 1988	Steel Pulse + Suns Of Arqa + The Scottsman
Saturday 19th November 1988	The Stone Roses
Tuesday 20th November 1988	The Richard Thompson Band
Saturday 26th November 1988	The Sun And The Moon + New Morning

1989

Saturday 25th February 1989	Gregory Isaacs & The Ryddim Kings
	+ Crucial Music + The Scottsman
Saturday 4th March 1989	Motorhead + Deathwish + Miss Daisy
Tuesday 7th March 1989	Stray Cats
Saturday 11th March 1989	Happy Mondays + M.C. Buzz B
Friday 17th March 1989	Steve Harley & Cockney Rebel
Saturday 18th March 1989	Vow Wow + Leatherwolf
Friday 31st March 1989	Roachford
Wednesday 12th April 1989	The Jeff Healey Band
Saturday 15th April 1989	Johnny Clarke & His Band + Sister Benji
Tuesday 18th April 1989	Mammoth + Torino

Friday 21st April 1989	Salif Keita
Saturday 29th April 1989	The Men They Couldn't Hang
Tuesday 2nd May 1989	Pixies + Wolfgang Press
Thursday 4th May 1989	The Godfathers
Friday 5th May 1989	Pop Will Eat Eat Itself
	+ John Moore & The Expressway
	+ Ned's Atomic Dustbin
Saturday 6th May 1989	The Stone Roses
Wednesday 10th May 1989	The Godfathers + The Claytown Troupe
Friday 12th May 1989	The Wolfetones
Tuesday 16th May 1989	Killing Joke
Saturday 26th May 1989	Toss The Feathers
Wednesday 31st May 1989	Fields Of The Nephilim
Monday 12th June 1989	Ghost Dance
Friday 16th June 1989	Fela Anikulapo Kuti
Saturday 24th June 1989	Transvision Vamp
Friday 3rd November 1989	Tiger + Leroy Smart
Saturday 4th November 1989	Beautiful South
Thursday 9th November 1989	Pinchers + Junior Demus
Friday 10th November 1989	Napalm Death + Morbid Angel
	+ Carcass + Bolt Thrower
Saturday 11th November 1989	Inspiral Carpets
Tuesday 14th November 1989	The Wedding Present + Thrilled Skinny
Wednesday 15th November 1989	The Wedding Present
	+ Thrilled Skinny
Saturday 18th November 1989	Omar + Unfinished Business
	+ Zushi + Fifth Of Heaven
Thursday 23rd November 1989	Dennis Brown + Freddie Mcgreggor
	+ Marcia Griffiths
Saturday 25th November 1989	The Bhundu Boys
Thursday 30th November 1989	Ziggy Marley & The Melody Makers
Saturday 2nd December 1989	The Macc Lads
Friday 8th December 1989	The Man From Delmonte
Tuesday 12th December 1989	Man O' War + Lizzy Borden
Friday 15th December 1989	Motorhead + Thunderhead
Tuesday 19th December 1989	Steve Harley & Cockney Rebel
Wednesday 20th December 1989	Bonfire

Bibliography & Permissions

Ankeny, Jason. Lost Souls Found – A history of Northern Soul. www.allmusic.com

Barnes, Mike. Captain Beefheart. Quartet Books. 2000.

Birch, Will. Rod Stewart The Graveyard Shift – Mojo. 1995.

Brewster, Bill, Broughton Frank. Last Night A DJ Saved My Life. Headline Books. 1999.

Cope, Julian. Head–On – Magog Books Limited. 1994.

Croasdell, Ady. The Soul of Sue – 2004.

Finnis, Rob. The Guy Stevens story – 2004.

Florek, Jaki, Whelan Paul. Liverpool Eric's – All the best clubs are downstairs everybody knows that. Feedback. 2009.

Gillett, Charlie. The Sound Of The City. Souvenir Press. 1971.

Hirshey, Gerri. Nowhere To Run. Southbank Publishing. 2006.

Lee, CP. Shake Rattle And Rain – Popular Music Making in Manchester. Hardinge Simpole. 2002.

Rawlings, Terry. Mod – A Very British Phenomenon. Omnibus Press. 2000.

Rylatt, Keith, Scott Phil. Central 1179 – The Story of Manchester's Twisted Wheel Club. Bee Cool Publishing. 2001.

Savage, Jon. England's Dreaming. Faber and Faber. 1991.

Scaggs, Austin. Interview with Rod Stewart. Rolling Stone magazine.

Scholtes, Peter S. Complicated Fun – October 26, 2004 Archives (Guy Stevens)

Welsby, Paul. The New Breed Interview with Roger Eagle. February 1999.

With thanks to...

BBC Radio 2 – 'Halls of Fame' documentary on the Eric's club with Steve Lamacq

Collectors Weekly – Ivor Abadi interview with Maribeth Keane and Brad Quinn

Edsell/Demon Records.

Guardian News and Media Ltd.

Independent Digital News and Media.

Liverpool Echo News Archives – Liverpool Library.

Manchester Beat – manchesterbeat.com

Manchester Evening News Archives – Manchester Central Library.

Melody Maker Archives – British Library, Colindale, London.

Mojo magazine – Chris Hunt.

Online Modernist Archive – Jack That Cat Was Clean – Roger Eagle interview. The Cat. 1985.

Radio Merseyside – Roger Eagle interview.

Roger Eagle interview with John Crumpton. 1994.

Times Newspapers Ltd.

South Manchester Reporter – Peter Bossley.

Twisted Wheel website. Ivor Abadi –
www. thetwistedwheel.com

Interviewees

Doreen Allen	27th June 2008. Liverpool.
Mike Badger	31st August 2009.
Mick Baker	28th June 2008. Whaley Bridge.
Bob Bellis	22nd October 2009.
Zane Branson	7th October 2008.
Neil Carter	13th October 2009.
Jayne Casey	4th September 2009.
Bernie Connor	13th January 2008.
Alan Cottam	6th October 2009.
Nicky Crewe	16th November 2007.
Geoff Davis	2nd February 2008. Liverpool.
Martin Dempsey	1st September 2009.
Mike Donn	16th August 2009.
Bill Drummond	14th January 2008. London.
Pete Dunn	28th June 2008. Whaley Bridge.
John Eagle	20th October 2008. County Cork, Ireland.
Martin Eagle	18th October 2008. County Cork, Ireland.
Roger Eagle	Spring 1994, interviews with the author, Whaley Bridge.
Dave Eaton	2009.
Roger Fairhurst	2nd March 2007. Preston.
Howard Fazakerly	2009
Allan Frost	25th March 2005 – Whaley Bridge.
Pete Fulwell	21st April 2007. Liverpool.
Charlie Griffiths	2007.
Bob Harding	1st September 2006. Manchester.
Steve Hardstaff	17th January 2008.
Les Hare	2nd February 2007. Manchester.
Penny Henry	14th November 2007.
Chris Hewitt	2007.
Stan Hoffman	29th August 2009.
Steve Hopkins PhD	10th March 2008.
Brian Jackson	18/24th October 2007.
Dougie James	17th July 2008.
Howard Jones	30th November 2007
Brenda Kenny	2nd March 2008. Warrington.
Jerry Kenny	2nd March 2008. Warrington

Norman Killon	2nd February 2008. Liverpool.
CP Lee PhD	30th September 2005. Salford.
Bruce Mitchell	16th February 2006. Manchester.
Henry Priestman	27th March 2008. London.
Dave Prosser	8th August 2008. Bangor.
Brian Rae	18th August 2008.
Val Randall	11th February 2009.
Elliot Rashman	1st September 2006. West Yorkshire.
Will Seargeant	21st February 2009. London.
Brian Smith	2nd February 2007 & 18th March 2010, Manchester.
Tommy Smith	20th July 2008.
Joe Strong	6th June 2008. London.
Ron Taylor	7th August 2008. Bangor.
Ken Testi	17th January 2008
Mark Thomas	24th July 2008.
Mike Tobin	24th October 2009.
John Watkins	9th August 2008, Bangor.
Judy Williams	13th August 2008.
Anthony H Wilson	29th May 2006. Manchester.
Alan Wise	27th February 2008.

The Author would like to thank each of the people interviewed about Roger Eagle for giving their time so graciously.

Index

OTHER MUSIC TITLES FROM EMPIRE

Morrissey's Manchester
by Phill Gatenby
ISBN: 1901746569 - £7.95

Out Of The Void - The Primal Scream
Story by Brendan Yates
ISBN: 1901746364 - £9.95

The Manchester Musical History Tour
by Craig Gill and Phill Gatenby
ISBN: 1901746712 - £7.95

All titles available from:
www.empire-uk.com